EPIMETHEAN IMAGININGS

Epimethean Imaginings

Philosophical and Other Meditations
on Everyday Light

Raymond Tallis

ACUMEN

*Dedicated with gratitude to Dr Samir Guglani,
physician, visionary, "unboxer" of medicine and friend*

First published in 2014 by Acumen

Acumen Publishing Limited
4 Saddler Street
Durham
DH1 3NP, UK

ISD, 70 Enterprise Drive
Bristol, CT 06010, USA

www.acumenpublishing.com

ISBN: 978-1-84465-825-1

British Library Cataloguing-in-Publication Data
A catalogue record for this book is available from the British Library.

Typeset in Warnock Pro.
Printed and bound in the UK by 4edge Ltd., Essex.

For Epimetheus I was called by my progenitors
He who muses on things past, and traces back,
In the laborious play of thought, the quick deed
To the dim realm of form-combining possibilities
(Goethe, *Pandora*)

M'illumino
d'immenso
(Giuseppe Ungaretti, "Mattina")

Contents

The Epimethean Vision

[Philosophy is a return] into that nearest, which we invariably rush
past, which surprises us anew each time we get sight of it.
(Martin Heidegger, *Between Good and Evil*, in Safranski 1999: 100)

If this book proves to be more hopeful and cheerful than its generally
hopeful and usually cheerful author (or anyone else come to that) is
entitled to feel, this is because it is in part a corrective.

After nearly forty years as a doctor, I feel a strong need to distance
myself from the message repeated to me day in day out by the practice
of medicine: that we are organisms as well as persons; that our living
is shadowed by rotting; and that the intricate structures of meaning
we so carefully erect over our lifetimes will sooner or later be erased.
Not that I want to deny that my fate, like that of every other human
being, is entangled with the general properties of a body, more or less
opaque to me (see Tallis 2004a), that sooner or later will utterly let me
down in some more or less spectacular way. But before we die, it is
proper to remind ourselves of the extent to which this fate is not the
final truth about us: that the rotting that shadows our living does not
prove that the distance we have placed between ourselves and our
animal bodies is an illusion; that we are defined neither by our helpless beginnings nor by our unchosen ends.

That, at least, is the chief motive behind this book. It is connected
with an impatience with those who seem oblivious of, or ignore, or

even despise, the achievements of this animal *Homo sapiens* that is not just an animal, this organism that is not just an organism; with those who overlook the extraordinary lives lived, the astonishing transformations wrought, by human beings. To this attitude, short on awe, vision and simple gratitude, this book is also a corrective. If at times I rather pile on the delight, I hope this will be forgiven as the understandable excess of one engaged in righting a wrong.

Humankind has been traduced by many thinkers who would presume to tell us what we are (for a critique of the antihumanist disparagement of humanity see e.g. Malik 2000; Tallis 1999a, 2011). If humans invented gods to give a home to self-loathing and, as a pre-emptive strike on fate, to tell us how contemptible and feeble we are, it is not surprising perhaps that, even in those societies where the gods have been pensioned off, the habit of self-hatred continues. The work of priests and theologians is continued by sociologists, cultural historians and a horde of scientistic quasi-philosophers. This matters for many reasons, not least because self-contempt sustained long enough eventually becomes justified.

A few words, first, on the title of this collection of essays, fictional essays and reminiscences. Epimetheus, the "after-thinker", was the brother of Prometheus, the "fore-thinker". In the standard account of the Greek myths, Epimetheus is presented as rather simple-minded compared with his trickster brother, who was able to outsmart the Titans. Epimetheus married Pandora in spite of his brother's warnings, and she let all the evils out of a storage jar where they were kept. More importantly, he was charged by the gods with the task of distributing their gifts. He began with the animals, giving strength to some, to some swiftness, the power of flight to others, and places of shelter to yet others. He also clothed them in thick coats and gave them appropriate equipment: tusks and trunks and so on. Unfortunately, he forgot to leave any gift for the race of men. When Prometheus found all the animals equipped and adorned and man naked and unprotected, he stole fire from the gods and the technology to use it. One might imagine Epimetheus, the "after-thinker", reflecting on the achievements of mankind, arising out of the ur-gift of fire made available to them courtesy of his brother the "fore-thinker" (see Servi 2001: "Prometheus, Benefactor of Mankind").

In invoking his name, I am mobilizing only one aspect of the Epimethean myth: the one that is captured in a phrase from Goethe's *Pandora*. In this play, Epimetheus is presented as more cautious and less rebellious than his sibling; for example, he urges Prometheus to accept Zeus' conciliatory offer of a tied cottage on Mount Olympus. I like to think that Epimetheus placed a high value on tranquillity because he wanted to be left alone to contemplate the mystery of the achievements of humans left to their own devices. This is, to put it mildly, implausible; even so, it is in this putative Epimethean spirit that many of the pages that follow have been written. At any rate, I imagine Epimetheus admiring the Promethean heritage, and wishing for this very reason to reflect and pause, for, in the end, achievements are truly achieved only if they are fully reflected upon.

Epimetheus' job description – tracing (in the phrase from Goethe I alluded to) "the quick deed to the dim realm of form-combining possibilities" – touches on the essential purpose of this book: unpacking some of the elaborately folded depths hidden in the seeming shallows of daily existence. I want to contribute to the project – sometimes explicit, more often implicit, in the work of innumerable artists and thinkers over the centuries – of making visible the richness of human consciousness. These depths are not matched in other sentient creatures. They are different in kind from the moment-bound experiences of beasts.

The emphasis on depths (which, inverted in the mirror of reflec-tion, give one a sense of the heights upon which humans are poised) explains why I originally titled this book *Epimethean Soundings*. Actually, "soundings" is not satisfactory. As my publisher pointed out, it awakens the wrong kind of association: with "sounding off" (although in Part II, "Tetchy Interludes", I do indulge in some sound-ing off). *Epimethean Studies* is a bit pedagogic, although it would have captured the analytical element in these pieces, most obvious in those in the first section. *Epimethean Investigations* would prom-ise something more measured, or at least more rigorous, than this book's butterflying visits here and there. *Epimethean Meditations*, with its Cartesian echo, is too grand. And so (at my publisher's gratefully received suggestion) it is *Epimethean Imaginings*.

Epimethean Imaginings endeavours to examine, and reveal, some of what it is that underlies (underpins, underwrites) the ordinary conscious moments of our human lives. It would be dishonest to pretend that the essays are other than random: a probe here, a drilling down there – no wise aiming at systematic coverage of the territory. The territory in question is the Atlantis of the subsumed, of the presupposed, of the incorporated, of the taken-for-granted in daily life. For I believe that the essence of the philosophical project is to wake us up out of the deepest, most incontrovertible assumptions of wakefulness, not necessarily to challenge them but at least to make them visible.

There are two complementary approaches to the Epimethean project of sounding the depths or counting the number of storeys – and stories – built into everyday light. The genealogical approach of a philosophical anthropology tries to express in the broadest terms our place in nature and measure the spaces that have opened up between ourselves and the rest of creation over those hundreds of thousands, indeed millions, of years that separate us from our closest animal kin. This is the approach adopted in the "Handkind" trilogy of books I published a nearly a decade ago (Tallis 2003a, 2004a, 2005a) and have developed further in recent years, most systematically in *Aping Mankind* (Tallis 2011). The opposite strategy begins from where we are now, starting from surface particulars and engaging in what we might call a "speleology of the ordinary". This was adumbrated in *The Kingdom of Infinite Space* (Tallis 2008), an examination of the human head, and is more explicitly exemplified in the final part of *Epimethean Imaginings*. In none of my philosophical books is either approach employed to the exclusion of the other, for the simple reason that they are not entirely separable.

Sadly, although *Epimethean Imaginings* and the "Handkind" trilogy adopt complementary strategies, they do not close the gap between, on the one hand, the here-and-now (in this room on a particular day) and, on the other, the great, pre-historic, indeed pre-human, events that made the here-and-now possible. Tracing the "quick deed" to the "realm of form-combining possibilities" leaves the form-combining realm to a great extent unilluminated in its dimness. The chains of events linking the first steps by which humans escaped from their biological heritage to arrive at such unprecedented ways of being-in-the-world are so long, so numerous and so bewilderingly intertwined that it is impossible to trace them. Completing the story of the connections between My Now and Our Origins – and thereby fathoming the depth and exuberant complexity of the human way of being – will require, I fear, a new kind of thinking, a new style of expression, a new mode of synthetic consciousness that escapes me at present. One does the best one can.

Epimethean Imaginings is, as I said at the outset, a work of hope, maintained against one rather intransigent countervailing sense of reality. It expresses a belief in the possibility of a delight in a life as deep as the suffering that, as so my years in medicine have endlessly reminded me, awaits us all – a delight that, if shared, might mitigate the pain of the solitude to come.

Acknowledgements

It is again a pleasure to record my enormous gratitude to Steven Gerrard at Acumen for his continuing tremendous support and enthusiasm for my writing. And my thanks are again due to Kate Williams for her excellent – painstaking and empathetic and knowledgeable – editorial work and to Jonny Pegg my agent. I would also like to thank Professor Flemming Steen Nielsen for his comments on the manuscript.

I should like to thank the editors and publishers for allowing me to reproduce material that has already been published. "Seeing and Believing", "Where Is that Itch?", "Draining the River and Quivering the Arrow", "Could the Universe (Even) Give a Toss?", a shorter version of "Causes as (Local) Oomph" and "The Shocking Yawn" are from my regular column in *Philosophy Now*. An earlier version of "Knowledge and the Subjective Qualities of Experience" was published in *Philosophical Investigations* 12(3) (1989), 217–23. "Does Rover Believe Anything?" began life as a lecture to the Philosophy Department at Birkbeck College. "The Fight Against (e.g. My) Stupidity" was based on a talk given at the Battle of Ideas Debating Matters Competition in 2013 and a review of *Being Wrong* by Kathryn

Schulz in the *Times Literary Supplement* (20 March 2011). An earlier version of "Colonic Material of a Taurine Provenance" appeared in *PN Review* 128 (1999), 35–42. Part of "Mission Drift" – "The Logos of Listmas" – first appeared in *The Times* (26 December 2012). "Reimagining the Wheel" was published in *The Reader* 14 (Spring 2004), 39–45.

I

Analyses

Most of what follows in Part I is stylistically and thematically conventional, and therefore requires least introduction, although I hope the reader will feel that I have discoveries worth reporting even when I take well-trodden paths. The topics covered belong to the traditional curriculum of philosophical anxieties.

The first two chapters deal with the problem of perception – and the relationship between sense experience and what, for the want of a better word, we call reality – and the conundrum of the location of raw sensations, those plebs of the human mind. Chapter 3 defends the claim that objective knowledge cannot capture or deliver the subjective quality of experience. This is a crucial element in the critique of scientism and of the claim that physical science is, or will be, the last word on everything, including conscious subjects such as you and me.

One mode of scientism is biologism, whose fundamental tenet is that the difference between humans and other animals is rather less than we humans have traditionally thought. Chapter 4, "Does

Rover Believe Anything?" affirms the reality of the wide gap between humanity and non-human animality by arguing that animals do not have propositional attitudes such as beliefs, which are the very fabric of human consciousness.

Another aspect of scientism is the mathematization of our portrait of what is there: the notion that reality is fundamentally quantitative. I examine two expressions of this: the reduction of time to a dimension on a par with space; and Zeno's paradoxes of motion, which claim that the mathematical impossibility of running for a bus demonstrates that running for a bus is impossible.

The final chapters in this section deal with two competing accounts of what it is that makes the world go round: statistical probability and causation. Neither makes sense, I argue, as constitutive features of the material world. They are inseparable from human consciousness. Chapter 8, "Causes as (Local) Oomph" offers an account that aims to avoid the Scylla of David Hume's reduction of causation to mere mental associations and the Charybdis of Immanuel Kant's locating it in the very processes by which our experiences are transformed into knowledge of a coherent or unified world. This, the longest chapter this section, may be one that the general reader may wish to reserve for another time. Or another life.

1

Seeing and Believing

Like many of the readers of this book (I guess) my first philosophical thoughts were provoked by questions about the nature of reality and its relationship with the way things appear to us in taken-for-granted everyday life. In my early teens, I was occasionally assailed by the queasy feeling that the phenomenal world might be a highly structured hallucination: that I was dreaming what I thought I was experiencing. Although these traditional Cartesian moments were transient, they triggered an abiding interest in the philosophy of perception.

This was reinforced by reading Bertrand Russell's "shilling shocker" (his own term for his classic popular introduction to philosophy) *The Problems of Philosophy* ([1912] 1959). I was captivated by its beautifully lucid chapter on "Appearance and Reality" from the opening paragraph:

> Is there any knowledge in the world which is so certain that no reasonable man could doubt it? This question, which at first sight might not seem difficult, is really one of the most difficult that can be asked. When we have realized the obstacles

in the way of a straightforward and confident answer, we shall
be well launched on the study of philosophy – for philosophy
is merely the attempt to answer such ultimate questions, not
carelessly and dogmatically, as we do in ordinary life and even
in the sciences, but critically, after exploring all that makes
such questions puzzling, and after realizing all the vagueness
and confusion that underlie our ordinary ideas.   (*Ibid.*: 1)

Russell conveyed, and awoke, the thrill of seeing how the basic problems in philosophy connected ordinary, everyday – indeed every
moment – experience with fundamental questions in epistemology,
metaphysics, and ontology.

I was reminded of that early encounter when I recently stumbled on a stimulating essay by Kent Bach, a San Francisco philosopher. Reading, and arguing with, "Searle Against the World" (2007)
seemed like homecoming. Bach's article triggered the thoughts (most
of them somewhat tangential to his arguments) in the present essay.

The philosophy of perception traditionally begins with what is
usually called the "argument from illusion" (although it also draws
on hallucinations). We can have apparent experiences of objects that
are not there or be presented with appearances, such as a stick seemingly bent by being plunged in water, that prove on further investigation to have been deceptive. It seems that there is a disconnection
between our perceptual experiences and the objects they purport
to be experiences of. More broadly, the gap between experiences of
appearances and our seeming knowledge of reality is even more puzzling, even vexing, because knowledge is both based on experience
and has to go beyond it.

Our unease is reinforced by the fact that actual things, things that
are really there, may have different appearances depending on from
where, or under what (internal or external) conditions, we are experiencing them. A demonstrably square tabletop may look diamond
shaped from many angles; a circular coin may appear elliptical. Our
tactile experience of the table varies depending on how, and how
firmly, we press on or otherwise handle it. This is not, of course, as

worrying as some philosophers would like us to think. When I look at an object I am aware not only of the object but also that I am looking at it from a certain angle, at a certain distance, in a certain light. In other words, our sense experiences come with warnings: "You are not seeing object O period but object O from a certain angle, at a certain distance, in the certain light". Unlike the intellectually challenged young priest Dougal in the television series *Father Ted*, we do not think that a person whose apparent size diminishes with distance is actually shrinking. We look *through* appearances.

The allowances we make for different conditions under which objects are perceived, as a result of which they have different phenomenal appearances, are underpinned by an assumption of what psychologists call "object constancy". This is our tendency to see objects as intrinsically unchanging in spite of the variations in the positions and in the conditions in which they are observed. This truly remarkable faculty requires a self-consciousness that builds into our sense experiences an awareness of the perspectives from which we perceive objects. We are conscious of the conditions under which we see things as well as the things themselves: we are self-perceiving perceivers. We are aware of the location of ourselves as perceivers in a particular relationship to that which we perceive. This is just as well, since there could be no experience corresponding to seeing an object "in-itself" from *no* particular angle, or distance, in no particular light.

So the diamond-shaped table and the elliptical penny are corrected for. And there is an additional source of checking. If seeing is tinged with doubt, touching may resolve uncertainty. Few headless horses, pink elephants, and bends in sticks plunged into water survive attempts to grasp them. At a more homely level, we can trace out the roundness of the penny with a pencil and confirm the rectangularity of the table by measuring its angles. It is, after all, ordinary everyday perception that exposes misperceptions for what they are: we realize we are deceived when we see the table as diamond-shaped because we have more reliable experiences that tell us that the table is in fact rectangular.

Even so, some still believe – or claim to believe – that our prone-
ness to illusions may imply that there is no connection between
perceptions and the existence or nature of their objects. *All* perceptions may be illusory or hallucinations. While perceptions may hang
together in some way, it is possible that what we think is out there
has no relation to a reality independent of our experiences; and our
thoughts about them may be (as John McDowell has put it) mere
"frictionless spinning in a void" (1996: 11).

This worry is reinforced (for some) by the fact that it is possible
to generate experiences by direct stimulation of relevant parts of
the nervous system – an observation that underpins the famous
thought experiment in which a brain in a vat of nutrient could, by
being stimulated in the appropriate way, imagine itself to be located
in a world, although the world in question is in fact created solely
out of its neural activity. The brain-in-a-vat thought experiment
should not trouble us, however. After all, setting it up presupposes
a non-illusory material object such as a brain located in a real material world that includes vats, nutrient, electrodes, scientists and the
entire paraphernalia that supports them.

And we have even more solid grounds for rejecting the possibility
that we are *always* deceived by our senses: namely, if illusion were
universal, there would be no reality to contrast it with. As Gilbert
Ryle pointed out, "there can be false coins only where there are coins
made of the proper materials by the proper authorities" (1954: 94).
The philosophical error is to conclude, from the fact that it is always
possible that we might be in error, that it is therefore possible we
might always be in error. And, finally, if perception were systematically in error, and thus disconnected from the world in which the
perceiver truly or actually is, it is difficult to see how the perceiver,
qua organism, could survive or, indeed, what use her perceptions
would be. To say that the very ideas of survival, of use and of the
organism may be regarded as themselves based in illusion shows the
unsustainable cost of maintaining the case for global illusion.

Even so, illusions reveal a gap between our perceptions and the
objects we perceive. Defining that gap has exercised the wits and

imagination of many philosophers. At the very least we can agree that there is no guarantee inside particular experiences that they really are *of* the things they appear to be experiences of. The relationship between the experience and its objects, that is to say, has an irreducible element of contingency. The reasons for this go very deep indeed.

At the heart of perception is an "aboutness": a reference to an object that is by definition something more than that which is directly experienced. This glass in front of me is not exhausted by any number of visual, tactile or other experiences of it – not yours, not mine, not anyone's, nor those of any sentient being. This follows from the fact that an object is not reducible to its presence as evinced in its phenomenal appearance to a subject. To put this the other way round (as did the American philosopher Barry Stroud [2000: 6]), our knowledge of objects is *underdetermined by our sense experiences* – the ultimate source of our knowledge. To reiterate what I said earlier: we look through appearances to that which we believe they are appearances of.

Some philosophers of a "phenomenalist" persuasion have concluded from this that what we take to be material objects are mere "logical constructs" out of experiences. This, however, would make it difficult to understand the role of the object in occasioning the experience of itself and providing the justification of the implicit claim of that experience to be true. If the object were built up out of experiences, how could the experiences owe their origin to, or be constrained by, the object? The suggestion that it is constrained by other experiences simply moves the question on.

This is an argument, perhaps, for another day and another essay. For the present we note that the mismatch between the *contents* and the *objects* of sense experiences – or between objects and the sum total of experiences – opens up some interesting lines of thought. A traditional way of characterizing a true perception, as opposed to an illusion, is that the former is *caused* by its apparent object. For example, if my perception P of a glass is not to be a hallucination or an illusion, P should have been caused by the glass itself. To put this another way: my experience P of a glass or, more generally object O, is truly *of* O if O *actually* caused it. (The notion of causation is far from clear, as we shall see in Chapter 8, "Causes as (Local) Oomph" but let us run with it for the present.) It is not sufficient that P should be exactly like the perception we would have if O *had* caused it. (Clearly, we cannot be expected actually to see this causal connection between true Ps and their Os; otherwise we could not be deceived in the way that, from time to time, we are – there would be no possibility of illusions and hyper-real hallucinations.) Given that the causal links between events are necessarily contingent, it is not surprising that the content of P is independent of the object O supposedly causing it – and that there is room for illusions and hallucinations.

The causal theory of perception, however, is beset with problems. For a start, it is misleading to think of an *object* – a standing, stable item – as a cause of an *event* such as a perception. It is events that cause events; so the putative cause of P cannot be O itself but something happening to O that sets in train a succession of events that finally impinges on the perceiving subject. In the case of vision, the most promising candidate is the incident light bouncing from O into the eyes of the person seeing it, eventually causing activity in the visual cortex. My view of O is due to the way O interferes with the light that bathes it and is deflected towards my eyes.

But the replacement of O with an event, or patterns of events, in or on O as the cause of P makes perception even more problematic. Somehow, out of an event (or events) in an object (let us call it E_{object}) causing an event (or events) in a subject ($E_{subject}$), there has to arise a perception P that is then *of* the object. O, of course, is beyond $E_{subject}$ – it is "out there" with respect to the subject "over here" – and transcends E_{object}, given that O is more than a subset of incident events that befall it. So we have an odd situation: if P is truly of O, P has to be caused by O, and yet, at the same time, O is more than anything that could cause P, and P (which postulates an object) is more than an $E_{subject}$ that any E_{object} could cause. There is a double dissociation between the object and the experiencing subject who is made aware of it.

These are not grounds for suspecting that the experienced world is an illusion – for reasons we have already given – but it is a valid reason for being deeply puzzled by perception, particularly since (as already noted) perceptions that have no basis in real objects may have an identical appearance to those that are truly of the objects they seem to be of: hallucinatory experiences can be qualitatively indistinguishable from true perceptions. There is no reason why a hallucination of O arising (say) as a result of spontaneous activity in the visual pathways of my nervous system should not have an identical content to a true experience of O occasioned by a causal interaction between O and my sensorium.

So we are driven to two conflicting conclusions. The first is that the criterion for a true perception P is that it must be caused by events in its object O – say the interaction between O and the light. There is, as it were, an audit trail leading back from P to O. The second is that O and P are *not* in a straightforward causal relationship. This is shown by the fact that P's being "about", its referring to, or being focused on, O seems to point in a direction opposite to any causal chain leading from O to P, from say the light interfering with the object and the neural activity in the perceiver's brain. This is why William Alston's aphorism "causality is no substitute for awareness" (1997, quoted in Bach 2007: 65) is so precisely to the point. While we maintain the fundamental difference between perceptions and hallucinations, and feel that the difference must somehow involve differences in the causal paths that lead up to them, there doesn't seem anything in the properties of the material object, or of the perceiving subject, that would make the former sufficient to induce perception in the latter.

Material objects, it seems, don't have the wherewithal to make their presence felt to a perceiving subject and it is not clear what, if anything, in the latter would confer the ability on material objects to make their mere existence into actual presence. We can see this more clearly if we try to make sense of the idea of the appearance of an object independent of any perceiving subject. It is an impossible idea. What would be the experience of a glass seen from no viewpoint – not from near or far, from above or below, in the dark or in light, from inside or outside? No answer is forthcoming and that is answer in itself.[1] Perception, in short, is deeply mysterious.

I began my philosophizing by brooding over the world of appearances and sense experiences. Fifty years on, this is still a place to which my philosophical thoughts repeatedly return. And the promise in the last paragraph of Russell's "Appearance and Reality" has been abundantly fulfilled in the intervening half century:

> Philosophy, if it cannot *answer* so many questions as we could wish, has at least the power of *asking* questions which increase the interest of the world, and show the strangeness and wonder lying just below the surface even in the commonest things of daily life. (*Ibid.*: 6)

NOTE

1. This is why the idea of sense data that Russell invokes in "Appearance and Reality" (having derived the idea from G. E. Moore) – as intermediaries between objects and subjects – is deeply unsatisfactory. He suggested that "whenever we see a colour, we have a sensation *of* the colour, but the colour itself is a sense datum, not a sensation" ([1912] 1959: 4). This seems to multiply problems unhelpfully. Instead of the single mystery of the relationship between objects and perceiving subjects, we have at least two mysteries: the relationship between objects and sense data and the relationship between sense data and perceptions.

2

Where Is that Itch?
Philosophy from Scratch

I am lying in darkness, trying to sleep. There is a tiny whining sound. It stops. I brace myself: the mosquito has landed. Shortly afterwards, a sting. In the confusion, the beast escapes my wildly swatting hands and I am left alone with my itch. Vengeance denied me, and the possibility of sleep made even more remote, I philosophize.

Where is that itch? Well, it's on my leg of course, where the beast landed, took out its hypodermic and injected its own saliva, prior to siphoning a minute aliquot of my lifeblood. Of this there can be no doubt because this is where, later, I see a little papule and where I have to scratch in search of relief. It's certainly not on my arm, in my liver, on the bed or in the next room. If I go to the bathroom in search of ointment, my itch goes with me.

Some of you will already be uneasy. An itch is a content of consciousness and such phenomena, we are told, aren't the kinds of things that can have locations in space, even bodily space. In the case of conscious contents such as thoughts, memories and mental images, it is easier to say why it's odd to assign them to a point in space: they have aboutness or reference; they point beyond themselves, so they cannot be *where* they can seem to be thought of as occurring. Itches don't seem to have that aboutness so perhaps it does make sense to locate them in space.

Let's stick with thoughts for the moment. Suppose I am thinking "There is a mosquito in the room". The thought has two aspects: it is a *token* that occurs at a particular time (say at 3am just before the little sod bit me); and it is also an instance of a type, an expression of a proposition. I alone have the token but many people can entertain the proposition about the mosquito. This is even more obviously true of a proposition such as "The Battle of Hastings took place in 1066". Indeed, I can have that token only *because* others have had the type it instantiates: it has, as it were, been "handed down" to the present, from 1066, when the events corresponding to the content of my thought were observations made by participants and eye witnesses. The token thought, in short, is a psychological phenomenon but the type is something else: it is the content or reference of the thought, which presents itself as a fact or possible fact, thought by any number of people. And the thought's status as an instance of a type from which it is inseparable, as a piece of intelligence or intelligibility, makes it something to which it does not seem right to ascribe a spatial location.

In possibly the most famous moment in Western philosophy, René Descartes came to the conclusion that he was identical with his thoughts because these were the only items whose existence he could not doubt since the very process of doubting that his thoughts were real would be a process of thought. What is more, if he *were* thinking, he could not doubt his own existence; because if he didn't exist, he couldn't think. Hence the famous formula *cogito ergo sum*. (It has never been very clear how much of the "I" his argument actually delivered safely from the jaws of doubt; for pitiless details see Tallis [2004a].)

What is relevant for our present purposes is that Descartes believed that his thoughts were parts of a "thinking substance" and this, unlike the material substance of his body, was not spatially extended or, indeed, spatially located. Avowedly anti-Cartesian, twentieth-century analytical philosophers would agree with him in this respect: influenced by the German philosopher Gottlob Frege, they believed that the essence of thought was the thought type – the proposition expressed in the thought – not the token thought, not the psychological event hosted by individual "bearers" of thoughts like me, and occurring (say) at 3am just before the mosquito struck.

More recently, however, some philosophers have focused on token thoughts and have argued that these items occur not only at a particular time but also at a particular place: they are located in the *brain* of the person thinking them (e.g. Bayne 2012). A thought *is* where a scan lights up when someone is having it. When we are sufficiently adept at brain reading, we are told, we shall become thought-readers. So thoughts are now reinserted into space, along with the mind of the thinker.

This won't do. First, there still remain aspects of thoughts – their meaning or reference – that (to use Hilary Putnam's phase) "ain't in the head". What's more, there is no such thing as a stand-alone thought: they are interconnected and inseparable from the worlds to which they belong. My thoughts fit together in something like what Wilfrid Sellars characterized as the space of reasons, whose denizens can be justified and, indeed, demand justification. This mode of connectedness is quite different from the causal connectedness of the material events evident on a scan.

Even when thoughts are reduced to words, as in the internal soliloquies of fictional characters, they are often elliptic, allusive and fragmentary. Single words can evoke a mini-universe of meaning. I can think something is *not* the case, idly entertain possibilities (which may be quite abstract, such as that Manchester United might have a lousy season), question what I have just thought, or recall thoughts others have had. Thoughts may be declarative or subjunctive, confident or tentative, tenseless or tensed, referring to past, present or future. The relationship between the themes of my thoughts and what I am thinking about those themes is not at all straightforward. Knowing what you are thinking requires both.

All of which is why, as Sarah Richmond points out, there are many philosophers – Wittgensteinians, externalists, phenomenalists and "extended mind theorists" – who doubt that "reading minds by 'decoding' images of brains" (2012: 114) even makes sense conceptually. Thoughts ain't in the head or localized in a bit of the brain inside the head. Or in the body. Or in the room where the body is currently sitting.

So much for thoughts. Let's go back to itches. Now they are quite unlike thoughts. Indeed, Descartes was rather sniffy about such sensations: they were, he said, "confused thoughts" incurably curdled by the body, from which they were inseparable. (What they were thoughts of is rather interesting to contemplate. The distance between the sensation of itch and the thought "I am itching" or "I have an itch" or "There is an itch on my leg" is vast – it gathers up much that separates mere sentience from human consciousness – and not one that can be crossed by the term "confused".) At any rate, they lack thought's double aspect of being a token psychological event *and* a proposition that the event refers to or instantiates. Itches are not about anything. Any temptation to think that my itch is *about* its cause, about the mosquito or its bite or its hypodermic syringe, may be resisted by recalling I can have an itch without having any idea of its cause, without its being an itch "about" a mosquito bite, or about the idea of it.

So itches lack the aboutness that prevents us (or should prevent us) from thinking of thoughts as being in any particular place. So is it OK then to grant location to them and other mere sensations? If so, where? According to the now standard view, the itch is not in my leg, where the bite can be seen, and where scratching brings relief. The itch is in my sensory cortex. Other parts of the brain may be involved – as when I think bitterly of the little beast that bit me – but it is the sensory cortex that is most crucially involved. There is, after all, a connection from the sensory nerve endings in the skin stimulated by the bite, up the spinothalamic tracts, thence through the thalamus, to the sensory cortex. It is there, we are told, that the itch is experienced, that is to say, comes into being. If the nerves between the sensory nerve endings in my leg and the cortex are cut or the relevant bit of the cortex is damaged, no itch is felt. So itches aren't really in the leg but, unlike thoughts, are in the brain.

The careful reader (every reader of this book) will spot some fancy footwork here. The argument that, because the itch is not felt unless there is activity in the relevant bit of the brain, it follows that it is *in* that bit of the brain, looks fishy. After all, if you asked me where my itch was I would point to my leg, where I was bitten, and not to my head. The bite and the itch are, surely, in the same place. There would be no itch if there were no relevant activity in my leg. Or, indeed, if my leg had been cut off.

This will not, however, prove decisive against those who maintain that the itch is really in the brain, not the leg. They will concede that it *seems* to be in my leg. But, they say, it seems to be there only because it is located in that part of my body image or schema that I take to be my leg, and the body schema is a construct of the brain. According to John Searle, "the match between where the sensation seems to be and the actual physical body is entirely created in the brain" (1997: 182). The proof of this, he says, comes from phantom limb sensations. I can experience pain in a limb that has been amputated. This is because I still have a two-legged body schema in my brain to which brain events, such as activity in pain pathways, can be referred.

Not so fast. We experience pains in limbs we no longer have only because we *usually* experience pains in limbs we do have. Phantom limb sensations are referred to non-existent legs only because of ordinary sensations that are felt in real legs prompted by real events. I feel an itch in my leg when I am bitten there; and I point to my leg when asked where the itch is because here is usually where I need to scratch or dab the soothing ointment. Yes, I could deactivate a bit of my brain and the itch would go but it is perverse to conclude that this – admittedly one of the necessary conditions of the itch – is where the itch is.

Besides, the claim that the itch is *really* located inside an image of the body created in the brain would have rather surprising consequences. Let me illustrate this with something that has bothered me since 1961. Ned Ellis, my physics teacher, once asked the class, between puffs on his Woodbine, where mirror images were. We gave the standard answer: as far behind the mirror as the object was in front of it. No, he said: they are in your brain. And he reminded us that if you looked behind the mirror, you wouldn't see the image. It is we who construct the image and locate it out there in the world. But this cannot be extended to objects as well as images. *We* do not locate the *mirror* in the world: it locates itself in the world without our help, thank you.

Whole-hog neurological idealism, however, holds that not only the mirror image but also the mirror (and the shop where it was purchased) – and all the objects reflected in it – are in some sense constructs of our brains. This is widely accepted. The distinguished neuroscientist Chris Frith (2007) expresses this succinctly: "the brain makes up the mind", which in turn models, or houses the model of, the world. But if this were true, the brain itself (and brain science and the equipment it uses) would be a somewhat problematic construct, somehow collaborating with a community of constructs to discover that, like everything else we are aware of, it is a construct.

Itches, of course, should be easier to think about than thoughts or mirror images. Unlike thoughts, as we have noted, they are not two-faced: psychological tokens instantiating general propositions. And they are not constructs like mirror images, although (*pace* Ned Ellis) the latter fit uneasily into the head because they are available to and confirmed by others. (I can ask others to look at a mirror image that we both see. For example, we can both look at the reflection of your face.) Itches are not shared like thoughts or mirror images: others can infer my itch from the bite on my skin or my scratching but not experience it. Even so, itches are problematic. The answer to "where" the itch is – in my leg, in my brain, in a mental model constructed by my brain, or as a despised inhabitant of a Cartesian thinking substance – will depend on what kind of space, and *what kind of "in"*, we are thinking of.

The space of sensations such as itches will be different from the dual space of thought in which the space of psychology is married to the space of logic and semantics, of meaning and reference. And it will be different again from that of mirror images. At any rate, the idea that the itch is "really" in my brain but is "referred to" my leg (by what means, by whom, is unclear) does not capture the sense that my itch really is in my leg. For the present, I will stubbornly insist that if it makes sense to locate a sensation, it is *where I feel it*, not in my brain or in some model of my body created in the brain.

Socrates famously described himself (reported in Plato's *Apology* 30e) as a "gad-fly" "arousing, persuading and provoking". My mosquito has provided the same service, causing much head-scratching as well as leg-scratching. But I want to sleep and I can hear the little pest returning. Time to reach for the hemlock aerosol.

3

Knowledge and the
Subjective Qualities of Experience

This essay is a contribution to a philosophical debate kicked off by a classic paper published by Thomas Nagel forty years ago. It is a debate that is still ongoing and, I suspect, is set to run for a long time yet. At its heart is the profound problem of seeing how subjective experiences fit into the material world revealed by objective knowledge.

In "What Is it Like to Be a Bat?" (1974), Nagel pointed out that, however complete our objective scientific knowledge about an organism, we should still not know *what it is like to be* that organism. We should not know what being that organism, and having that organism's experiences, is like *for* the organism. Behind Nagel's argument is his intuition that the subjective experience lies beyond the reach of scientific enquiry and is irreducible within any scientific theory; more generally still, that there is an unbridgeable gap between objective knowledge and subjective experience. For him, this demonstrates how the laws of nature as revealed by physical science will not account for human beings, for whom subjective experience is central.

In their responses to Nagel's essay, philosophers have utilized a series of thought experiments – usually involving deaf or blind super-scientists – to examine the gap between objective knowledge and subjective experience (see e.g. Robinson 1982: 4). We may, for example, imagine a deaf scientist who knows everything there is to know about the physical – and in particular the neural – processes involved in hearing. There will still be something that this scientist will not know: namely, *what it is like to hear*. The physicalist account of the world does not, therefore, capture its subjective aspect.

Not everyone is persuaded. The American philosopher Michael Tye thinks he can counter these arguments by showing that there are no subjective experiential *facts* that physical information cannot encompass. Tye (1986) imagines a twenty-third-century congenitally blind super-scientist Jones, who has "exhaustive knowledge of what goes on in us when we see colours and use colour words". Jones is about to undergo an operation to give him sight. Won't post-operative Jones know something that pre-operative Jones did not: namely, what it is like to have the experience of seeing red, blue, green and so on? Yes, Tye says, post-operative Jones will know what pre-operative Jones could not know: that a particular experience e has a specific phenomenal content which may be rigidly designated R. Importantly, it has to be appreciated that this is not the same as knowing (in general) what it is like to undergo any experience with content R since this kind of knowledge can be possessed by persons who hold no belief about the particular experience e and could, theoretically, be available to pre-operative Jones.

By concentrating on token experiences rather than types of experience, Tye claims to strengthen the anti-physicalist force of the argument from knowledge: the argument that objective knowledge falls short of subjective experiences. He then attacks this strengthened version of the argument. He concludes that of course Jones *will* learn something about e when he gains his sight: he will discover what e is (phenomenally) like. But there is, Tye maintains, a conceptual distinction between discovering a new fact and discovering what a new experience is like. Jones's post-operative revelations fall into the latter category. Since he does not acquire new facts as a result of his operation, his case presents no difficulties for the

19

physicalist; and neither, more generally, does the subjective character of experience.

We shouldn't get distracted by the validity or otherwise of Tye's proof that discovering what a new experience is like does not add to one's store of factual knowledge. (Nagel's own anti-physicalist case would be consistent with this belief.) Instead, I shall examine Tye's assumption that if Jones's post-operative discoveries are non-factual, then subjective experience does not present a threat to physicalism. Now I believe this is a very peculiar assumption indeed – more precisely that it is false. If we think of "factual knowledge" as the kind of objective information made available by scientific investigation, then *of course* Jones is not in possession of any new fact as a result of his operation because it is assumed, in setting up the thought experiment, that he already knows all that there is (factually) to know about sight pre-operatively. The scarcely surprising discovery that Jones does not learn any new *facts* when his sight is restored is damaging for Nagel's argument against physicalism only if it is interpreted as an argument about *factual knowledge*. But it is crucially *not* about such (objective, factual) knowledge, and therein lies its whole point.

That anti-physicalism does not require the subjective quality of experience to be itself a new set of facts is something Tye seems not to grasp. He cannot, however, be held solely to blame for this. For Nagel's own essay asserts that his "realism about the subjective domain … implies a belief in the existence of *facts* beyond the reach of human concepts" (1974: 437, emphasis added). These are facts that embody a particular point of view. Nagel's argument, later further developed in his book *The View from Nowhere* (1986),[1] is that scientific facts are precisely those facts that are *not* rooted in, or contingent upon, a particular point of view. Science, or objective knowledge, approximates to "a view from nowhere". I therefore feel uneasy about Nagel's use of the word "fact" in relation to the subjective character of experience and it may have been at least in part responsible for Tye's thinking that Nagel's argument can be answered by showing that, if post-operative Jones discovers no new facts, then subjective experience does not present a threat to physicalism.

Behind Tye's misunderstanding of Nagel – and even perhaps Nagel's lack of full understanding of his own position – is, I suspect, a deeper and more fundamental error based on an inversion of the relationships between subjective experience and objective factual knowledge. And it is this that makes Tye's essay particularly important, because this inversion is widespread. Its nature may be best shown by an even more ambitious thought experiment.

Let us postulate a twenty-sixth-century super-super-scientist who is not only blind but also deaf, dumb, having no sense of smell, and lacking proprioception and taste – in other words totally sense-less. Can we imagine that, despite these disabilities, it would be possible for him to have exhaustive factual knowledge of what his fellows with normal senses know so that when sense experience is made possible for him by a spectacular neurosurgical coup he learns nothing new? Of course not; for he would have no means of gaining pre-operative access to scientific, or indeed any, knowledge; his colleagues would have been unable to communicate with him. This illustrates a more general point I wish to make about the relations between subjective experience and knowledge.

While it is possible to conceive of an individual or organism having experiences in the absence of factual knowledge (enjoying "brute" or "low-grade" awareness, mere sentience), it is not possible to conceive of the opposite: to imagine an organism being knowledgeable in the absence of any sense experiences whatsoever. The inconceivability of my twenty-sixth-century super-super-scientist is an indirect reminder of the obvious fact that sense experience is a *precondition* of knowledge. This gets overlooked in single-sense thought experiments – such as Tye's one involving the blind super-scientist – where the missing sense may be bypassed, from the point of view of factual knowledge, by those that are intact. Such single-sense thought experiments give the misleading impression that subjective experience is something merely tacked on to, or at least additional to, factual knowledge.

And this is perhaps how Tye interprets the argument behind Nagel's original example – the subjective experience of a bat – since

Nagel's paper deals with a particular, although exemplary, area of knowledge/experience. When we are dealing with specific areas of the outside world, knowledge may precede experience. There are many – perhaps they are in the majority – cases where we *know* of something before we *experience* it. But the fact that we often know empirical realities "by description", to use Russell's term, before we have sense experience of them "by acquaintance" or unmediated presentation does not alter the overall priorities of factual knowledge and sense experience. Whether or not objective knowledge is a relative latecomer in human consciousness is uncertain; but what is certain is that it can be conceived as emerging only against the background, and out of, necessarily pre-existing sense experience. This is why my sense-less twenty-sixth-century super-super-scientist, infinitely knowledgeable about a world he cannot experience, is unimaginable.

Tye's demonstration that "a person who knows what it is like to undergo a characteristic experience of seeing red does not thereby know any further fact than a person who has all the relevant physical information" (1986: 16) actually *supports* the anti-physicalist case by reminding us that the subjective quality of experience is not something that is tacked on to knowledge as a supplementary store of facts: is not an additional piece of knowledge. To someone who already knows everything, the *experience* of what is known cannot count as more knowledge. But this only shows that experience is not the same as objective or factual knowledge, which is precisely what the argument from the subjective qualities of experience is all about and how the point of Nagel's paper should be interpreted.

It is important, however, not to fall into the mistake of thinking that subjective experience is merely something that goes beyond or, in some mystical way, "transcends" factual knowledge. Of course, subjective experience may seem to have this character when we are thinking of our knowledge of an entity, such as a bat, that has experiences of its own but which we approach through the lens of objective knowledge. We appear to be able to get closer to its subjective experiences, with our increasingly precise and detailed objective knowledge about its nervous system, as if by successive approxima-tions, but never actually reaching the goal of "complete knowledge" in whose tightly drawn net subjective experience can then be cap-tured. It was this view that Nagel opposed with his assertion that, however exhaustive our knowledge, we would never arrive at the subjective experience of an object of our knowledge such as a bat.

But an anti-physicalist who starts from the idea of the subjec-tive quality of experience as something that eludes knowledge has already conceded too much to the physicalist by *localizing* subjec-tive experience, so that it is either "out there" (as in the case of the bat) or a mere missing ingredient (as in the case of the blind or deaf super-scientists). Subjective experience, then, begins to look like a further territory (perhaps the last territory) to be captured by, for or in objective knowledge. But this is to see things upside down, for sense experience is prior to knowledge; it is the ground out of which knowledge grows. The idea of the subjective quality of experience either as something that at present lies beyond objective knowledge or something that can be captured in it is totally mislead-ing. Although Nagel is right against Tye – there *is* more to experi-ence than can be captured in objective science – both of them are wrong in seeing experience as merely going "beyond" knowledge. Experience is not merely "knowledge plus", something to be added on to knowledge.

The fundamental error – that of inverting the relations between knowledge and subjective experience – is widely subscribed to in both physicalist and anti-physicalist camps. Behind the arguments about whether or not subjective experience could become a domain of objective scientific knowledge – so that "experiencing e" becomes "knowing what e is phenomenally like" and the latter passes imper-ceptibly into "factual knowledge of e-like experiences" – is the idea that objective factual knowledge encloses subjective experience. Precisely the reverse is true. By making us aware of this, Tye has, as I suggested at the outset, performed the unwitting service of show-ing the real basis, and hence bringing out the true strength, of the anti-physicalist case and Nagel's contribution to it in particular.

Just how important these issues are has become clear in Nagel's most recent book, where he correctly sees that the difficulty physicalism encounters in making sense of consciousness and subjective experience is "not just a local problem, having to do with the relation between mind, brain, and behavior in living animal organisms, but ... invades our understanding of the entire cosmos and its history" (Nagel 2012: 3). That knowing everything there is to be known or could be known about a bat's nervous system and behaviour would not tell us what it is like to be a bat is something worth being reminded of.

NOTE

1. The argument for physicalists, and those who identify conscious experience with neural activity, has been made easier than it should be by allowing the notion of "knowing all there is to be known about the nervous system" to pass on the nod. Does knowing all that there is to know about the neurology of vision include, or automatically deliver, that which the visual system knows or is supposed to be aware of – which is clearly part of "knowing all there is to know about the nervous system"? Can we, by looking at a nervous system know what the owner of the nervous system knows? The answer is clearly no. A nervous system does not see a particular world unless it is embedded in a body with a particular history in a particular location in the world. In short, even if the nervous system were the entire basis of consciousness, it would still require a world to be conscious of and a body to pick out that world. The nervous system remains only one of two or more *relata*, the others including the world it relates to.

4

Does Rover Believe Anything?

Whether animals do or do not have beliefs is a more significant question than might appear at first sight. Beliefs are propositional attitudes (henceforth PAs) – indeed key ones – and I believe that they are not merely unique to human beings but are a central manifestation of what is fundamental to human consciousness, which I have characterized in an earlier book as "propositional awareness" (of which more presently; see Tallis 2005a). In this essay, I shall challenge two opposing errors: the first is that PAs in humans are not real entities but hangovers from a pre-scientific "folk psychology"; and the second is that animals have them. What motivates both errors is the desire to close the gap between humans and animals.

Most of the essay will be devoted to denying that it is valid to ascribe beliefs to animals. I shall begin with some of the standard arguments put forward by philosophers such as Norman Malcolm, Donald Davidson and George Graham. While these arguments are fine as far as they go, I do not think they dig deep enough. I shall therefore try to specify what is necessary for a creature to be capable of having PAs, identifying *the ability to propose explicit possibilities* as the key to having PAs. Possibilities go beyond the actual. I shall examine this in the relatively primitive or basic case of our intuition of material objects that are posited to transcend sensory experiences. I argue that this intuition – the ground floor of "propositional awareness" – is ultimately rooted in the existential intuition: the unique sense humans have of their own status as embodied subjects.

PROPOSITIONAL ATTITUDES

First a few words about PAs. This was a term introduced by Bertrand Russell. Examples of PAs are: my belief that this essay will make sense to those who read it; my desire that it should be enjoyed by those who read it; my hope that its arguments will be accepted; my intention that it should be as clear as possible; and so on. PAs are *about* the world: they have semantic content, although this may be at least in part implicit and certainly not fully verbalized. A PA is an attitude (thought, belief, intention, hope, desire, etc.) targeted on or *towards* a proposition.

As for propositions, they are horribly slippery things and I am sufficiently aware of the extent and depth of the philosophical literature they have provoked, and of the extent and depth of my ignorance of it, to wish to keep things very simple. I am going to dodge difficult questions about the actual status of propositions: how they relate to sentences, assertions, facts, and so on. This is in part because I believe that we shall never sort this out since these terms have had their own history and have grown up independently of each other. To vary Kant, "out of the crooked timber of human discourse no straight thing was ever made". But more importantly, I believe that what is significant about propositions is that they are manifestations of *explicitness*: they may be seen, when they are materialized in token sentences and asserted, to be the most developed form of a more general "propositional awareness". What matters for my present purposes is what might be called the "general form" of propositions.

In the *Tractatus Logico-Philosophicus* Wittgenstein characterized the general propositional form as: "This is how things stand" (1961: §4.5). I would prefer another way of expressing this: "That X is the case". Either way, the form applies more easily to some PAs than others: more easily to belief, knowledge and thought than, say, to intention, desire, hope, expectation and so on. Nevertheless I think it highlights something central to all PAs: their connection with the unique explicitness of human consciousness.

So much for proposition. What of the attitude? I have indicated the targeting of the attitude on the proposition by the word "that". Although, as I have indicated, I believe that the "that" belongs with the proposition, I separated it out to ensure that it is not lost. "That" is what is common to all kinds of PAs: my desire *that* something should be the case, my intention *that* it should be the case (by bringing it about, etc.), my hope *that* something might be the case, my knowledge *that* something is the case and so on. It is not surprising, incidentally, that "that" – which itself makes explicit the making-explicit of a PA – is lost in Wittgenstein's definition; and in much of the anti-psychological analytical tradition that he inherited from Frege and which he was so influential in transmitting – a tradition in which the philosophy of the concept dominated over the philosophy of consciousness. But that is another story and a big one (Tallis 1997).

Some readers may be uneasy with Russell's reworking of hopes, intentions and beliefs as PAs because it may be taken to imply that they are inextricably connected with language, more specifically with human language. This may seem to reduce any thesis about humans possessing and animals not possessing beliefs and so on to a banal reiteration of the obvious fact that animals do not articulate them, or not, at least, in ways that we might understand or recognize or be prepared to acknowledge.

The danger of this simplification is illustrated in the reason given by Malcolm in his essay "Thoughtless Brutes" (1972–73) for denying PAs – in this case thoughts – to animals: "The relationship between language and thought must be so close that it is really senseless to conjecture that people may *not* have thoughts, and also really sense-less to conjecture that animals *may* have thoughts" (1972–73: 17–18). Malcolm allows that animals might think but not that they have thoughts.

As well as raising all sorts of questions about whether it is possible to think without having thoughts or to have thoughts – or other PAs – without language, it does not address the deeper question: what is it about human beings that enables them to have language? Or, indeed, what language actually is. I do not, of course, deny the intimate relationship between PAs and language in the narrow sense: a PA is best captured, or most sharply characterized, in a sentence. Or, to put it another way, we know of no more precise way of discriminating a belief that is held or a piece of knowledge that is known than by casting it in sentential form. But this is not the whole story: as we steer ourselves through the world, we do not articulate all the beliefs that enable us to pass from one more-or-less-chosen situation to the next. Such "auto-pandiculation" would be incompatible with the normal business of daily life. To think this is how we operate would be to fall into the Cartesian trap, which Malcolm identifies, of over-intellectualizing daily life. Propositional awareness in the widest sense cannot be reduced to talk.

On the other hand, we have to be very careful when we loosen the connection between PAs and language. We might open the floodgates and allow all sorts of things – such as inarticulate, or at least unarticulated, pieces of behaviour that can be placed under certain descriptions – to count as expressions of PAs, or *implicit* PAs. The idea of an implicit PA (belief, knowledge, intention, etc.) parasitizes that of explicit PAs and it is the latter that wear the trousers. If we forget this and think of implicit, as opposed to explicit, PAs as the basic, paradigm, kinds of beliefs, we shall find ourselves at the top of a slippery slope, to which I shall return presently.

DENYING PAS TO HUMANS: FUNCTIONALISM

Neo-behaviourist functionalists, who aim to assimilate the mental and its contents to the behaviour of material organisms in a material world, don't like PAs because they seem to have phenomenal aspects: the *feeling* of thinking, believing, knowing, intending something. The fewer mental contents there are to eliminate, the sooner they can declare mission accomplished. They want to reduce minds to causal way stations between sensory inputs and behavioural outputs: internal discriminative states tuning outputs to inputs. This is, of course, only a first step to getting rid of them altogether. Since the same piece of behaviour could be explained equally well by invoking direct causal relations between input and output as by invoking causal relations between input and output *plus* a PA in the middle, the principle of economy, they believe, demands that we should dispense with the middleman, the PAs. PAs will give way to something more readily handled by biomaterial science, and will go the way of "vital spirits" and other intuitive pre-scientific constructs.

The reduction of PAs to causal intermediaries between inputs and outputs of the nervous system fails on several counts. First, it has not proved possible to explain or even describe very complex (i.e. ordinary, bog-standard, everyday) human behaviour without recourse to explicit PAs. For example, I have yet to see a plausible account of something like my visiting a friend in a neighbouring city that does not assume that my behaviour is steered by a variety of *explicit* beliefs, desires, and so on, the listing of which would take me many hours. In other words, the assumption that causal–neural accounts could explain how I could arrive at my friend's house – several months after he invited me to do so – assisted only by synaptic weightings that do not require a many-layered network of explicit PAs is just that, an assumption. It has become no more well founded for being endlessly reiterated for a quarter of a century or more. One of the key difficulties for the PA-eliminators is the absolute singularity of the goals in question: without my knowing what I am doing, why I am doing it and so on, it is difficult to see how I could have been brought successfully to this particular, chosen spot.

Second, there is introspective evidence that we do have PAs and that for the most part we are able, when challenged, to say what they are. The minority of occasions when we are self-deceived only serve to highlight the majority when we are not deceived: when we know what we are doing and why we are doing it. The further claim that the undeniable and irreducible phenomenal aspects of belief, knowledge and thought are the artefacts generated by introspection bewitched by language remains just that, a claim. (The connected assertion that the phenomenal aspects of PAs have no causal efficacy – that they are merely epiphenomenal – renders them totally inexplicable, and even more embarrassing for scientistic functionalism than if they had causal powers.)

Third, while PAs are necessary to steer our behaviour, they cannot be translated into the kinds of rigid causal relations between inputs and outputs to which functionalists would like to reduce the mind, because there is no fixed pattern of relationship between our PAs and our behaviour: no PA could be defined by a particular range of behavioural dispositions, independent of other mental states. This is particularly obvious in the case of factual beliefs or pieces of knowledge such as "The Battle of Hastings took place in 1066". What behaviour corresponds to this? Some have claimed that our belief that "The Battle of Hastings took place in 1066" *is* fully cashed-out behaviour. The behaviour in question includes most prominently our tendency to assert that "The Battle of Hastings took place in 1066" in response to the challenge to say when the battle took place. This desperate attempt to rescue neo-behaviourist accounts of PAs hardly deserves attention. Suffice it to say that it does not capture all, or only, the circumstances in which I might entertain the belief or assert it or choose not to. My very use in this essay of "The Battle of Hastings took place in 1066" itself illustrates the looseness of the association between beliefs (and other PAs) and patterns of behaviour. More broadly, the fact that we can mention or cite our beliefs as well as acting on them shows how far we are from being merely

in the grip of them or their boiling down to the tuning of uncon-
sciousness neural mechanisms linking sensory inputs with behavioural outputs.

In summary, it seems that functionalists are in the grip of a special
subtype of PA: namely, a pious hope. Ironically, the overall effect of
the attempts to eliminate PAs actually highlights what is undeniable
and irreducible about them, what makes them resist reduction to a
quasi-hormonal tuning of neural propensities to behave in a certain
way: namely, that they are *explicit*; that their phenomenal aspect is
no mere surface or trivial aspect of them; and that this cannot be
reduced to a link automatically fine-tuning the relationships between
sensory stimuli and discriminative behavioural responses. Indeed –
to anticipate a later argument – the dissociation between PAs and
any particular patterns of movement is connected with something
profound and important about them: that they are an expression of
the *loosening* of the connection between the conscious human and
the immediately surrounding material world. Functionalism tries
to conceal this, or wish it away, making of humans and beasts alike
organic machines effectively wired into their environments by their
nervous systems.

This is why it is important not only to be tough on functionalism
but also to be tough on the intellectual framework of functionalism.
The dominant, supposedly Darwinian, version of functionalism aims
to give an account of all living creatures, including human beings, as
being effectively plugged into their material environments in such a
way as to maximize the chances of replication of the genetic material. This – Darwinitis rather than Darwinism – supports a network
of beliefs informing evolutionary ethics, evolutionary psychology
and evolutionary epistemology, whose overall purpose is to natu-
ralize not only the human organism but also human behaviour, and
human consciousness.

And this brings me back to a point I made earlier. If you believe
PAs are important maps by which we steer ourselves though the
world, the bases on which we *lead our lives* as opposed to merely
living as animal organisms do, we must not allow beliefs to become

too implicit, to lose their phenomenal content. While it is important not to fall into the error of making linguistic formulation narrowly construed as a condition for having a PA – such that PAs exist only in so far as they are articulated – it is equally important not to relax the entry criteria too completely, otherwise they will disappear into the open maw of functionalist philosophers of mind waiting to assimilate them into a nexus of biological causes and effects.

ASCRIBING PAs TO ANIMALS

Let us now turn to a second strategy for eliminating the difference between us and beasts: namely attributing PAs to non-human animals. Crediting all sorts of beasts with, for example, implicit, unexpressed PAs is attractive to neurophilosophers because it downgrades PAs and the humans (including neurophilosophers) who have them. I shall presently argue that what distinguishes PAs from the kinds of things that functionalists allow humans to have is the "That", as in "*That* X is the case". The "that" which links the attitude with the propositional content of the PA is the most profound marker of the gap between human beings and causal nexus described in biology. Let us first address the standard arguments about animal beliefs and thoughts.

An important thread in the contemporary discussion of animal PAs begins with a story recounted by Malcolm in his essay. A dog is chasing a cat. The cat runs full tilt towards an oak tree, but suddenly swerves at the last moment and disappears up a nearby maple. The dog misses this change of direction, races past the relevant tree, and stops at the one the cat had seemed to be heading for. He waits at the base of that tree, barking. He is literally barking up the wrong tree. Are we entitled to claim that the dog is barking up the wrong tree because he has the belief, or even the thought, "*That* the cat is hiding in this tree ..."? For Malcolm, as we have seen, this description is unacceptable because of the intimate relationship between thought and human language. But this, as I have already remarked, does not dig deep enough for our present concerns. Malcolm does not ask what it means to say that a dog has no language. In the absence of such an account of language, his argument may be vulnerable to the objection that dogs do have a language of sorts; indeed, a language of barking, which, with the help of a good deal of implicit existential deixis, communicates that there is a cat up a tree. Some refinement of Malcolm's claim is necessary.

Davidson – whose agreement with Malcolm is signalled by his position "Thought requires talk" – suggested one such refinement in his 1982 essay "Rational Animals". If we want to say that an animal believes or thinks something, you must be able to say what it is that it believes or thinks. If you ascribe to the dog the thought or belief "*That* the cat is hiding in this tree" – if, in other words, you present it as a PA – you will, wittingly or unwittingly, imply that the canine is in possession of an entire network of beliefs and concepts that are linked with, and underpin, that particular PA. Consider certain *concepts* that make up that PA: "tree", "cat", "hiding", and so on. Now these concepts are manifestly rooted in general ideas that no dog could have. For example, the concept of a "cat" is not at all straight-forward and incorporates a good deal of knowledge that it would be absurd to attribute to a dog. PAs can be *individuated* only within a dense network of concepts and related beliefs: each belief implies, requires and is rooted in a world of further beliefs to give it specific content and distinctive identity. As soon as we claim that the dog has the contents of the PA corresponding to the sentence "The cat is up this tree", we find ourselves ascribing more than seems plausible to its canine mind.

This conclusion may be linked with the observation that there is no such thing as an *isolated* belief. Wittgenstein made this point in *On Certainty*: "When we first begin to *believe* anything, what we believe is not a single proposition, it is a whole system of proposi-tions. (Light dawns gradually over the whole.)" (1974: 21e, §141). Or, as Davidson expressed it, "the identity of a thought cannot be divorced ... from its place in the logical network of other thoughts" (1982: 321).

The argument that every individual belief is possible only as part of a network of beliefs, however, may seem vulnerable to a counter-argument, put forward by Graham (1998). It goes as follows. It is unfair to require a dog to be in explicit possession of all the components of a belief-network or all that is implicit in the components of a belief-network or all that is implicit in the concepts that make up a belief before we can grant that it really does have the belief that a cat is up a tree. After all, when *I* believe a cat is up a tree, my concept of a cat is quite blurred, as is illustrated by the fact that there are many things I do not know about cats in general and this cat in particular. I know very little about the taxonomy or metabolism of cats, or the number of hairs they typically have. As for the particular cat, Felix, up the tree, I might well be unaware of some quite fundamental things about it: its sex, its precise location in the tree, the identity of its owner, and so on. Nobody is going to suggest that I am unable to hold the belief that Felix is up the tree just because there are many things I neither know nor understand about cats and trees in general, or this cat and this tree.

While it is obvious that you don't have to have *all* this information in order to be in possession of the concepts necessary to put together the belief or thought that "The cat is up the tree", it is not possible to say how much one needs to know in order to be able truly to have the belief that "The cat is up this tree". Unfortunately, there is no principled way of separating those parts of the belief–knowledge–concept-network I need to have in order to entertain a belief about a cat and those that are quite unnecessary. It is not possible to identify a point at which belief vanishes and we have only inputs of stimuli and outputs of behaviour. I cannot, therefore, say with confidence that a dog lacks, while I have sufficient, background knowledge and understanding to be able to host the belief or thought that the cat is up the tree.

In fact, Davidson seems to have anticipated this argument in his essay, when he makes the following point:

There may be no fixed lists of beliefs on which any particular thought depends. Nevertheless much true belief is necessary.

Some beliefs of the sort required are general ... some are logical ... To have a single propositional attitude is to have a largely
correct logic, in the sense of having a pattern of beliefs that
largely cohere.   (1982: 321)[1]

Thus Davidson, the moderate holist. While we cannot place a clear
boundary to the nexus of beliefs to which a particular belief or PA
belongs – to say how much you need to know, understand and believe
in order to have a given belief – there will be a necessary conceptual
and epistemological hinterland around any belief and this will contain things that we could not expect a dog to know, understand or
believe. To press the point home, there is no way of characterizing
a dog barking up a wrong tree as having, and acting in accordance
with, a thought or belief without being drawn into ascribing to the
dog other parts of a network of PAs that would seem implausible.

Those who are wedded to the notion that animals really do have
PAs just like us may counter-argue as follows. Yes, it is obvious that
the dog does not have *explicit*, individuated thoughts such as "That
cat is up this tree": such thoughts would require talk. What Rover
does have, however, is a matted tangle of implicit, pre-linguistic
thoughts and beliefs woven into what the German philosopher-
biologist Jakob von Uexküll described as an *umwelt*. By treating
beliefs as *propositional* attitudes and so casting them in linguistic
or pre-linguistic form or exaggerating their proximity to language,
we are loading the dice against dumb animals: we are merely saying what Malcolm said – that "languageless means thoughtless". If
we refrained from formulating the dog's belief in human language,
which is inseparable from a nexus of knowledge and concepts, all
of which belong to a space of reasons, which extends infinitely in all
directions, might we not then be able to ascribe it to the dog without running into the problem of attributing to it concepts that lay
beyond the scope of its canine mind? Could we not, to revert to the
earlier view, be satisfied with the notion that beliefs and other PAs
are just as real if they are implicit in behaviour as if they are avowed
by someone listing them?

Unfortunately, once we accept that it is possible to have implicit beliefs in the absence of having *any* explicit – formulated, reflected upon – beliefs, we are at the top of a slippery slope, at the bottom of which lies a good deal of lunacy. (The coefficient of friction on the slope is reduced almost to zero by liberal application of what I have elsewhere called the "fallacy of misplaced explicitness" [see Tallis 2004c: 46].) It becomes possible to justify attribution of PAs to all sentient creatures: for example, to argue that the spider spins a web in the hope, belief, expectation and knowledge that this will trap flies and hence ensure its own continuing health and well-being. Indeed, we need not stop there. We could find ourselves being unable to resist seeing beliefs implicit in an amoeba's migrating along a certain pH gradient: it does this because it believes *that* this will promote its survival.

Since there is no defensible cut-off between implicit-belief-expressing or implicit-belief-steered behaviour, on the one hand, and simple behaviour on the other, it seems wise to withhold the attribution of implicit beliefs and other implicit PAs from creatures that do not also entertain explicit ones. The price of attributing PAs to animals that have no explicit, reflected upon or articulate PAs seems to be that of emptying the notion of belief and other PAs of any distinctive content worth having or defending. To this, functionalists – who happily slide down this slippery slope – would cry exultantly "result!"; but for those who can see what a disaster functionalism is, it is a warning to avoid the slope altogether.

CLARIFYING PAs: ON "THAT"

We need, in short, to find a way of characterizing PAs so that we can justify not ascribing them to animals without relying on the criterion of language to differentiate them, which latter would make the whole issue both more contentious and less interesting. In order to do that we need to look more closely at PAs.

Let us tease out their structure:

Attitude

(hope, believe, intend, know, etc.)

That

Proposition

(*X* is the case, might be the case, is something I shall make the case, etc.)

The part that tends to get overlooked is "that" and it is this that I want to spend much of the remainder of this essay discussing. Indeed, it is the heart of my concern; so much so that I would have called this essay "The Rediscovery of 'That'" or "Affirmative Action for 'That'" had it not seemed wilfully enigmatic. What "that" does is designate explicitness and this is easily overlooked; and importantly so because "that", I shall argue presently, marks the difference between human and animal consciousness.

The failure to appreciate the importance of "that" is evident in Malcolm's (1972–73) claim that "Animals think but do not have thoughts", so that:

It is OK to say that "The dog thought *that p.*"

but

It is not OK to say that "The dog had the thought *that p.*"

I believe animals neither think nor have thoughts; and that it is as illegitimate to say that "The dog thought that *p*" as to say that "The dog had the thought that *p*". Malcolm's position – which fails to restrict "That" to thoughtful humans and extends it to thoughtless brutes – betrays how he misses a fundamental point about the nature of PAs and about human, as opposed to animal, consciousness. It is captured in Davidson's assertion in his 2004 essay "What Thought Requires" that while some animals can learn many things, "they do not learn *that* something is true". The entire passage is worth quoting:

Animals show by their behaviour that they are making fine distinctions, and many of the things they discriminate we do too. They recognize individual people and other animals, distinguish among various sorts of animals, find their way back to places they have been before, and can learn all sorts of tricks. So it is important to reflect on why none of this shows they have propositional attitudes: beliefs, desires, doubts, intentions, and the rest. Dumb beasts see and hear and smell all sorts of things, but they do not perceive *that* anything is the case. Some non-human animals can learn a great deal, but they do not learn *that* something is true.   (2004: 136, original emphasis [but I would have put it there too!])

Beliefs, knowings, thoughts, hopes, desires all make certain states of affairs explicit. They all have the form:

"That X is the case ..."

attached to different degrees of certainty. More precisely, they have the form:

"That X is (or might be or come to be) the case".

This flags up how, at the heart of PAs, is the entertaining of explicit *possibility*: possibilities that might be the case (as in knowledge or belief); or might come to be the case (as in the case of hopes, intentions, fears, desires, etc.).

A proposition, after all, proposes something. In the narrow technical sense in logic it proposes that something (a predicate) is affirmed or denied of something (a subject); this is where PAs are most closely identified with concepts. But in the wider sense, it proposes a possible state of affairs that may already exist or be brought about. Crucially, that which is proposed *may or may not be the case*. Hopes and desires are more aware of this than beliefs and knowings. All, however, are subject to being tested and confirmed or refuted (or dashed, or disappointed) in the light of experience. To say this is to be reminded that the possible *exceeds* the actual. And the extent to which possibility is entertained, explicitly proposed, is the extent to which the conscious creature is uncoupled from the necessarily actual, material environment to which it relates. This applies equally to possibilities that happen to be realized – beliefs that are true, intentions that are fulfilled, hopes that are undashed, desires that are satisfied – as to those that are not realized. In either case, explicitly entertained possibilities are side by side with material actuality.

Let us momentarily go back to Malcolm's example of the dog chasing the cat. The initial temptation to attribute to it thoughts or beliefs, in short PAs – which Malcolm correctly disapproves of – is awoken by the fact that the dog is *wrong*. There seems, in other words, a disconnection between the dog's behaviour and the world; or a discrepancy between the actual world the dog inhabits (where the cat is in one tree) and the possible world in which the dog's behaviour would have been appropriate (where the cat is in the tree the dog is barking up). It is the dog's *error* that has seduced people into thinking that he is in the grip of a PA. We would be less inclined to say of a dog barking up the right tree that he is in the grip of a (true) belief. He is just chasing after a cat, which we can think of as instinct-driven and cue-directed rather than PA-steered. We are inclined to ascribe PAs to an actor when there is an uncoupling of behaviour from the environment; and while it is wrong to infer the PA in the case of the dog, it does highlight a fundamental character- istic of genuine PAs: they propose possibilities that, realized or not, are side by side with the actual.

PAs, PROPOSITIONAL AWARENESS AND POSSIBILITIES

The significance of propositions, of individuated possibilities pro- posed in PAs, whose connection with actuality is not guaranteed – indeed is entirely contingent – becomes apparent when we think, by contrast, of the picture of highest-level consciousness offered by functionalism. For functionalist philosophers, human beings are essentially organisms; their minds are identical with neural activity;

and they are wired into their environment exceptionally tightly because they are especially well adapted to survival. This "tightness of fit" model has been expressed with exemplary clarity by Paul Churchland, whose functionalist form of eliminative materialism is one of the best examples of what happens when Darwinism mates with neurophilosophy and Darwinitis results. According to Churchland, higher mental function expressed in intelligence is simply a means of ensuring that organisms are "more intricately coupled to the environment":

> If the possession of information can be understood as the possession of some internal physical order that bears some systematic relationship to the environment, then the operations of intelligence, abstractly conceived, turn out to be just a high-grade version of the operations characteristic of life, save that they are even more intricately coupled to the environment.
>
> (1988: 174)

According to this account, thoughts, beliefs, hopes, desires, intentions, plans and the like – all the characteristic manifestations of human intelligence – exist to ensure ever more "intricate coupling" to the environment.

It is difficult to see how this could be more wrong: it elides the gap that PAs open up, or mark, between the conscious human being and the world(s) of which he or she is conscious. Humans are uncoupled precisely to the extent that they are able to propose explicitly states of affairs that have only a probability or possibility of existing. And humans are, of course, perpetually engaged in entertaining possibilities – the possibility *that* X is, or might be, or might be caused to be, the case. It is this that justifies characterizing human consciousness as "propositional awareness", a supersaturated solution of possibility precipitating locally or focally into distinctive PAs that may or may not be articulated or individuated as full-blown propositions.

It is entertained possibilities – which in humans are often but not always articulated – that make what actually is the case explicit. The possibilities that are not realized form the contrasting background against which those that *are* realized are made visible. "That X is the case ..." is itself highlighted by a background of what is not the case. The latter is the necessary context for the *assertion* of what is the case; for saying "of what is that it is or what is not *that* it is not", to quote Aristotle's definition of truth (*Metaphysics* Γ 7.27, quoted in Blackburn & Simmons 1999: 1). "That", in short, opens up the space for both truth and falsehood; for affirmation, confirmation and correction; and for being right or wrong. It is in propositions that possibility is individuated to the point where it can be most specifically confirmed or corrected directly or indirectly by sense experience.

This has profound consequences. It is only within propositional awareness that there is the distinction between truth and falsehood; the distinction between appropriate and inappropriate behaviour is not enough. And we can connect this with another distinct faculty of humans: the capacity to doubt, to entertain doubts, to cultivate doubt and to engage in that "active uncertainty" elaborated whose most glorious manifestation is experimental science. Rover's not being able to doubt (which is not the same as mere hesitation) is the other side of his not having fully fledged beliefs.

Because the consequences are so profound, we are prompted to ask this question: what is it about human beings that makes them uniquely possessed of the ability to have, and be motivated and steered by, PAs? More precisely: what is it about humans that makes them such lavish entertainers of possibility such that what there is becomes "*That* which is the case"? In addressing this question in this essay I am conscious that I shall leave a vast number of trailing ends, which will look like unsupported assertions. And I shall have to glide over certain things that really warrant much closer examination and to allude to ideas that deserve more careful elaboration. I have dealt with the most important of them in more detail in a trilogy of books on human consciousness that readers may wish to look at (Tallis 2003a, 2004a, 2005a).

Given that *possibility* is the background against which what is the case become explicit in this way, what kind of creature is it that can entertain possibility? More precisely, what is it about human beings that makes them uniquely bearers of possibility? Given also that the scope of possibilities exceeds what actually turns out to be the case, what kind of creature is able to intuit, or be explicitly conscious of, specifically propose, what only *may* be the case and indeed may turn out *not* to be the case? More precisely still, what is it about us that enables us to have as objects of consciousness entities that exceed our sense experience with the remarkable consequences that flow from this? Here are a few: (a) even what does turn out to be the case appears as something that realizes a previously entertained possibility; (b) that of which we are conscious may be categorized as "true" or as "untrue" or as underpinning truth or falsehood; (c) seeming states of affairs are items that are the case and are susceptible to being confirmed, refuted or denied.

INTENTIONALITY, OBJECT PERCEPTION AND PAs

To take this further, we need to clarify the ways in which objects perceived, intuited or known by conscious humans exceed the sense experiences through which they are presented. In order to do so, we have to link the creation of possibilities with the intentionality or aboutness of PAs. In pursuing the foundation, or conditions, of intentionality, it is necessary to step back a little from the comparatively sophisticated intentionality of the propositional content of PAs and look at simpler forms of intentionality, such as those associated with the perception of material objects. In this way, we remove the discussion about PAs from arguments about the possession of language.

The argument that follows rests on two linked assumptions:

(a) that the "aboutness" of PAs is like the "aboutness" of object perception;
(b) that the fully fledged intentionality of human perception is an essential precursor of the intentionality of PAs.

The first assumption will, I presume, be allowed "on the nod". The link between the intentionality of propositions and of perception has often been made, and emphasized by writers such as John Searle, for whom it justifies treating the philosophy of language as a branch of the philosophy of mind (Searle 1983a). The second assumption, which is just as important for my argument that animals do not have PAs, may meet more resistance. The claim that the intentionality of PAs is ultimately rooted in more primitive intuitions connected with the intentionality of perception of material objects may seem questionable. To pursue this, we need to grasp what is common to both of them, which will enable us to dig deeper than language in considering human propositional awareness and by this means placing the claim that animals do not have PAs on a firm basis.

In both forms of propositional awareness – perceptions and more traditional PAs such as beliefs – we have an intentional object that is *proposed* to exist: *that* it is; or *that* it is the case. This requires further examination. Importantly, the intentional object is differentiated from, is other than, transcends, the conscious contents – the sensations or qualia – of the experiencing subject. Indeed, this is the very force of the "aboutness" or *of*. In the case of perception of a material object, the object is only partially disclosed through sensations; in the case of the propositional contents of a PA, the relevant object or objects may not be disclosed at the time that the PA is entertained – as when I believe, hope or desire something that is not present before me. It or they are present only in so far as they are proposed. In both cases – and this is the important point – *possibility* is opened up. While the object of perceptual awareness – let us say a material object such as a cup – is located partly in the space of possibility and partly in physical space, the intentional object of the PA is located solely in the space of possibility. To put this another way, in the case of perception the material object has sensible properties located in space and opens up possibilities that are not thus located: in the case of PAs the object is not located in space. The object of a belief or hope, for example, is located in the space of reasons; or in a realm of intelligibility that may be partly located in the future.

What is important for the present is that in the case of both perceptions and PAs, their intentional objects exceed what is given in sense experience. They are "proposed" to exist. This exceeding of what is given in sense experience – which begins with material objects – has been presented traditionally as a gap between what we think we know – our beliefs about the world and its contents – and our sense experiences. This gap has been a conventional starting-point for philosophical doubt about the scope of certain knowledge, as discussed in Chapter 1, "Seeing and Believing". In the past 250 years, the doubts have been targeted mainly on knowledge that exceeds sense experience, which has been seen as an incorrigible, if inadequate, foundation for knowledge. As David Hume argued ([1739, 1740] 1985: bk 1), since there is nothing in sense experience that directly reveals, say, matter (or substance) to us, so much the worse for matter. Our belief that objects continue to exist when we are not perceiving them, while it may be true, is a matter of faith. W. V. Quine echoed this discomfort when he said that: "Our only avenue of information about external objects is through the irritation of our sensory surfaces ... There is thus a wide gap between our data and our knowledge of the external world" (1969: 75). And Barry Stroud put it even more succinctly: "our knowledge of the world is 'underdetermined' by whatever it is that we get through that source of knowledge known as 'the senses' or 'experience'" (2000: 6).

All attempts to close, or indeed to deny, the gap have failed. Phenomenalism, the notion of objects as logical constructions out of sense experience and the supplementing of the receptivity of the senses with the spontaneous activity of the mind have all proved unconvincing. And importantly misconceived. For to remove doubt and close the gap between undeniable sensory experience and the world we think we know, we would have to remove *possibility* and leave only actuality understood as sensations that posit nothing other than themselves: that is to say would have no intentional objects. It would be to remove: the very conditions under which it could be asserted *that* anything is the case; explicitness; and hence the very conditions that, remotely, have made it possible to have everyday discussion about what is true and what is false. To try to close the gap between incorrigible sense experience (which doesn't claim anything about the world beyond itself) and corrigible beliefs or assertions *that* something exists or is the case is to fail to grasp the need for that gap, in order that there could be possibility and actuality, truth and falsehood, and the *that-is-the-case* of the contents of the world. Because sensations are incorrigible does not mean that they are above correction, but that they are beneath it. They have no truth-value; they do not assert or deny the existence of anything; they cannot be right or wrong. The passage from sense experience to belief-that or to what counts as knowing-that opens up a space – beyond the cognitive universe of wall-to-wall sensation – for possibilities that may or may not be realized; for things that might be the case or might not be the case; or for true or false assertions that propose possible states of affairs. No one can gainsay that I have a feeling of warmth. Dubitability starts when I attribute it the action of the sun on my arm – or, indeed, when I call the feeling "warmth". Or when I say to someone (in expectation that they will confirm my observation) *that* it is warm.

THE EXISTENTIAL INTUITION AND THE
ORIGIN OF FULL-BLOWN INTENTIONALITY

Even in material object perception, then, human consciousness overreaches itself by positing objects *that are the case,* that transcend it. What kind of creature proposes such objects and opens up the space of possibility where the actual is made explicit as the realization of a possibility? What kind of creature arrives at the idea of a reality that goes beyond what he is currently experiencing; a reality behind the appearance of objects; and a reality outside the current sensory field? Or (to declare my hand) why did man, uniquely, become the believing, doubting or knowing animal, informed by the intuition that there is a world that transcends what he senses? Answering this question takes us a long way back, to a point several million years ago when humanity forked off from other forms of animality.

In the first two volumes of my trilogy *Handkind* (Tallis 2003a, 2004a), I link the emergence of a unique degree of self-consciousness, other-consciousness and agency in humans to the possession of a fully developed hand, interacting with other biological features such as bipedalism and subsequent developments such as tools that are not assimilated into the body scheme. Irrespective of whether that Just-So story is true – I happen to believe that it is true – no one, I presume, will deny that human self-consciousness *is* uniquely intense, uniquely sustained and uniquely elaborated. Self-consciousness in us has evolved into a multiply layered, folded sense of self.

At the root of self-consciousness is what I have called the "existential intuition" – "That I am this ..." – analysis of which occupies the entire second volume of the trilogy (Tallis 2004a). The complement of "am", the "this", is, in the first instance – in newborn infants and, one may suppose, in early hominids – the engaged body, interacting in a meaningful way with the surrounding material world. Ultimately, the this that "I" "am" gets progressively more elaborated and enfolded and encompasses, for example, social roles and is subject to a variety of judgements by one's self and others as to the kind of thing I am. Let us, for the present, however, stay with the body as the primordial "this" that I am.

First of all, the existential intuition makes me obtrusively present: the body that I am sticks out like a warm, fat thumb in my sensory field. Not all the time, of course. We lose ourselves in what we sense, but we recover ourselves as well. Again and again, we find ourselves located in the field of our experience: I not only see but see that I am seeing, and see that I am seeing from a certain position or angle. This awareness, that is aware of my aware body standing in explicit relation to that of which I am aware, is an absolutely basic level of distinctively human awareness. In *The Knowing Animal*, I described this as indexical propositional awareness: it is awareness that points to itself (*ibid.*: §4.4, 106–17).

This explicit relation to that of which I am aware changes the nature of my awareness of it. That of which I am aware becomes an entity that is explicitly disclosed from a certain viewpoint *to* me through my senses: I am aware that it has a multitude of alternative appearances, as seen from different angles, at different times, under different conditions. This lies at the heart of our intuition, already discussed, of the objectivity of the object: that its appearance at any given time explicitly falls short of what it is, understood as the sum total of its appearances. Actual sensation is haunted by the John Stuart Mill's *permanent possibility of sensation* ([1865] 1979): there's plenty more where that came from. There is also something that exceeds all possible as well as actual appearances, such that any given appearance will be merely an *appearance* of the object.

This sense of an intentional object transcending the experiences through which it is disclosed is formalized in the concept of substance, which was later elaborated into the scientific conception of matter with its intrinsic properties. This bolder intuition, a more radical awakening out of sentience, to the intuition of something that is the putative ground of sense experiences, of all actual appearances, but is never entirely present in any of them, and could not be exhausted by any of them, is also, I want to argue, rooted in the existential intuition; and, more particularly, in the relationship the human being has to his or her own body. How can this extraordinary claim be justified?

While, following the awakening of the existential intuition, I *am* my body to a greater or lesser degree; my modes of identity with it are multiple. At any given time, there are: bits of my body that I simply or transparently am; bits that I suffer; bits that I possess; bits that I flaunt; and bits that I access indirectly (as when I catch sight of my face in a pool). More generally, we might say that I colonize my body with immediate awareness to varying degrees. I am very often my tongue bathed in warm saliva and never my bone marrow and am other bits to varying degrees at a given time.

This is the peculiar situation of a human being. While animals – lacking the existential intuition – are essentially sentient organisms, humans are subjects within their bodies, which they "am" to varying degrees and at different times. This variable "am" is not selective haunting of the body by a Cartesian ghost – an *à la* Descartes, as it were. It is the condition of being what Maurice Merleau-Ponty called an "embodied subject" (see Matthews 2002). As Merleau-Ponty emphasized, the embodied subject is ambiguous, and I have just described that ambiguous relationship the subject has to "its" body.

What does our peculiar, delightful, vexed relationship to our own body have to do with object knowledge, that is to say with our intuition of intentional objects that exceed and (systematically) elude the sense experiences that disclose them? Simply this: that our intuition of ourselves as living bodies that are only partly disclosed to us gives us an exemplar of a thing of which we are aware but which is incompletely exposed to us. It is an exemplar we live out. It is not surprising, therefore, that it is generalized to the notion of an external material composed of things that are only partially disclosed.

The inscrutability, or incomplete scrutability, of our bodies, I am arguing, is the basis for our sense of the hidden, of undeclared possibilities, that are the key features of our sense of a material world and its objects – of our indexical awareness and subsequently of the deindexicalized awareness instantiated in the propositional content of PAs – a content that is not understood as spatially located with respect to us. This feeling, along with the intuition that there are appearances always potentially at odds with reality, awakens our feeling of ourselves as knowers, in possession of forms of consciousness of objects that (a) actualize possibilities and which (b) may therefore be either true or false. In the case of material objects out there (including the bodies of our fellows), of course, inscrutability is more complete, if only because my sense of being *this* body underlines my sense of *not* being *that* body. The material obstance – to use the nice old-fashioned philosophical term – of physical entities out there is a projection of the cognitive impenetrability of the bodies that we both are and are not: bodies that we "am" and "am not". The inscrutability of matter is an intuition projected from the intuited inscrutability of that of which we are ourselves composed: of our ambiguous first-person being.

In some ways, this theory turns Arthur Schopenhauer's thesis in *The World as Will and Idea* on its head. Schopenhauer argued against Kant that we do, after all, have access to the noumenal world – the world of things-in-themselves as opposed to the phenomenal world of our sense experiences – namely, through the individual we ourselves *are*.[2] Whereas everything else is mediated to us through our senses and is presented as an idea, or a representation, that which we ourselves are is given to us immediately and consequently as what it is in itself: according to Schopenhauer as the will. I have been arguing precisely the reverse: our sense of being something that we are incompletely, of being a body that we both are and are not, gives us the intuition of an only partially scrutable world to which we have only indirect access, a world of possibility, in which we are capable of error. This is a world in which it is possible to have knowledge (and ignorance), and certainty (and doubt); in which there is space for falsehood and hence for truth; a world of incompletely transparent physical objects and forces: a world picked out by beliefs and other propositional attitudes.

Propositional awareness – the sense *that X is the case* – is inseparable from possibility and hence from the possibility of error. Illusions are cognitively offensive because we have the sense of a governing principle – matter and hidden forces, linked by laws – in accordance with which things cohere in a way that goes beyond mere successions of experience. As Quine once put it (although after this he and I part company): "illusions are only illusions by contrast with genuine bodies with which to contrast them" (1975: 67). For him this supports the case for a radical empiricism, part of which is a naturalization of knowledge and of human beings; for me, this is a case for seeing how knowledge – and knowledge of physical objects, the ground floor of propositional awareness – is something that always reaches beyond the sentience that humans share with all other creatures to something that no other creature possesses. The contrast between illusions and genuine bodies is the contrast between mere sentience on the one hand and, on the other, knowledge of putative objects. In judging something to be a stick – or a body with an independent reality – I am proposing more than I sense.

A LITTLE EMPIRICAL EVIDENCE

This, then, is the basis of the intuition that underlies the sense of possibility, of a world that exceeds sense experience, of a world that exists explicitly, of *That*. Is this peculiar to humans? Increasingly, the animal evidence suggests that it is. There isn't space to do justice to all the evidence, but the most compelling relates to research in our nearest animal kin, the primates (Povinelli 2003; Wynne 2004). Some of the most relevant work has been carried out by the primatologist Daniel Povinelli, who has demonstrated how chimps do not entertain the notion of the invisible. At the most basic level, they appear not to have the intuition that objects have intrinsic properties separate from their visible and tactile appearance. They do not have a full-blown sense of objects capable both of being perceived and of existing unperceived. Nor do they have the sense of hidden intermediary forces governing the connectivity of events; and have only an inchoate sense of the possibility of bringing things about, using causal connections (Wolpert 2003). They have the merest glimmers of the minds and viewpoints of others and do not point things out to each other, which is another reason for denying them the PAs whose propositional content is at least in part the produce of a community of minds (Tallis 2010). Their trial-and-error-shaped acquisition of practical skills is not driven by a notion of general, abstract principles in the way things come about.

Animals appear, in short, to have no fully developed sense of anything – not even physical objects – that transcends their own sentience. They are no more ontologically advanced than human infants and do not achieve the capacity of positing objects existing independently of themselves that humans have by the second half of the first year of life. This is linked with chimps' limited sense of being the organisms that they are, the faintness and intermittence in them of the existential intuition. They are living organisms but not embodied subjects.

Some primatologists believe that non-human primates have capacities that bring them closer to humans than Povinelli has suggested. Most notably, Josep Call and Michael Tomasello (2008), have argued that chimps ascribe beliefs to other chimps. However, they have admitted that there is no evidence whatsoever that they can understand that their fellows can have false beliefs. A world in which there are true beliefs but no false ones is like a world in which true exists in the absence of false; but, in the absence of falsehood, the notion of truth is empty. If animals are truly to have beliefs, they have to be able to entertain the idea that their beliefs might be false. There is no belief without the possibility of doubt.

CONCLUSION

I hope I have persuaded you not only that animals do not have the PAs – beliefs and the like – that humans have but that the reasons for this are rooted in the profound differences between our mode of consciousness, our way of being in the world, and theirs. These differences are founded on a sense of possibility; on a sense of the explicit existence of objects and states of affairs, beyond sense experience: on the sense *That* X is, or might be, or might be caused to be, the case. This is the underlying basis for the propositional awareness of human beings whose awakening out of sentience ultimately leads to sentences that express PAs. Man, the "knowing animal", unlike all the other sensing animals, is precisely a creature whose consciousness reaches beyond its phenomenal experiences. That is why he can get things explicitly (as opposed to merely behaviourally) wrong, not only barking up the wrong true but doing so in the belief that it is the right one; that is why he can doubt; why he can get things right; and why there is purpose in assertion and why there is denial.

And why, incidentally, we are comparatively free agents, incompletely wired by our nervous systems into the particular parishes of the material world that constitute our biological environments. Why we are offset from the physical world, operating in a logical space of possibilities that is distinct from the material or biological space of nature. Why, contrary to what evolutionary psychologists and epistemologists and ethicists, and other sufferers from Darwinitis, would claim, we are partly uncoupled from nature; being creatures in whom, as the German philosopher Schelling said, nature opens its eyes and sees *that* it exists.

I rest my case. If I am barking up the wrong tree, at least I hope you will acknowledge that the tree in question is a sequoia rather than a sapling.

NOTES

1. What is more, the network is, as Wilfrid Sellars (1956) pointed out, made up of pieces of knowledge, or belief, set out in logical rather than physical space; in a space of reasons rather than a sensory field.
2. The key ideas are: "Our *willing* is the one opportunity which we have of understanding simultaneously from within any event which exhibits itself outwardly, consequently the one thing known to us *immediately*, and not, like all the rest, merely given in idea", and the will "reveals itself to everyone as the in-itself of his own phenomenal being" (quoted in Gardiner 1963: 58).

5

Draining the River and Quivering the Arrow
Against the "Flow" and "Direction" of Time

The most radical expression of scientism is the claim that the last word on the nature of the world we live in is, or will be, spoken by physicists. One aspect of this is the belief that the truth about time is to be found in the fundamental theories of physics such as relativity (which seems to deny the reality of tenses) and quantum mechanics (some versions of which lose time altogether). A key step in the assimilation of time to physical theory – and its subsequent impoverishment – has been to reduce it to a dimension. I have argued elsewhere (Tallis 2012b) that placing time on a par with the three dimensions of space as the "fourth dimension" misrepresents it, howsoever useful this may prove for predicting and manipulating the material world (and I shall address this issue in more detail in a future book). The idea of time as a dimension analogous to space is particularly tenacious because temporal relations in science are universally represented as lines. For example, time is typically the x-axis on graphs portraying the unfolding of physical processes, and histories are presented as "timelines".

The metaphor is so powerful that it can live alongside other quasi-spatial images of time, even though these additional images are directly at odds with the very idea of time as a dimension. Time, we are told, flows; or, if it does not actually flow, is unidirectional, pointing one way rather than another. Thus the origin of the "rivers" and "arrows" of time. But flowing and pointing are odd things for dimensions to do. "Length", "height" and "breadth" don't flow; nor do they have a direction. While together they permit a movement to have a direction, in themselves they don't move or point one way rather than another. If spatial dimensions do have a "direction" it is simply a relative one in which each is at 90° to the other two.

These "dis-analogies" should, therefore, bring comfort to those who want to rescue time from the uncongenial company it has fallen into. Alas, no comfort is forthcoming from these dis-analogies because the distinctively unspatial properties ascribed to the fourth dimension – flow and direction – are illusory and I want to consider why.

We often speak poetically of the "river of time". This is clearly wrong because rivers, unlike the water in them, do not flow, otherwise maps would be continually out of date, with all rivers disappearing into the ocean. But couldn't time move like the water in the river? Let's leave aside the question – not as daft as it may seem – of whether "water" means all the water in the river or the water at a specific place, and focus on the more obvious problems. If time flows, what does it flow in? Stuff such as water flows in space, relative to other stuff in space (such as banks) that flow not at all or more slowly. This is clearly not something that time could manage: time could not flow in, or relative to, time in the way that spatially extended, located matter such as water flows between other bits of spatially extended matter. Besides, how quickly would it flow? The obvious answer – one second per second – demonstrates the vacuity of the very notion of "time on the move". Velocity or rate cannot have the same dimension on the numerator and the denominator.

Nevertheless, the idea of "flow" is irresistible. It gets a bit of a boost from the way the calendar makes us think of time in lumps. On Friday, my doctor's appointment next Wednesday is five days away. On Saturday, it will be only four days away. Wednesday, it seems, is coming nearer, bearing the dreaded appointment in its belly. Doesn't this show time on the move? No; in order for Wednesday to come a day nearer to "now", now has to move by a day towards Wednesday. Friday and Wednesday remain separated by an unchanging amount. So there is no genuine, or net, movement, unless we allow the peculiar and self-contradictory notion of time moving towards itself in two opposite directions.

There are other ways of retaining the notion of time as "dynamic" without resorting to an idea as self-evidently vulnerable as that of flow. For some, what is on the move is not time itself but "now", which picks out successive moments. With characteristic floweriness, George Santayana speaks of "the essence of 'nowness'" that "runs like fire along the fuse of time" (quoted in Williams 1951: 463). This only multiplies the problems of the dynamic idea of time. It separates "now" from time, in order that time-in-waiting can be picked out by "now" skipping along it. The notion of the present as "a moving spotlight", giving successive instants their instant in the sun, is even more problematic. It requires time to move in a dimension that is both distinct from itself and inseparable from it.

There have been many attempts to construct objection-proof dynamic ideas of time. Some writers have replaced flowing with "growing". Time is like a tree that gets bigger but overall stays in the same place. The present is "the growing tip" of time. This raises the question of what it is growing into. It can hardly be growing into the future, which doesn't exist until it has been grown into. Others think of time as "a growing block", reflecting the apparent observation that, as time "passes", there is more of it, preserved in an increasing accumulation of events. Every year that passes adds another year's worth of the Past. This, of course, confuses time itself with events that have happened in time, or rather with the record of them. The diary of my life will get fatter as I get older because more pages will be filled *and these pages can coexist.* The days in which the events happened do not, however, coexist, any more than the events themselves. So time does not increase like a growing heap of days and their contents.

There is a last-ditch position for those who can't entirely shake off the notion of the "passage" of time; namely, that although time doesn't actually move, it at least has a direction; that (unlike, say, a straight line) it is *asymmetrical*. Even when it is not moving, an arrow is differentiated into the head pointing to where it might be going and the tail marking where it has come from. This has prompted a search for the so-called arrow of time, to explain why there is an irreversible passage from something that was once future to something that will be past.

The basis of such arrows has been sought in overall trends in the physical world. The thermodynamic arrow reflects the fact that overwhelmingly we see a move from lower to higher states of entropy or disorder. The radiative arrow (probably another manifestation of thermodynamic asymmetry) is constructed on the observation that outgoing waves from a source – such as a pebble dropped on a still pond – are coherent whereas we do not see coherent incoming waves converging on a source. The supposed observation that an unknown, indeterminate future becomes a known, determinate past is the basis for the arrow of information expressed in a one-way accumulation of facts. The causal arrow draws on the fact that earlier causes bring about later effects but not *vice versa.*

All these attempts to derive a time-asymmetric world from the time-symmetric physical laws that govern it fail to deliver, as Huw Price (1996) demonstrates in his indispensable, magisterial study of this issue. This is a topic for another day, but it is sufficient for the present to note Price's rigorously argued conclusion that there is nothing objective about temporal orientation; if you take a genuinely atemporal viewpoint, time would not be asymmetric. To put this another way, finding directionality in time requires us to establish independently *in advance* that states of the universe are "earlier" or "later" before we could notice that, say, the universe has a temporal trend towards increasing untidiness as we move from one state to the next. We cannot ground time's arrow in something other than time.

It is not difficult, therefore, to demolish ideas of time that see it as dynamic or even unidirectional. And given also that "flow" and "direction" are actually at odds with the idea of time as a quasi-spatial dimension, it may seem surprising that they are so adhesive. Perhaps it is because they express something absolutely central to experience; what Donald Williams has described as our being "immediately and poignantly involved in the whoosh of process" which we then translate into "the felt movement of one moment into the next" (1951: 467). Time is, as it were, the inner whoosh inside the outward and visible whoosh of process and event. We project into time the dynamism of our restless universe and in particular the most fundamental and ubiquitous mode of that dynamism: motion.

This is not entirely irrational. Time can be seen as that which permits the universe to be restless; it permits change, by heading off the logical impossibility of parts of the world having two or more incompatible properties. An object cannot be at both position 1 and position 2 (let's leave quantum mechanics out of it for today) unless it is at position 1 at time t_1 and position 2 at another time t_2. So perhaps it is because time is the very condition of the possibility of change that we are inclined to ascribe to it the dynamism of change itself. This is, however, self-contradictory for many reasons. The most obvious is that, if time were not only the possibility of change but were in itself a change or in some sense changing (flowing or whatever), time would be required to make time possible.

Even so, the idea of the "flow" of time is difficult to shake off. Once we divide time up into parts – whether they are extended parts like days or notionally unextended parts like "nows" – we are even more inclined to ascribe the properties of the changing universe to it. Successive days, or successive "nows", or successive moments such as t_1 and t_2 borrow the character of events. The arrival of Wednesday noon and the arrival of my doctor's appointment seem like two comparable, even analogous, happenings. Don't we say, "And then the great day/the appointed time *arrived*"? And we reinforce the misunderstandings implicit in this idea of "times as happenings" with the calendric view, which makes days into event-containers moving towards "today" like cable cars towards the stop.

It is also difficult to shake off the ideas of "flow" and "passage" and "arrows" because we have no alternatives to replace them and our minds abhor a vacuum. The fact that time is not dynamic does not mean that it is "static": that, for example, the universe is really frozen and change is an illusion. Of course, there are many entities that are neither moving nor still; for example, prime numbers. (The seeming stillness of the block universe of the Einsteinian four-dimensional manifold, by the way, is, as J. J. C. Smart [1955] pointed out, only a reflection of the fact that it is an imagined sum-total of all events over all time. Nothing, no additional event, can, by definition, be added, to a total.)

If I seem to have taken what are only metaphors too literally, or too seriously, this is because we take them more literally and more seriously than we would like to admit. To break their spell, we need, as Wittgenstein put it in *Philosophical Investigations*, to teach ourselves "to pass from a piece of disguised nonsense to something that is patent nonsense" (1958: §464).

Nonsense they may be; but the dynamic metaphors are not entirely empty. The "passage of time" captures our sense of the loss of the past – passage is passing away – and of the implacability of change that propels us from birth to death, in respect of which we seem like logs on a river surging towards a cataract. Ridding ourselves of spatialized time, and quasi-spatial notions, therefore, requires constant vigilance against long-established habits of thought.

6

Mistaking Mathematics for Reality
Where Zeno Went Wrong and So Many Followed

Antisthenes the Cynic, unable to answer [Zeno's arguments against the reality of motion], got up and walked, deeming a proof by action more potent than any logical confutation.

(Elias, sixth-century commentator, quoted in Barnes 1982: 296)

Zeno put forward his paradoxes of motion in order to support the claim by his teacher Parmenides that movements (and indeed all changes) are logically impossible and hence illusory. As an illustration of the dire consequences of mathematical literalism – the belief that mathematical representations of reality are reality itself – it would be difficult to improve on his famous paradoxes. While they purport to demonstrate that there are paradoxes in our ordinary experience of the world, they in fact demonstrate that we should not imagine that mathematics tells us what is real and what is not. We should resist mistaking the mathematical image of aspects of the world for the reality beneath the way things appear to us.

I am running for a bus. The kind-hearted driver has signalled that he will wait until I arrive. According to Zeno, his kindness will be ill rewarded. In order to cover the distance between myself and the bus, I have first to cover half the distance; in order to cover half the distance, I have to cover half of half (a quarter) of the distance; in order to cover this ... Well, you can see which way it is going: *ad infinitum*. Since the process of halving (or dichotomizing) can continue forever, it would appear that I would have to complete an infinite number of tasks in order to cross the gap between myself and the bus. Given that it is not possible to complete an infinite number of tasks, I will never reach the bus. The driver will wait for me in vain.

Something has obviously gone wrong. After all, I usually catch the buses that wait for me. Zeno, however, does not even allow me to get started on my run for the bus. After all, to complete the first step, I have to complete half a step, and a quarter of a step, and an eighth of a step and so on. It's worse than that: not only am I stuck *at* the starting-point, but I couldn't get *to* the starting-point in the first place unless I was there already. This would remain impossible even if I were born in the very place where I started chasing for the bus, since my mother would somehow have had to get to that spot in order to give birth to me, unless she, too – and indeed my father – came into being at that point. A journey *to* a starting-point, therefore, is seemingly as paradoxical as the journey *from* a starting-point. And the driver, by the way, is in the same boat. He could not get to the bus stop to await me with thinning patience. In short, not only would the journey be impossible to complete, but it could not be set up as a task to be completed. If no one can get from A to B, nobody can get *to* A or *to* B either. (This is, of course, the result that Zeno, as an obedient disciple of Parmenides, sought. Not only motion between locations, but also separate locations, are banned by Parmenides. The universe is an unmoving, undifferentiated, indivisible, unified blob.) In Zeno's famous example of the race between Achilles and the tortoise, they could not meet to compete against one another.

The commonest way of dealing with the paradox is to suggest that Zeno made a *mathematical* error. He fails to notice that, as the distances to be covered are divided into smaller portions, the time taken to cover them also falls proportionately. As a consequence, although the number of portions of time into which my race for the bus can be divided is infinite, they belong to a converging series that adds up to a finite quantity. Let us suppose that I intend that my dash for the bus will take 10 seconds, then ½ the journey will take 5 seconds, ¼ the journey 2.5 seconds, ⅛ the journey 1.25 seconds and so on. As this series extends, it gradually converges on 10 seconds, even though the number of steps is infinite.

This mathematical solution does not deliver what is required. As Peter Cave says, "To converge is not to reach" (2007: 108). We could put this differently: not only does mathematical convergence not result in arrival, but it does not count as journeying at all. Mathematical convergence to a mathematical limit is not convergence on a particular point in space, such as that occupied by my bus. Zeno makes walking seem like a *mathematical* problem – one of completing an infinite series – by making real movement a matter of mathematics. The fundamental mistake is to think of locomotion as an act that involves, or even consists of, passing through mathematical stages. So the idea that Zeno's paradox can be sorted by getting the maths right is a mistake.

We should be alerted to the invalidity of mathematizing my dash for the bus by the fact that Zeno's take on travelling would yield the same number of mathematical steps irrespective of whether the bus was 10 metres, 100 metres or a million light years away: an infinite number. Every destination, however near or far, would have the same number of mathematical divisions. Not only could I not get closer to the bus if it involved accomplishing an infinite number of steps, but also the notion of "getting closer to the bus" would have no meaning because all distances would have the same number of components: every point would be an infinite number of steps from every other point. Zeno's argument undermines itself by collapsing the fundamental quantitative (that is to say mathematical) distinction between large and small distances. The gap between my index finger and my thumb and that between my index finger and a distant star can both be divided into an infinite number of fractional components. Spatial division infinitely continued leads to individual spatial points and the number of points in the line signifying any distance between two points is the same: namely an infinite number. In short, mathematics loses its grasp on real extension and, given that points are not located in space (since they do not occupy space; see Tallis 2012c), it has also lost its grip on location. One could even say that the mathematization of distance in this way has emptied it of actual spatial content, of space that can be inhabited, traversed or lived in. My running for the bus is in one place and the mathematical story is elsewhere.

What is more, if a distance were to be understood in mathematical terms, in other words to be *identical with* its mathematical description, then it would seem to be in conflict with itself: at any given moment, I would be "at" an infinite number of different descriptions of my location: say both ⅓ and ⅔ way through my journey, or a recurring decimal proportion of the distance, namely 0.3333333…, and so on. The source of all these problems is the failure to appreciate that when I walk, I walk through *lived* not mathematical space, *taking steps not fractions* (½, ¼, ⅛, etc.). That inhabited space is not mathematical is demonstrated indirectly by the fact that the completed journey could be described mathematically in an infinite number of ways (two halves, a million millionths, and quintillion quintillionths). If my journey were identical with any particular mathematical description, then I would seem to be doing many incompatible things at once.

The same observation applies to *times* as to distances. To hold your breath for a second you would have to hold it for half a second, a quarter of a second, an eighth of a second, and so on. It might be argued that *seconds* – unlike distances crossed – do not have to be *accomplished*: they happen of their own accord and a second will come to an end in a second without anyone's assistance. The mathematics of the action of holding one's breath, however, is the same: it can be dichotomized without end. The slightest pause has an infinite number of micro-pauses.

And the same mathematics applies to events other than actions; for example, to happenings such as the fall of stones. Or to other changes, such as the alteration of the colour of an object from red to green. The trajectory, presented as a quasi-mathematical, quasi-spatial distance to be crossed, would comprise an infinite number of intermediate places or states, discovered through the perfectly legitimate mathematical operation of division. Zeno would be happy with this, of course, because his paradoxes were intended to demonstrate the illusoriness not only of all motion, but of all change.

We should not look to more, or more advanced, or better, mathematics to solve a problem that has arisen as a result of an inappropriate mathematization of the material or lived world. Zeno's fundamental error is not due to his primitive mathematics but to a false belief that the space through which we chase buses, or the world in which changes take place, is mathematical so that the mathematical description of motion, or indeed of anything else, trumps the experienced or lived reality of it; that the failure to match a mathematical description of a piece of the world as we usually conceive it proves that we conceive it, indeed *experience* it, incorrectly.

This becomes evident when we consider the difference between mathematical steps and walking steps. Taking an infinite number of footsteps would be difficult enough but would be even more difficult taking each of those steps separately. The nimble-footedness required to keep within the bounds of one step at a time would be beyond my capability long before I got to divide the journey into an infinite number of discrete steps. I could not run (literally) into the mathematical difficulty Zeno envisages because I cannot help walking in strides rather than in indivisible fractions. As Cave puts it, "Divisibility differs from constitution and composition" (2007: 117). Zeno is guilty of "mistakenly transforming abstract fractions generated endlessly by mathematical rules into physical divisions that must be traversed when physically traversing" (*ibid.*: 119).

This is why attempts to resolve the paradoxes mathematically are misguided. "Don't worry," say the mathematicians, "a series can be infinite and yet have a finite sum. All those fractions – ½, ¼, etc. – simply add up to 1. More precisely, the series converges on '1'." Cave's retort that "convergence does not reach" takes us only halfway there, although it shows one deficiency in the mathematical "solution": we would still not get to the end of the journey; or indeed to the end of any journey, however small; so we effectively do not move. The same number of mathematical steps in a converging series would not bring us any closer, in terms of remaining mathematical steps, to the end of a journey of 1 mm than it would to the end of a journey of 1 or a 100 million light years. If I have to "converge" on a bus 100 metres away, I would have also to "converge" on the next stage in the journey to the bus 1 millimetre away.

But there is another way of making this point that bears more directly on the relationship between mathematical space and the inhabited space of our lives and actions. The infinite series that converges to 1 does not add up to 1 *actual journey* (or any number of whole journeys). The "1" upon which convergence converges is "1-anything". We have to add something in order to make "1" into a completed journey; into, say, "1 bus chase". We could add, for example, a unit of actual distance, for example "metres of pavement". Then the steps would no longer be purely mathematical steps but real steps or stages. My dash to the bus would be divided into 50 metres of pavement + 25 metres of pavement + 12.5 metres of pavement and so on, until we get down to tenths and millionths of metres of pavement, at which stage the issues of nimble-footedness would come in. And we can then see that the problem of the impossibly many steps of Zeno's paradox relies on their actually being taken (separately) despite being impossibly small. As Cave says of another paradox, Achilles and the Tortoise, "In some races, the smallest distance ... Achilles could run in his hobnailed boots may be one yard ..." (*ibid.*: 120). The mathematics of converging series could not capture the difference between walkable and unwalkable fractions of a journey. There is nothing in the maths to reflect the cut-off between steps that are large enough to be taken separately and those that are too small to be taken separately. What's more, the maths does not specify those that are too big to be taken as a single action – for example, the first 50 metres of a 100-metre race.

In short, to fall foul of Zeno's paradox in real life would require impossible things of us. Covering a journey one millionth of a metre at a time would need fancy footwork well beyond the limits of our ambulatory acuity. And it is no good Zeno arguing that one footstep is made up of an infinite number of fractions of a footstep because beyond a certain number of divisions, it is impossible to perform the resulting components separately. To quote Cave again: "What is and what is not possible with regard to abstract mathematical series do not carry over to what is and what is not possible in the world of wood, runs and restings" (*ibid.*: 122). So we could not get into the mess Zeno envisages: "That an infinite series can be summed does not mean that it can be walked through" (*ibid.*: 110) – or that it *has* to be walked through. Walking is not the completion of a mathematical series. The mathematics is a latecomer, applicable in some sense to walking after the fact, but not, as it were, retrospectively, exposing its true nature and consequently demonstrating its impossibility.

What Zeno reveals is not that mathematics proves the impossibility of movement through a finite space in a finite time – and hence of movement – but that mathematics does not capture movement. The mathematical description of space is not the story of lived space and our journeys through it. You cannot walk in mathematical space (or space-time); in such a space, we cannot start a journey never mind finish it; nor can we even get to the start of a journey from some other place; nor can we hurry or dawdle. In the actual world, we walk in strides not in mathematical fractions that are not fractions of anything. The walker is a living being, not a mathematical point making a mathematical journey along a one-dimensional line from one mathematical point to another.

Numbers – like mathematical points – do not of themselves specify real locations or real distances. They seem to do so only by borrowing locations from outside the mathematical scheme of things, by means of axes that have an implied frame of reference, an implied viewpoint, placed there by individuals with definite viewpoints. Without such an extra-mathematical implicit reference, the numbers do not count as locations or distances. This becomes clear when we think of mathematical locations. Consider a third of the journey in decimal notation: 0.3333333333 …. It is a point that has such precision that its mathematical description is infinite. But this is true of any mathematical point – for example 1 – which has no extension, no penumbra, no blurring.

And changes of (mathematical) locations would not count as movements. Under such circumstances, no object would have a definite location and the difference between movement in space and remaining still would be lost, which is what, of course, happens when we mathematize the entire world. The result is the unchanging space-time continuum: a conceptual totality of all that has taken place somehow added up, although observed from no viewpoint.

It will seem obvious that that cognitive *parvenu* mathematics – which appeared on the scene billions of years after animate and inanimate objects began moving – cannot retrospectively prove that the restless universe is in fact, and always has been, still: that no movement is possible. Instead, we conclude that Zeno's paradoxes merely demonstrate the limitations of mathematics or, rather, reveal what eludes mathematical description, namely actual events. From the standpoint of one kind of maths, all changes are the same: the seeming outcome of a convergent mathematical series adding up to "1" where "1" is the completed change, although this has to be specified *outside* the mathematics. Purely mathematical journeys are not real journeys: they have no purposes, of course; but neither do they have distances or duration or direction. And purely mathematical changes – changes that are entirely reducible without remainder to mathematics, to the passage, say, from one number to another – are not like any changes in the real world. This is why every change seen through the mathematical lens Zeno applied to motion in generating his paradoxes would be the same as every other change: consisting of halves plus quarters plus eighths and so on, or thirds plus ninths plus twenty-sevenths. They all share the same impossibility. My running for a bus, Achilles chasing after a tortoise, Zeno proceeding from the beginning to the end of an explanation of his paradoxes, the sun setting and shadows lengthening, or a stone falling towards the earth, would be equally caught up in the Parmenidean paralysis. By this means, Zeno has talked himself out of existence: he could not have come into being.

If we accepted the consequences of the paradox, the very conditions under which the paradox can arise, never mind be stated, would also be ruled out. This applies to the other well-known dichotomy paradox: Achilles and the Tortoise (rather similar to my trying to catch a bus, with a slightly less kind driver, so that it is very slowly drawing away from the stop). Achilles challenges a tortoise to a race but decides to give him a head start of 100 metres. Off they go and Achilles, leaving position A_1, attempts to reduce the distance between A_1 and the tortoise's starting position T_1. In trying to reduce that distance, he runs into the dichotomy paradox. Every reduction in the distance appears to require him to traverse an infinite number of fractions of that distance. However, the tortoise, too, is susceptible to the same mathematical paralysis; this therefore factors out and the race is back on. After all, while they all have to traverse the same number of mathematical distances, whatever distance Achilles has to cross, the tortoise will cross it more slowly. It is this difference that the race in real, as opposed to mathematical, space will pick up. But there is a twist in the tale: by the time Achilles has reached T_1, the tortoise will have moved to T_2 and Achilles has more work to do. But during the time he passes from T_1 to T_2 the tortoise will have moved to T_3. The creature will, it seems, remain permanently just out of reach: the tortoise's position will be something towards which Achilles approximates ever more closely but never reaches. Again, this would apply only if "catching up with the tortoise" were a mathematical rather than a physical operation. In practice, as Achilles gets closer to the tortoise, he will have increasing difficulty avoiding treading, or leaping over, the beast. There will come a point at which he cannot take a step small enough to avoid overshooting the target.

That this is obvious should prompt us to wonder how or why Zeno's paradoxes have exercised philosophers and mathematicians for so long (and, indeed, have had many fruitful methodological spin-offs). The confusion between mathematical steps and ambulatory ones, or between the movement in mathematical space and movement in real space is central to the paradox. It is an instance of the more widespread confusion between mathematical and physical space, at least in part rooted in the belief, already touched on, that mathematics reveals the ultimate truth about physical reality or, even, that mathematical objects are the fundamental stuff of the world or, at least, its primordial materials

There is something else at work behind the scenes here, in addition to the error of confusing mathematics and material or lived reality. This is a civil war within mathematics. Look again at the idea that completing the first half of the journey is a separate act from completing the second half of the journey; the first half of the first half separate from the second half of the first half; and so on. In short, it takes (a) space, (b) the mathematical representation of movements through space and (c) real live locomotion as all being *discontinuous*. The paradoxes arise not just because this is an unrealistic – or incomplete – representation of space but because it is at odds with another (mathematical) representation of space. Let us examine this.

When space, trajectories and real live movements figure in mathematics, they can be represented either arithmetically or geometrically. The geometrical representation of movement is a line that is manifestly continuous. Even if the line were considered as being composed of discrete points, those points are buried in the manifest image of the line. The arithmetical representation of movement, by contrast, is discontinuous, saltatory. The moving item passes from one position to another and the positions are interruptions to space: they are locations *in* it. The numbers that mark them are discontinuous: there is a gap between one number and the next. This is true, irrespective of whether the numbers are so-called "whole" numbers, integers, or whether they are fractions or even decimals. There is an obvious gap between 1 and 2; but there is an equally real gap between 1.1 and 1.2, between 1.11 and 1.12, and between 1.111 and 1.112, and so on *ad infinitum*. This follows from the fact that between any two neighbouring numbers, there is always room for another number. Consequently, numerical space, or space conceived through numbers, is also discontinuous. This suggests an alternative understanding of the aetiology of Zeno's motion paradoxes. While the consternation they cause is the result of confusing the mathematical representation of the world with the world itself, the particular form they take may result from a fundamental incompatibility between two kinds of mathematical representation of reality: geometrical and arithmetical.

In order to accept Achilles' problem, we have to imagine his journey as a line. In other words, we have to assume that real journeys are reducible to movement along a single dimension, which in turn reduces them to pure quantities. To put this another way: Zeno's paradox arises at least in part from our reducing real movements to that which can be extracted from them mathematically as a line. This line has no properties other than extension. Its location, and the actual experience of any journey – effort, sweating, stumbling, sense of purpose – are irrelevant. (That is why the paradox applies equally to Achilles or a falling pebble.) The second step is to rethink that line arithmetically as something that can be halved not merely in principle but in fact. It is broken up into distinct aliquots: halves that can be halved and halved and halved; thirds that can be trisected and trisected and trisected; and so on, right down to notionally indivisible points. There is a tension between these two views of the journey represented by a line: geometrical, which sees it as continuous (and it is portrayed as such); and the other, arithmetical, which sees it as composed of distinct, and hence as discrete, components.

This conflict between a discrete number system and continuous geometry, with the latter seeming to be closer to the perceived and lived reality of the world, has been characterized by Tobias Dantzig as "staccato" versus "legato":

The harmony of the universe knows only one musical form – the *legato*; while the symphony of number knows only its opposite – the *staccato*. All attempts to reconcile this discrepancy are based on the hope that an accelerated *staccato* may appear to our senses as *legato*.   ([1930] 2007: 176)

The greatest advance in the endeavour to get continuity – and continuous change – and hence change (given that, at the experienced level, all change is continuous) out of arithmetized reality is the calculus. But that still seems like a mathematical fiddle. The real world, of course, requires no calculus to be continuous. And the irreducible approximateness of any endeavour to recover continuities (such as continuous movements) from a mode of representation that is intrinsically discontinuous demonstrates that, while there is a mathematics of motion, motion is not itself mathematical.

The particular form that Zeno's paradoxes take is ultimately a result of the projection into the world of a domestic dispute within mathematics that treats an abstracted representation of movement in two ways – as a continuous line and as a (granular) series of numbers – and cannot reconcile them. They are incommensurate. Any given number is seen as being separated by a virtual space from any other number. To reiterate, this virtual space is realized by the numbers that can be interpolated between two neighbouring numbers. Between 1 and 2, we may insert 1.1, 1.2 and so on. And between 1.1 and 1.2 we may insert 1.1.1., 1.1.2 and so on. The process has no limit.

Let me end this discussion of Zeno's paradoxes by explicitly linking it back to our earlier reflections on the nature of spatial and mathematical points and the sin of taking them literally as locations. Zeno repeatedly divides the distance that separates me from the bus until it cannot be divided any further. That which cannot be divided – because it has no parts – is, of course, a Euclidean, or more generally a mathematical, point. There is an infinite number of these so, if my journey requires – as Zeno thinks it requires – that I visit each of them in turn, I will have to make an infinite number of visits. However, even if I were able to make this infinite number of visits, I would not make any progress. There is, by definition, no gap between points: any gap is filled by points. Passing through a point is no passage at all since, again by definition, there is no interval between the entrance to and the exit from a point. What is more, since points are not extended, ticking off an infinity of them would not add up to a finite distance crossed: an infinity of extensionless points does not add to any extension at all. This is betrayed by the fact that, if the infinity of points *did* add up to a distance, that distance would be as likely to be 10^{10} cm as 10^{-10} cm because we can extract an infinite number of points from any distance, large or small. The fact that they do not add up to one distance rather than another reveals that they do not add up to any distance whatsoever.

In short, dividing a journey into an infinite number of steps makes it no journey at all, even if all the steps could be accomplished. The treatment of the journey as an arithmetical transition that can be divided indefinitely, however, commits us to reducing it to an infinity of infinitesimally small constituents. Once we are embarked on the mathematical division of the journey, there can be no stopping until we have reached the unextended point. And we are embarked on this earlier than we may be aware. As soon as we think of the journey mathematically, as a line – which can by definition be divided – we are on the path to paradox. The original sin is to envisage the journey as a line and consequently as one-dimensional. This it cannot be because I the traveller – and my feet – are three-dimensional, as are all objects.

Real journeys are not reducible to abstract lines and there *is* a limit to the smallness of the steps anyone can actually take. Most mathematically possible fractions of distances are not ambulatory possibilities. After a certain number of divisions, we spill out of the mathematically defined path constrained by divisions. Hobnail-booted feet do not occupy mathematical points on a one-dimensional line and my position at any time is not a mathematical position. Mathematics crash-diets – and hence misrepresents – my position to an unextended point at the notional centre of the place I occupy; in fact, however, I am extended. I am inescapably located at more than one mathematical place at once: indeed, at an infinite number of mathematical places. Neither I, nor Achilles, nor a falling pebble is a mathematical point on the move. The very fact that we exist means that we are not zero-dimensional points moving along one-dimensional lines, although the mathematics that separates the journey (a line) from the one who journeys may deceive us into thinking this.

You may think that Zeno has anticipated this move and has another paradox up his sleeve to deal with it: the paradox of the Flying Arrow, which is extended (as I am), occupies space (as I do), but still does not move. Let us look at the arrow and ask why it is (fallaciously) supposed not to move.

At any given point in time, or instant, Zeno tells us, the arrow occupies a space identical with itself. It cannot, that is to say, exceed its own boundaries, cannot "put out" beyond itself. But, Zeno argues, the whole of time consists of instants; so the arrow must remain confined within the boundary it has at an instant. It cannot therefore fly. Since arrows *do* fly and St Sebastian did not merely die of fright (*pace* George in Tom Stoppard's play *Jumpers*), something must have gone wrong in our formulation of what is happening. What is it?

At the most obvious level, there is the problem of judging the velocity of an arrow at an instant. The notion of "instantaneous velocity" is perfectly respectable but it is not one that can be arrived at by dividing how far the arrow moves in an instant (that is to say in no time at all) by the time in question. It is obvious that an arrow cannot move any distance at all in *no* time. If it did, its velocity would be infinite. Any distance greater than zero travelled in zero time would give an infinite velocity and this would apply to all moving arrows, whatever their apparent speed. Velocity has to be measured over an interval of time. Indeed, if an arrow maintained a particular velocity over only an instant, which is to say over no time, one would say that it had not achieved that velocity at all. All that one can have at an instant is a position. The very notion of the arrow-at-an-instant is the product of a freezing glance and it is this that arrests the arrow in the position occupied by itself. The Flying Arrow paradox merely asserts that an object cannot occupy two positions at a given instant in time; or that it cannot get from one position to another in no time at all.

When mathematicians talk about instantaneous velocity, they are not really talking about movement in no time. In the case of uniform motion in a straight line, it is simply derived from the measured total distance travelled over a measured period of time. In speaking of "instantaneous" velocity, mathematicians are not mobilizing a self-contradictory notion that somehow manages to combine being *at* an instantaneous position with *passing through* that position at a certain speed. In the case of variable velocity (as in uniformly or non-uniformly accelerated motion), "instantaneous velocity" is an idea – an unreachable goal – of ever more precise tracking of velocity over smaller and smaller intervals of time to the point at which inaccuracies are unimportant.[1]

Instantaneous velocity, therefore, is a very useful notion but must not be taken literally as a measure of the velocity *at* an instant. An arrow has a *position* at an instant but velocity requires something definite (extended) on the denominator: a period of time exceeding an instant. Instantaneous velocity must not be thought of as something derived from, or requiring, movement of the arrow in a zero period of time, for any movement in zero time would be at (the same) infinite speed. All velocities *at* a literal instant are the same: zero distance units divided by zero time units. Instantaneous velocity is something that can be tracked with ever increasing precision but the result is not a measure of velocity sampled at a randomly chosen instant (no time at all) but a measure of velocity over ever shorter periods of time.

The flying arrow seems to be at rest only if we consider it at, or over, a period of time – zero – too short for anything to take place. Its stillness over zero time does not translate into stillness over any period of time more than zero. Its seeming paralysis is the result of merging the notion of *at* a time (when the arrow occupies a position) and *over* time (when it occupies a succession of positions). We could express this distinction by noting that the flying arrow does not *maintain* stillness, it does not *keep* still. It is not still over any actual stretch of time. Not moving in an instant, over no time at all, does not count as *staying* still. Both instantaneous velocity and instantaneous stillness (zero velocity) are contradictions in terms.

The flying arrow flies, given time; and it is given time because it does not have to put together time out of instants. If we fail to grasp this, it is because our conception of an instant – a mathematical artefact – hovers from between "no time at all" and "a very tiny stretch of time". If we are inclined to think of an instant as a vanishingly small stretch of time that has not completely vanished it is because we are able to allocate it a location and, as is the case with spatial points, we think that something that has a location must somehow lay claim to one place rather than another: it has a toehold, even though it has no toes or indeed anything else. We can specify an instant as a value of "t" in a coordinate axis. The instant at which $t = 2$ is a mathematical conception. Like spatial points, temporal instants (moments, points) exist only as numbers in a coordinate scheme.

Although this was not his intention, Zeno has done us the service of demonstrating that the notion of a point in time is a purely mathematical construct and maths, unlike arrows, does not move. More generally, he has reminded us – if we needed reminding – that mathematical space is not the space in which you and I and Achilles and arrows and pebbles move and have their being. Mathematical space is a world of spatial and temporal points made visible through numbers that have no intrinsic extension, even less mobility. That is why it can bring movement to a halt: the result Zeno wanted to obtain on behalf of his master Parmenides.

The fact that, according to Zeno, a change such as standing up from sitting down is as impossible as lifting oneself up by one's bald head at a speed greater than that of light, should lead one to conclude that Zeno has nothing to say about the real world. (For a discussion of this, see Tallis 2012c.) He might have been happy with this, arguing that what we take as the real world is an illusion. This, however, would then eliminate science, which is full of moving bodies, as well as the deliverances of common sense, as a source of truth. Since Zeno gives logic (or his version of it) the last word, it follows that if things cannot move in theory, they cannot move in practice. The wrong counter-argument is to say that if we can walk in practice, there must be something amiss with the theory. The better counter-argument is to say that theory is not the last word because, if it were, there would be no word (and hence no theory) since speech, too, requires movement.

The broader conclusion we may draw from Zeno's paradoxes is that we should not confuse the mathematical representation of change with change period. The apparent problem of demonstrating motion mathematically does not mean that motion is impossible but that the mathematics of motion is not identical with, or constitutive of, motion. We should not confuse mathematics, which captures an aspect of things that cannot stand alone, with the things it refers to.[2]

NOTES

1. If we move at an apparently constant velocity of 2 mph, the instantaneous velocity will be 2 mph. In reality, velocity will always vary, however slightly, from moment to moment even when it is thought to be uniform. The more closely you look at it the more change you will see. And the shorter period of time over which it is observed, the more constant the velocity within that period because of the limits on the rate of acceleration or deceleration. We could imagine that a velocity that is sustained roughly over an hour could be sustained more precisely over a minute, even more steadily over a second, even more over a millisecond, even more over a nano-second. (There is less time to change velocity even in the case of accelerated motion.) So we are licensed to imagine an "instantaneous" velocity that absolutely constant over a moment. (Thus the theory of infinitesimals: dx/dt is unchanging, and in a straight line, or near as dammit, over the period under consideration. But neither dx nor dt is zero, a distance corresponding to a spatial point over an interval corresponding to a temporal instant.)
2. In "The Perception of Change", Lecture 2, Henri Bergson argues that Zeno's paradoxes arise out of confusing indivisible movement with the space traversed by completed movement. This is not quite right. The confusion is between continuous movement on the one hand and on the other a line purporting to represent that totality of the movement – with the beginning and end present simultaneously – that is open to endless division because it consists ultimately of points. For Bergson, the division between discontinuities and continuity is the difference between the intellect, which breaks up the unfolding of the world into frozen moments, and intuition, which feels them from within as smooth and unbroken.

7

Could the Universe (Even) Give a Toss?

A little while back, at the Hay Festival of Literature and the Arts, I gave a talk "Has Physics Killed Philosophy?", arguing that physicists need philosophers. Afterwards, I had a conversation with a remarkable man, Raja Panjwani, who, in addition to being trained in physics and philosophy, is an international chess champion. We got talking about one of the most striking and disconcerting features of quantum physics: the replacement of causation by probability. At the subatomic level, the last vestige of "*A* causes *B*" is replaced by patterns of events whose statistics can be predicted with stunning precision, although – outside the "many worlds" interpretation of quantum mechanics, in which *everything* happens in some world or other – no *particular* quantum event is obliged to occur. However, there is a constraint on the frequency of certain outcomes within a given range of values over large numbers of events, this frequency being what the most famous quantum equations predict. Raja, perhaps sensing that I was getting out of my depth, turned the conversation to the staple of probability theorists – the tossing of a coin – which subsequently provoked the thoughts that follow. The confusions, I am confident, are mine, not his.

When you toss a coin, there are two possible outcomes: heads (H) or tails (T). (In the real world, of course, it is possible that a coin could land on its side. When we use the example of coin-tossing in discussions of probability, we are talking of ideal coins.) No outcome should influence its successor: there is no influence exerted by toss 1 on toss 2, as there is, say, from the movement of the thumb to the movement of the coin. The chances of H on a particular occasion are therefore the same irrespective of whether its predecessor was H or T. Improbable sequences – such as a hundred straight Hs – do not defy or even bend the laws of mechanics. But if the outcome of toss 1 does not influence the outcome of toss 2, such that there is no gathering pressure for a T to follow a long run of Hs, why don't we easily accept that the series H, H, H, ... could be extended indefinitely? Why would an unbroken sequence of a hundred Hs raise our suspicion of a bent or even two-headed coin?

Let us look a bit more closely at the properties of a genuinely random sequence. As we extend the series of tosses, the number of possible patterns increases enormously, but the *proportion* of those that are significant runs of Hs or Ts are vanishingly small. There is a one-in-four chance of HH (the other possibilities being HT, TH, and TT), but twenty-five Hs in succession would be expected to occur by chance only once in 33,554,432 throws. The longer any run of Hs or Ts, the less frequently it will occur; so the most likely outcomes will be those in which runs of Hs or Ts are soon broken. This is how we reconcile the 50–50 chance of getting H on a particular toss, irrespective of what has gone before, with the growing suspicion that appropriately greets a very long series of Hs and the mounting expectation of a T. While all outcomes are equally rare, not all are equally interesting. Twenty-five Hs in a row is no rarer than a mixture of Hs and Ts, but is more salient to human interest. Hence our suspicion.

This is all basic stuff; but let us dig a little deeper. We'll start by focusing on the expectation that has been the ruin of many a gambler. The key point relates to the *history-so-far* of Hs. It is this history that makes us feel that the coin sooner or later will feel obliged to come up T. We must not, however, see the history-so-far as a kind of pressure bringing about affirmative action for Ts, so that they match the number of Hs: a history of coin-tosses is not in itself an event, even less a cause. Random *sequences* do not have the kind of reality, even less the causal efficacy, that individual events have. A sequence, in short, is neither an event nor a cause that can influence what follows it. This may seem counter-intuitive, but it's true, because 50–50 equipoise or symmetry is an intrinsic property of the (idealized) coin, and that's not something affected by its history.

What makes a sequence seem like a cause is our subjective expectation, which turns a lengthening run of Hs into the idea of a kind of pressure to produce a T. Our expectation is, however, in no sense a force "out there". Rather, as David Hume pointed out in *A Treatise of Human Nature* ([1739, 1740] 1985), our habits of expectation often translate "how things usually turn out" into "how they are obliged to turn out". (But see Chapter 8, "Causes as (Local) Oomph".)

While it is clear that our subjective assessment of probability is not "out there", we still retain the idea of there being objective probabilities "out there" based on the expected relative frequencies of certain kinds of events or sequences of events. However, even understood in this way, probabilities cannot entirely shake off their mental dependence. This is because a *sequence* of events is not "out there" in the material world.

Firstly, it is only by remembering past tosses, and gathering them up into a series, that we are able to place actual sequences into a fraction with a denominator corresponding to the sum total of possible sequences – a 1 in 33,554,432 chance of twenty-five tosses all turning up heads, for instance. Moreover, collecting tosses for the sequence will require ring-fencing of the population we are drawing from: the series we have just started, or all the tosses in the history of the world, or something in between. It is the gathering together of tosses that tells us that certain combinations ought to be common or rare, so that we should expect them to occur frequently or infrequently. But the present existence of no-longer-existent tosses is entirely mental. They are not even present by proxy as a *cause* of a present state of affairs, because, as we have said, toss 1 does not have any influence on toss 2. (Probability exerts no causal pressure. Frequencies have to be in place in order for probability to emerge. Probability, however, feels like an explanation because we retroject frequencies observed *post hoc* into a kind of *ante hoc* force that brings them about.)

What's more, coin tosses have had to be shorn of their material features and classified simply as H or T in order to be gathered up into a sequence that feeds the calculations of probability of what we think is going to happen in future. Importantly, those future possibilities have to be defined as the branches of a fork, as the mere instantiation of the logical alternatives "H" or "T". This crash-dieting of a physical event to one of its characteristics also warrants further examination.

Any actual coin-toss must have numerous features additional to, and irrelevant to, the dichotomy H or T: when the coin lands head up it does so via a unique trajectory, and is propelled by a unique force to a particular height, to land on the ground, all courtesy of a particular individual. None of these additional elements counts as a criterion for H or T. But in order for there to be an H, a toss has to occur, and any actual toss will have to have more characteristics than simply being H. Without these additional features, the coin couldn't land *either* H or T. Furthermore, for the coin to fall either H or T, something has to be bent in order to break the 50–50 equipoise or symmetry between H and T: not the coin, but necessarily the event. (Since nobody is bending the outcome, no caller has an advantage, so the ethics are not bent: contingent influences are inescapable, but that's okay if they're hidden and cannot be manipulated.) But this only highlights the fact that describing any particular toss as H or T is stripping it of numerous features necessary for the full-blown event to happen: to *be* an H or a T. More broadly, material events in a material world cannot be reduced to forking branches of possible outcomes; just as a victory for a football team like Arsenal is not just a featureless "V(ictory)" as opposed to a featureless "D(efeat)".

Any particular toss that instantiates H or T will have a vanishingly small probability of occurring as that specific event. Actual events, specified precisely in advance, are highly improbable. The circumstances that produce a real event, even a little one like a coin falling H, are in fact unique, because each event, each instance of H, has unique characteristics. The more fine-grained the description of an event, the more the improbability of that event increases. If events had a million either/or features, and each of the features had a 50–50 chance of happening, then each event's individual probability would be $\frac{1}{2}^{1,000,000}$, the denominator being a number greater than that of the number of atoms in the universe. And there is no principled limit to the grain of the description, as no description captures an actual event completely. However, this uniqueness and improbability applies equally to all Hs and all Ts – any actual H is as unlikely as any actual T – which is why H and T are equally likely to occur. In short, probabilities apply not to specific actual events but to *types* of events – reduced, in the cases of tosses, to the dichotomous possibilities H vs T. The mathematics of "either H or T" applies only to a future reduced to branching logical possibilities: a material future reduced to a logical one.

While the 50–50 chance of Hs and Ts is built into the job description of coin-tossing, its realization – and the apparent pressure for it to be realized – is in events that are in possible *futures* reduced to either H or T. In addition, the *past* also has to be *present* in the gathering up of these strictly stand-alone events into a (retrospective) series pointing to this prospective future. The mobilization of all three tenses of time – which do not have a foothold on the material world – itself betrays that with probabilities we are a long way from the material world. Material events are what they are, and not what they were or will be.

In short, the mathematical logic of probability deals with events crash-dieted to forks of logical branches, and draws on retrospective and prospective views that have no place in the material world. Could this be a source of some of the problems quantum mechanics has with change? When causation is replaced entirely by probability, defined logically or mathematically, there is no obligation for anything in particular to happen, because actual events – macroscopic, real events like real coin-tosses – are beyond the reach of probability. A 50–50 chance of a type of event such as H is not a 50–50 chance of any real, messy, fat event corresponding to a coin toss. The latter is necessarily more than logically defined possibilities (although it can be logically reduced to one such), more than tines in a dichotomous fork, and real events do not exist in sequences that encompass past and present.

Many physicists trying to unite probabilistic quantum mechanics with general relativity lose time and change altogether, instead envisaging a frozen four-dimensional universe in which nothing happens. Physicist Carlo Rovelli has even welcomed the prospect of quantum mechanics becoming "a theory of the relations between variables, rather than the theory of the evolution of variables in time" (2008: 1): in short, a theory of the eternal relations between kinds of possibilities rather than between actual events in time. If this were correct, we would be justified in concluding not only that the universe couldn't give a toss about us, but that it couldn't give an actual toss. The lack of contamination by actual events is the necessary condition of the purity of a mathematical vision of the world based upon probabilities. As mentioned, a minority of physicists invoke a "many worlds" version of quantum mechanics, in which every fork of possibility is taken. This seems a very expensive way of melting a universe frozen as a consequence of replacing causation with probability. It may be why a few physicists now think physics needs philosophy; although many more would add "like a hole in the head".

8

Causes as (Local) Oomph

The law of causation ... is a relic of a bygone age, surviving, like the monarchy, only because it is erroneously supposed to do no harm. (Russell [1953] 1992: 171; later in life he was more sympathetic to the notion of cause)

It is easy to sympathize with those philosophers who have come to regard causes as, well, a lost cause. The venerable idea that everything that happens is *caused* to happen by other, previous happenings – going right back to the first cause, the mysterious uncaused cause (God or the Big Bang, according to taste) that got happening to happen – has been under increasing attack for nearly a quarter of a millennium. While it has fought back valiantly – mainly by redefining itself – things are looking pretty bad for the (efficient) cause.

There are many reasons for this. They include the fact that "cause" is a rather slippery concept that serves a multitude of explanatory needs. (And this is true even if we confine ourselves, as I shall do in this essay, to physical causes, bypassing questions about historical, social or mental causation.) It draws on a several overlapping inchoate notions. Among them is the idea of (material) necessity: that how things are is how they had to be. Material (as opposed to logical) necessity has a rather complex and unhappy relationship with natural laws as they are usually conceived, not least because those laws betray their contingency in the seemingly arbitrary values of fundamental constants built into and derived from them. While a

higher-level law may seem to be an explanation of a lower-level one
– so-called "nomological subsumption – at any given level of generality, we still have an appeal to a naked uniformity: "Things happen like this because they always happen like this". Or the principle
of precedence, in accordance with which "Nature tends to repeat
itself". If this repetition is not obvious – and novelty seems to be
the order of the day – this (it is assumed) is only because of our
epistemic limitations, which prevent us from seeing past superficial
differences to underlying similarity. Causation is woven into our idea
of automatic *mechanisms* that ensure what happens shall inevitably
happen. And the notion of a cause is also appealed to as that which
has the power to bring things about. The fundamental attraction of
the idea of causal efficacy is that it holds an explanatory promise in
which powers and reasons, raw energy and intelligibility, converge.

At any rate, there are numerous untidy intuitions behind the
notion of causes as explanations. To get to the bottom of this, we
need to reflect on why events require explanations or, more generally, why happening needs something else to make it happen, and
why this something else should be prior happenings – in the last
analysis *immediately* prior happenings. By this means we shall discover the origin of the felt need for causal explanation: namely, that
it lies in the relationship between conscious subjects and the physical
world and the role of such subjects in creating localities in the latter, which otherwise lack them. The idea of causation is an attempt
to heal the fragmentation, indeed granulation, of the physical world
arising out of the irruption into it of explicit, enduring subjects with
their points of view and their knowledge that partially transcends
their individual points of view. Before we arrive at this conclusion,
there is a good deal of ground to be covered.

PSYCHOLOGIZING CAUSES

The most famous attack on the link between causes and effects as
a necessary and universal connection and on the belief that causes

are fundamental constituents of reality, intrinsic properties of the material world beyond the mind, was David Hume's reduction of the causal relationship to expectations:

> In reality, there is no part of matter that does ever, by its sensible qualities, discover any power or energy, or give us ground to imagine, that it could produce any thing, or be followed by any other object, which we could denominate its effect. ...
>
> (Hume [1748] 1975: 64)

> It appears, then, that this idea of a necessary connexion among events arises from a number of similar instances which occur of the constant conjunction of these events; nor can that idea ever be suggested by any one of these instances, surveyed in all possible lights and positions. But there is nothing in a number of instances ... except only, that after a repetition of similar instances, the mind is carried by habit, upon the appearance of one event, to expect its usual attendant ... This connexion, therefore, which we *feel* in the mind, this customary transition of the imagination from one object to its usual attendant, is the sentiment or impression, from which we form the idea of power or necessary connexion. (*Ibid.*: 75)

If we have observed that B has always followed A, he argues, we come to believe not only that (i) B will in future always follow A but that (ii) B *must* follow A because A causes B; that, if A happens, B cannot help happening as it will be brought about by A. It will also follow that, other things being equal, if A does not happen, neither will B. Our experience, which exposes us to patterns of events in the universe, forges mental habits that turns what is in fact a matter of the contingent succession of one thing after another into something that feels like causal necessity. It may even feel like a *rational* sequence: if A is always followed by B, then it is unthinkable that B will not follow A and if it is unthinkable then the relationship of A and B feels necessary – irrespective of whether or not it is – and has a sufficiency of reason. The reflection of the patterns of the events to which we are exposed in our mental habits turns what is a mere matter of the contingent succession of one thing after another into a universal law: if B in our experience invariably follows A, we intuit that it will always follow A because the latter has the power to bring B about. There is, however, no basis in experience for extrapolating from experience hitherto – however extensive – to experience in the future. Only necessity could guarantee universality and there is nothing in experience to show that the way things turn out is how they will always, how they must, turn out – "that the course of nature continues always uniformly the same" (Hume [1739, 1749] 1985: 137).

There are problems with analysing causes as mental constructs. The most obvious is that it seemingly draws on something that it denies: a real causal relationship that cannot be assimilated into the mind, because it is between the material world and the mind of the subject. Hume effectively presupposes the reality of a cause-and-effect relationship connecting the *experience* of B-always-follows-A with the *idea* that B necessitates A: the stable pattern of events, the constant concomitance of A-type and B-type events, *causes* our sense of necessity. In other words, Hume sees our notion of causation as being itself a mandated (mental) effect of a non-mental cause. What's more, since causal necessity is apparently universal – all human beings see it at work throughout the universe – this body–mind causation is a manifestation of a (universal) causal law.

There is an additional difficulty: how do we ground the seemingly valid distinction between pairs of events that are causally related and those that are merely constantly associated, as would be the case if they were successive parts of the same process (as in stretches of the flight of a flying arrow) or if they were time-staggered effects of a common cause? More generally *post hoc* requires something more to justify being regarded as *propter hoc*. "B always follows A" is not sufficient to make A in our minds a sufficient reason of B. It is implausible that the difference between "one damn thing after another" and the relationship between a flash of lightning and a clap of thunder has no objective reality and is entirely cooked up in our minds. The painfully acquired methods we have developed to distinguish causation from mere succession, however tightly correlated – and to expose seeming causal relationships as accidental associations – suggest that this difference is real: that there are justified and unjustified expectations.

Nevertheless, Hume's critique was profoundly damaging. It was a key element in the empirical tradition – unhappy with the idea of "hidden powers" – that he inspired. But it also provoked a different kind of reaction that led to idealist philosophy. Kant accepted that the idea of a necessary causal relationship between events could not be directly observed:

> The very concept of a cause so manifestly contains the concept of a necessity of connection with an effect and of the strict universality of the rule, that the concept [of cause] would be altogether lost if we attempted to derive it, as Hume has done, from a repeated association of that which happens with that which precedes, and from a custom of connecting representations. (Kant [1781] 1964: B5)

He appreciated the profound significance of this and was stung into a radical response. Yes, there was no justification within experience for the imputing of a necessary connection between cause and effect, nor could there be. Mere observation of contingent associations could not be an adequate basis for *universally* valid objective laws (extending beyond, necessarily local or limited, actual experience) and of true necessity linking events. Empirical rules of association would not provide the very cornerstone of our sense of a coherent world. Hume was right in one respect: causation as a necessary connection was indeed contributed by our mind; but this was not a mere effect of experience on the mind. It was an aspect of the *a priori* intellectual structure of experience, of pure understanding: the necessary connection of perceptions was the very ground of possibility of experience, underpinning our sense of a coherent world. Causation, like space and time, was necessary for the unification of perceptions to deliver a sense of a unified world – the phenomenal world of both everyday experience and of science – populated by material objects and operating in accordance with physical laws. Subjective perceptions become objective knowledge by their "*necessary* unification": the condition for there being experiences of an "outside" world accessible to all and everyone and ultimately to a science that would reveal the world as a connected reality going under the name of nature.[1] In short, Kant was at one, therefore, with Hume in the latter's view that the sense of causal necessity as "the cement of the universe" could not be justified in or by experience; but for Kant this was because it was that in virtue of which experience held together sufficiently for the very notion of justification to have any meaning.

Kant's view of causal necessity (and of space, time and substance) amounted to a world picture that many have found deeply unattractive. The noumenal reality hidden behind the veil of phenomenal appearance was unwelcome to the empirical spirit that Hume has done so much to foster in philosophy and beyond the English-speaking world in the centuries since his death. Less costly ways of rescuing some aspects of the notion of causation – of seeing what it might mean, given that the idea of an intrinsic "power" or "necessary connection" between events is seemingly untenable – have therefore been sought.

CAUSATION DISPLACED BY STATISTICAL PROBABILITY

A more modest notion of causation is one in which A (the cause) does not *make* B (the effect) happen but simply increases its probability of happening. The strength and salience of A *qua* cause is reflected in the mathematical measure of the extent to which the probability of B's occurrence is raised. This is reflected in the strength of a statistical correlation between type A and type B events, which is more or less resistant to changes in circumstances, helping to distinguish between causally related and causally unrelated sequences.

This mathematization of cause is a halfway stage to the complete replacement of causation by probability. More recently, and most importantly, physical science – to many, including many philosophers, the ultimate authority on what is really there – has discarded causes entirely in favour of statistical probabilities at the subatomic level. The "smallist" assumption that the nature of the physical world is defined by the properties of its smallest components meant that causation, rejected by quantum mechanics, must also be expelled from our picture of the world entirely. All we have is the brute reality that nature has the habit of repeating herself. This is expressed not in a guaranteed definite (local) effect of a definite (local) cause but in a constant statistical distribution of data. If you measure the location of an electron orbiting, say, a hydrogen atom you will not get the same individual results each time but a spread of results that will remain constant over time (I owe this way of expressing the idea to Joe Boswell).

The image this gives is of a universe that is true to its habits without being *obligated* to this fidelity to itself by causal pressures requiring B to follow A. There are many reasons why this is unsatisfactory (see Chapter 7, "Could the Universe (Even) Give a Toss?", in this collection for some of these). The one that is closest to the concerns of this essay relates to the question of whether or not we can retain anything of the idea of a cause if we empty it of the idea of necessity. For at the heart of our intuitive sense of cause is something that goes beyond mere timeless or eternal habits of the material world: it is a kind of *pressure* that the past applies to the future; that what is now happening is obliged to do so by what has already happened, and what is happening now will oblige what will happen to happen next. This sense of cause as a kind of *power*, and causation as the transmission of power, is missing (not always by oversight) from several alternative accounts. Let us look at one of these before we reflect on why we think we need this, or something like this, to make sense of the unfolding of the universe.

CAUSES AS COUNTERFACTUALS

Consider what is possibly the current front-runner among philosophical accounts of causation: the idea of causes as counterfactuals, first suggested by Hume and developed by John Stuart Mill but most particularly associated in modern philosophy with David Lewis (1973). The theory has been developed with great sophistication but at its heart is the idea that event A is to be identified as the cause of event B if it is true that, if A had not happened, B would not have happened: a cause is something that makes a (salient) difference to what happens. While the discussion of counterfactual theories of causation has tended to focus on token or singular events, rather than types of events, the patterns seen in types of events underpin ascribing causal connections between singular events. We are justified in saying that A caused B if we can say with confidence, on the basis of repeated observations, "If A had not occurred, B would not have occurred".

One of the challenges facing the counterfactual theory is that of establishing a secure basis for the difference between causes and conditions. It is accepted that causes as counterfactuals operate against a background or causal field. If I had not been in London (A), I would not have been knocked down by a London bus (B). It is perfectly obvious, however, that A is a necessary or background condition of B but not a sufficient condition of it, rather than a cause of B. The vast majority of people in London are not being knocked down by London buses. Many events additional to A or, more precisely, many existing states of affairs, are required to ensure that B happens. The counterfactual theory does not offer a satisfactory basis for singling out the event that counts as completing the prior conditions to make B inevitable. Not that this is a problem peculiar to the counterfactual theory. As Mill argued, "Nothing can better show the absence of any scientific ground for the distinction between the cause of a phenomena and its conditions, than the capricious manner in which we select from among the conditions that which we choose to denominate the cause" (1846: 198, quoted in Schaffer 2013), a sentiment that has been echoed by many philosophers since.

This, however, highlights the fundamental problem with counter-factual theories of causation. Conditions are, as it were, permissive rather than active: a mere platform, a passive stable background upon which the cause can stand, which positions the cause to bring about its effect. The failure to offer a satisfactory distinction between causes and conditions underlines how counterfactual theories are rather negative. "If A had not happened, B would not have happened" is equally true where A is a static or stable background condition of my being injured (such as my being in London) or something that looks like a cause (such as my colliding with the bus). To say of an event A that its absence may result in another event B not happening does not seem to capture the feeling, germane to the idea of a cause, that it should be something that brings something about.

The counterfactual theory, that is to say, seems too remote from the admittedly naive – but nonetheless stubborn – intuitions upon which our idea of cause is based, and which makes us protest against Hume's reduction of cause to our sense of causation and our sense of causation to mere mental habits. The counterfactual theory lacks what causes seem to bring to the party, namely the *oomph* to bring about events. Without this, the privileged relationship between a cause (as opposed to mere conditions, etc.) and an index event that is identified as its effect seems to remain undefined. Various attempts to modify the theory will seem unsatisfactory for a fundamental reason: that it is a *negative* definition of cause. If we set aside the idea of causes as *pressures* obliging their effects to occur – the necessity in the necessary connection between events – we may as well give up on the idea of cause entirely.

This intuition of causes as pressures is most readily realized in the notion of an impetus – energy, momentum, velocity – imparted from one item to another, evident in the push–pull, moving-billiard-ball vision of the physical world, in which one moving object runs into another and donates something to it of its own motion; of causal power as being instantiated in the transfer of momentum or energy or both from one object to another object, in accordance with the law of the conservation of inertial energy. Object A collides with object B (cause) and A slows down and deviates a bit (effect 1) and B is set in motion (effect 2). The movement of object A seems to have within it the (causal) *power* to bring about the movement of object B.[2]

The question we now need to address is where this intuition comes from and why we have the feeling that events won't happen unless they are caused by previous events. Whence, in short, is the origin of this notion that *an event is always made to happen by other events;* that happening *has to be made to happen by prior happening.* What is it that underpins our notion that the universe is, or has to be, self-driven by its own contents, so that what takes place at time t_1 shapes what takes place at time t_{1+n}? Kant, as we have discussed, had his answer: it lay in the structures of understanding necessary for our perceptions to add up to a coherent, shared, public world. There are other possibilities. One of the most important is our sense of ourselves as actors in the world. Let us now look at this.

CAUSATION AND MANIPULABILITY

A popular analysis of our intuition that there are causal powers driving the world forward is that it is deeply connected with our ability to make, or prevent, events from occurring, to make happen things we want to happen. We are allowed to think of A as the cause of B if an agent could bring about the occurrence of B, or at least increase its probability of occurring, by bringing about the occurrence of A.

Let us examine this theory as a halfway house to the fundamental reason behind our causal sense; between locating causation within ourselves – so that we are as Georg Christoph Lichtenberg called us "the cause-seeking creature" ("Man is a cause-seeking creature; in the spiritual order he could be called the cause-seeker. Other minds perhaps think things in other – to us inconceivable categories" [quoted in Berlin 1956: 276]) – and what it is that underpins our notion that the universe is self-driven by its own contents at time t_1 shaping its contents at time t_{1+n}. This, the manipulability theory, sees causes as being defined by "handles" for manipulating what happens or, more precisely, bringing about effects.

It has criss-crossing connections with the counterfactual theory (lucidly teased out in Woodward [2013], to which I am greatly indebted). If A is the manipulation (I clap my hands) and B is the manipulated result (you wake up), then A is a cause of B (your waking at that moment) because, had it not been for A, B would not occurred. Rooting causal ascriptions in our powers of manipulation, however, deals with one issue that the counterfactual theory does not seem to cope with: namely, defining what it is that separates causes from conditions or from other conditions – the viewpoint-dependent differentiation of foreground from background. According to the agency theory, that which can be, or ought to have been, manipulated in order to bring about a desired event is the cause and the rest is background. The desired event or effect is the basis for picking out the cause. So clapping my hands stands out against the rest of the universe at the time at which this event takes place because it is linked to the result that is required and which is also singled out from the universe: namely, your waking up. In other words, the desired effect picks out the cause by highlighting the set of events that can bring it about and by selecting, within that set of events, the particular ones that I can influence, and then by selecting within that subset the one that I have chosen.[3] What counts as cause and what counts as effect single one another out: the desired effect confers salience on the cause.

This view of causation is attractive because it is importantly connected with many things, notably the allocation of individual responsibility for significant events. It captures the intuitions that are mobilized when, for example, we consider issues of personal blame and legal liability. When we think of the cause of a crash, we tend to focus on circumstances that are unusual, such as a slippery road and poor visibility. But when we look for salient causes we pay particular attention to circumstances that are both unusual and avoidable so that they could or should have been avoided: carelessness, drunkenness or sleepiness in the driver. This in turn reinforces the connection between the ideas of causation and of agency or liability: causes are events we can and (if they are importantly desirable or undesirable) *should* change. That is why when I look for the cause of your waking up, I focus on something that some*one* does or allows to happen. (For example, not keeping the children quiet or forgetting to close the curtains.)

The translation of causation into manipulability, however, is attended with difficulties. The most obvious is that many events that count as causes are not *done* by anyone and perhaps could not be done. You might be woken up by the contractions of your bladder, not by something that I, or even you, might do. (Of course you might use this phenomenon to ensure that you do wake up early by deliberately not going to the toilet last thing at night in order to be able to count on a full bladder to act as your morning alarm: a high-risk strategy perhaps but a viable one and a striking reminder of the subtle ways we use the biological givens to our human ends.) We shall return to this. But let us look more closely at causes that I can exploit.

Supposing I bring about B (waking you up) by doing A (clapping my hands). How do I bring about A? Doesn't A itself have to be caused to happen? In other words, the notion of causation seems to extend beyond the relationship between a manipulation and that which is manipulated. In order for me to clap my hands, certain neural activity has to take place and I do not *do* them. What is more, the internal relationship between manipulator (hand-clapping) and manipulated (you waking up) appears to have embedded in it many causally related elements, many intermediate steps with their causal connections, which are hardly brought about by my agency. They tend to get overlooked, indeed are effectively invisible, because they are below the level at which the (causative, agentive) action and its intended effect are described. They are nonetheless just as real as the coarser-grained interaction between my hand-clap (seen as a single event) and your awakening (also seen as a single event). In order for the sound of my clapping to wake you up, the air between my hands and your ears has to vibrate and there has to be a certain kind of response in your brain. I *do not* do any of these things either. The things we *do* are riddled with things that merely *happen*, that are, it appears, seeming effects of seeming causes.

The spaces between the deliberately enacted or "doing" component of actions and their (merely) happening element are filled by mechanisms, some of which have been teased out by natural science. In other words, there is a large element of any actual manipulation that is not itself authored by agents – and indeed is unknown to them – even though they depend on the kind of certainty we associate with causal connections. What is more, agents rely on their actions having guaranteed consequences beyond the reach of their manipulations: I do A in order that B may happen so that C will happen. Agents can set things in train and beyond this it appears to be down to non-agentive causal mechanisms. The causative action controls only a limited part of its (desired) effects. Part of this reliance of agency on mere happening is the knowledge that the effect will be proportionate to the cause – perhaps based on the law of conservation of mass-energy or more generally a law that some quantity is conserved in the passage from cause to effect – although provision is made for the amplifying or damping effects of the conditions in which the cause is operating. (This is one of the points of connection between the laws of nature and moral luck; at any rate, it is another way of highlighting the intimate relations between causes [and effects] and conditions.) And where the effect is on a conscious individual (as when I wake you up) what succeeds this intended effect is related in a much more complicated way to the cause.

These are the most intimate challenges to the manipulability theory and they are perhaps more damaging than others that its critics have tended to focus on: namely, that there appear to be causal relationships between events where no agency is, or even could be, present. The limited reach of manipulation, and the fact that the scope of manipulations falls short of the scope of what we usually consider to be causal relationships, is a powerful objection. Causes seem to operate outside the territory that is potentially exploitable for the purposes of controlling the way things unfold. While it is true that, if A causes B, I can bring about B by bringing about A or prevent B by preventing A, it seems odd that causes should be defined as, or restricted to, a distinct class or subset of material events that are defined by our powers (enhanced by our knowledge and knowledge-based technology) to change the world. Part of that oddness is that it makes the scope of causality dependent on the range of our powers.

More generally, there seems to be a problem with rejecting causation outside human agency, or the practical or theoretical possibility of such agency. It defines causation in too anthropocentric a way that would withhold applying the notion to, say, the interactions between planets prior to the emergence human beings, or prior to the development of the relevant technology, which lie beyond human agency. For example, few of us would doubt that the gravitational forces operating in the early years of the universe were responsible for shaping the planets and that, if we accept that there is such a connection as causation, this should qualify, even though there could be no possibility of any agent being present to influence it. While it is not *logically* impossible to think of an agent having a manipulative role in the first million years of the universe, it is a matter of fact that no agent could, as it were retrospectively, visit those years to shape what happened.[4] As James Woodward (2013) has put it:

> If the only way in which we understand causation is by means of our prior grasp of agency, then it is hard to see what could justify us in extending the notion of causation to circumstances in which manipulation by human beings is not possible and the relevant experience of agency unavailable.

Such extrapolation to the universe at large would seem to be a serious case of magic thinking on the part of the species *Homo sapiens*, if not the philosophers trying to tease out the origin of our causal sense.

There are many ways of dealing with this objection, the most popular being the so-called "interventionist" versions of manipulability theories, according to which an occurrence can count as an intervention, and hence as a cause, even if it does not involve human agency, action or intention. For an event to count as an intervention, however, it would have to have been picked out by another event, which counts as its effect. But without the idea of human agency – or human wishes, needs or aspirations – there would be no basis for picking out the relevant event.

Most unsatisfactorily, the manipulability theory of causation seems to give agency independence of, or priority over, causation. And this is assumed even though it is accepted that the operation of our freedom is limited, its limits being defined in part by the laws governing the interactions between our bodies as physical objects and the world as a physical system. It makes it difficult to understand how there could be a subgroup of events that can be manipulated, a subgroup that can be expanded by pooling our powers either directly or via technology. This exacerbates the puzzlement often expressed by philosophers that we can exercise agency at all: that we can redirect the course of events in what is frequently described as a "causally closed" world. How can we, or our wishes, alter anything given that we and they are the effects of causes whose origin lies beyond our very existence, never mind our control, unless whatever it is that occasions our actions is somehow sealed off from the causal net?

We can now turn the question on its head. This is a good moment to anticipate the thesis of this essay. Our freedom not only requires that we can rely on a causally connected world – so that when we do A, the B we expect from previous experience *must* follow, other things (conditions at both ends of the cause–effect pair) being kept constant – but has the same source as our causal sense, the very feeling that our freedom is constrained. This sense of our freedom, as something limited or constrained, far from being the marker of a world closed against our manipulation, is the result of an opening up of the world of an embodied subject in the material universe, of the irruption of conscious selves into unconscious reality, of points of origin, of centres, and of localities in a reality that otherwise has none of these things. Causation and freedom are not opponents, but partners in an opened-up world. Of this, more presently.

ABSENCES AND NON-HAPPENINGS AS CAUSES

The manipulability theory is more attractive than the counterfactual theory because the idea of a cause as a handle seems to make a cause something positive. The notion that A counts as the cause of B if the non-occurrence of A would result in the non-occurrence of B, or a reduction in its probability of occurring, is unattractively negative. What is more, the counterfactual theory shares the anthropocentricity of the manipulability theory. A counterfactual exists only as a possibility that is entertained – and rejected. This requires something – more precisely someone – to entertain that possibility. Counterfactuals seem like an absence whose only contribution to happening is not to stop it not happening, which seems doubly parasitic. However, some particularly generous versions of the manipulability theory share the negativity of the counterfactual rival. Some have argued that absences may be causes.

Here is an example. The fact that you did not turn up to our meeting made me cross. Does this mean that your absence or an event that does not happen has causal power? No. You are absent at many other times in my life and it does not have the power to make me cross – or indeed to experience any other emotion (because I scarcely know you). The origin of my crossness lies with: the undertaking you made to meet me; the trouble I took to arrive at the venue in the reasonable expectation that you would be there; the time and effort I took to reschedule another meeting; in short, events that actually happened. Absences, like a vacuum, rely on their filled surroundings to have any identity and to have even the similitude of causal efficacy. The desperate suggestion that absences could operate as causes given the right circumstances only underlines the fact that absences, things that don't happen, borrow causal efficacy from presences, things that do happen. My failure to water the flowers in the past twenty-four hours does not cause them to wilt. The sun's heat, resulting in transpiration that exceeds the plant's ability to draw water from relatively dry ground, caused them to wilt and my failure to water them – an abstract singular idea, not an event or a negative event – meant that they were not prevented from wilting. Causation by omission may have legal status – culpable negligence is a punishable failure – but cuts no metaphysical ice. A universe that was composed entirely of absences – of non-events, of things that do not happen, of nothing – would not be very lively and manifestly not causally wired.

What is more, absences have no material existence and (connected with this) no definite intrinsic character. Just try listing the characteristics of a failure to water the flowers. Here are some possibilities: my forgetfulness; my being out of the country; my not being in the garden; and so on. There is no limit. Indeed, there is no reason why we should restrict the absences to my failure to water the flowers in the past twenty-four hours. I could cite an additional counterfactual for each second of the past twenty-four hours and for each person who might be considered as a potential candidate to water the flowers. (And defining the field of candidates would take us into very complex territory indeed regarding the notion of responsibility.) They are pure possibilities whose existence is entirely mental. There is no reason why we should think of any single one of these possibilities as *the* cause of something happening; and, given that there is no compelling reason for choosing one out of the millions of things that did not happen and could be thought of as salient, there would be an unresolvable competition between those many things to count as the cause. In short, the wilting of the flowers would be crushingly overdetermined. To think of any of them as causes – unmediated by, or independent of, an actual person who entertains them – is magic thinking.

The invocation of absences as causes at least honours the fact – to be discussed presently – that lies at the heart of this essay: that the world in which we invoke causes is one in which there are gaps opened up in the world by consciousness, so that the world is presented as discrete events that have to be reconnected. This, however, is a "holiness" too far. There cannot be any role for unrealized possibility in the shaping of the material world, except in so far as those possibilities are envisaged by conscious human beings that may act as agents.

CAUSES AS OOMPH

The notion of causation is a response to the intuition that whatever happens is, indeed has to be, *made to happen.* This need to be made to happen is, I want to argue, a response to the fragmentation of the world of the conscious being, which extracts individual events from the intrinsically undivided flow of becoming. This image of a causally propelled unfolding of the universe is associated with the idea that the universe at any particular time can be differentiated into standing conditions (a relatively static theatre) and occurrent events (the dynamic drama in the theatre). It is the latter that are charged with carrying the causal pressures and the former are merely the context in which those causal pressures can operate. While the standing conditions do change – of course – they change more slowly than the succession of events: that is why they are able to provide the platform out of which events spring, the theatre of their causal effects.

This way of looking at the material universe provides the background assumptions of the notion of causation as the work of discrete events providing the necessary oomph to make the occurrence of other discrete events seem to have sufficient reason.[5] Crucially for our argument, this is not the only way of looking at the material world. There are other ways of conceiving it that do not require us to invoke discrete causes of discrete effects. We may envisage the universe as unfolding seamlessly from its origin to the present. Its history is, as it were, an unrolling carpet of states of affairs that is guaranteed by the initial conditions and the laws of nature that operate on them to generate subsequent conditions. The laws do not have an independent force; they are simply the general shape of what in the broadest sense, and beneath the immediate appearances to us, actually happens. They are the most capacious description of what is happening. There is a notional "vanishing point" at which the scientific process by which individual laws are progressively subsumed under laws of greater generality reaches its terminus and we have some kind of statement to the effect that what is happening overall is happening overall because it is happening overall. While the passage from a lower-order law to a higher-order law may seem like explanation, as when the behaviour of gases according to Boyle's law is revealed to be a manifestation of the laws of motion as applied to gaseous atoms, at the highest level we have simple brute fact: this is how things (most generally) are. The brutality of the brute mega-fact that "The universe is how the universe is" highlights how laws do not have legislative power; more specifically *the power to bring particular events about*. (They lack even the negative power of constraint, of keeping the universe on the rails. If they seem to have this negative power, it is only in relation to possibilities postulated by human beings, that are not, and cannot be, realized.) The intuition is that what happens must happen according to general laws of happening that, moreover, these capture the habits of the universe, and that these particular laws are different manifestations or expressions of a single law capturing the sum total of happening, gives priority to generality. Particularity is underdetermined: something else is needed to make any actual event happen; or, indeed, to have a particular manifestation of the law(s) of nature.

The causal sense, of course, precedes anything corresponding to a scientific notion of a law of nature. But it is worth noting at this stage that the global view implicit in the expectation that the world will unfold according to a fundamental law does without – indeed finds it difficult to accommodate – the idea of the local oomph that prior events (causes) provide to ensure that posterior events (effects) come about. Successive states of the universe are not frogmarched into happening by their predecessors that have been similarly frogmarched. Once the universe is brought into being, once it is it set unfolding according to its intrinsic properties, nothing more is needed to bring about the events, evident to a viewpoint, at

t_2; certainly not specific causal powers operating at t_1. This is in part because the universe thus conceived is a continuum, not chopped up into discrete events that have to be causally connected. In order to understand the origin of our causal sense, we shall need to look at the nature and provenance of the conception of a granulated universe in which causation is invoked as a kind of cement. We shall return to this presently.

Let us first illustrate the grand narrative of an unfolding universe, unified under laws of the highest generality, with the metaphor of an arrow in flight. At t_1 the arrow is at position P_1; at t_2 it is at P_2. Reaching P_2 at t_2 is not the *result* of anything happening at t_1: it is simply a continuation of what is happening at t_1. Of course, the movement of the arrow can be seen as the result of an event at t_0 when the bowstring sent it on its way. In the case of the universe as a whole, there is no distinct bowstring: the universe is not sent on its way by anything. The idea of a first cause or original oomph would be an illegitimate backward extrapolation of the causes we identify in particular parts of the world. Indeed, the very idea of causation sits uneasily with the vision of the universe as an unfolding continuum, so densely interconnected as to put the very idea of a connection (between discrete parts) into question.

Identifying a particular cause-and-effect pairing is highly artificial. If we accept the objective reality of causation, there is no limit to the causal ancestry of an event or its causal descendants. When we see or say that event A is caused by event B, both events are picked out by considerations of saliency. It is this that enables us to quarantine the pair from their limitless antecedents and their endless consequences and to separate them from background conditions. In the case of our earlier example, the salient event is an individual waking up: of negligible importance in the universe but of great importance in our parish. This is the index event that triggers the search for causal ancestors and fixes its scope, determining where we stop in tracing the chain of linked events. Saliency also accounts for the apparent asymmetry between causes and effects; the fact that the consequences of a discrete event identified as a cause are far from discrete. Take a simple example: I drop a pebble into a pool. The splash, the ripples, the trembling of the reeds and so on would exhaust any attempt at description. But this asymmetry is misleading: the causal ancestry of my dropping the pebble into the pool is also extremely complex and it, too, would defy complete description. The closed system defined by the cause and its consequences would show the asymmetry and the tendency to increasing untidiness that seems to be in line with the second law of thermodynamics; but the system is closed only by a description defined by our interests, creating an apparent starting-point that does not correspond to anything in the material world itself.[6]

CAUSES, VIEWPOINTS AND LOCALITIES

We have two rival accounts of the evolving universe. The first is of the expression through time of an unfolding from initial conditions in accordance with a multitude of laws that are ultimately expressions of a single law of the highest generality. This is a universe without interruptions, discrete events or granulation: it is a continuum. The other is a universe in which there are discrete causes that bring about discrete effects. What is it that separates the two universes? It is that the former is one in which there are no viewpoints, no localities. There is no here and there, no far and near, no centre or periphery, no hidden or revealed, no knowledge or ignorance. The latter, the world of causation, by contrast, is one that is broken up into localities picked out by a point of view for which there is here and there, far and near, centre and periphery, the hidden and the revealed, knowledge and ignorance. The point of view, as it were, places an interruption in the seamless unfolding of the universe (which latter has no points of view within itself). The present interests of the viewpoint identify a beginning and an end, or a starting-point (the cause) and an end (the effect) – the index event which is of interest and an end that in some cases will be a goal or a fulfilled purpose. It is because the world(s) in which certain salient events are seen as immediate, or mediated handles – are provided by self-conscious subjects who pitch, create and light up personal and collective localities in the universe – that the notion of causation as manipulability is so attractive despite its anthropomorphism. Without the conscious subject, the unfolding of physical reality would not be divided into causes and effects, into beginnings and ends. Self-evidently, the universe seen *sub specie aeternitatis* is not divided into *localities*. But neither is it differentiated into (prior, discrete) causes and into causes and contexts; nor into relevant contexts and the rest of the universe. It is entirely interconnected. The disconnections come from the viewpoint of the subject inserted into the interconnected world. It is this that provides the spatial separation and asymmetry in time that characterizes causation as it is usually thought of.

This account of the origin of the causal sense is anthropocentric in one respect but not the respect in which the manipulability theory is anthropocentric. The idea of the universe as a network of causes whereby events have to be brought about by preceding events, in which happening doesn't just merely happen but is made to happen (or needs to be made to happen) by local causal oomph, is the result of our situation as embodied subject operating in a locality in pursuit of our local needs. But this does not mean that causation is confined to those things we can, or could possibly, or could in principle, manipulate. Causation has to be universal once the seamless flow of events has been arrested by our viewpoint: once the flow of events is confronted and localities are created. The oomph to resume the flow is required not universally but wherever we look: wherever the universe is broken up by the gaze of an embodied subject.

I have dug beneath the rival theories of causation to see what motivates the very idea of cause. I have argued that the idea has its roots in something deeper than an idea: in the fact that we are situated; that we have viewpoints that divide the world in complex ways. Out of this fundamental existential reality of conscious beings originates a world that is granulated into events some of which have a characteristic that is preserved even in the most deflated account of cause: namely, saliency or privileged importance, foregrounded against a background of what is also happening. Behind saliency is the viewpoint of a subject whose existence is of concern to itself. Of this, our ultimate target, more presently. This is a world in which there are stories that have a beginning, a middle and an end. And, as Hume said, "Whatever has a beginning has also a cause of existence" ([1739, 1740] 1985: 72). And whatever has an end, has to be caused to end. Causation is necessitated by interruption, which opens a space for beginnings, or constitutes endings, in turn the consequence of the irruption of consciousness.

LAWS, CAUSES AND PARTICULAR EVENTS

One way of viewing physical science is to see it as an endeavour to rise above the parochial viewpoints of embodied subjects. (This is never complete, of course, because science will never entirely shake off the pre-scientific consciousness, the interests, and the modes of imagining and the language of human beings.) The most obvious fruits of this endeavour are general laws that purport to encompass ourselves and the material world we are in, things that matter to humans and things that don't, within a single descriptive gaze. As already noted, despite their names, laws do not legislate or mandate what happens: they have no power. This is most evident when the laws are expressed in the form of an equation, such as $F = ma$ (force = mass × acceleration). There are no localities – in space or time – in these equations. What is more, this quantitative correlation between variables has no spatial or temporal direction. The equation could just as well be expressed in the opposite direction as $ma = F$. The retrospectively discovered pattern of what happens is not a constraint, even less an external or prior one, on what happens. The laws are not, as it were, continuous interventions. Nature's habit of repeating itself is not a *pressure* to repeat itself. Laws *are* the habits not that which secures the habits: not something from without that necessitates those habits. Nature is not *obliged* to repeat itself; indeed, it is misleading even to think of nature repeating itself because this would imply that its unfolding was broken up into slices that are then observed to copy one another.

If laws seem to legislate on what happens or is possible, this is only in relation to possibilities that we conceive and the intentions we form that can then be fulfilled or frustrated. It is our wishes and needs that translate the habits of the material world into an inevitability, into something implacable or ineluctable, into something we need to align ourselves with in order to achieve our goals or pre-empt something we don't want to happen. Otherwise the unfolding of states of the universe along certain lines seems simply that: it is not an *imposition* of certain constraints on the universe – most obviously because that would *per impossibile* require an outside from which the imposition was imposed. The laws of nature are not outside the material of nature. The universe does not disobey its own laws but it does not obey them either.

Causes, on the other hand, seem to bring things about because they operate within localities that do have outsides. Once you have dropped the egg on the floor you cannot stop it smashing when it lands: the cause operates with the implacable law of gravity to bring about the effect. This inevitability is exploited in manipulability when we bring about a desired event by aligning the state of the universe with an invariable predecessor of that event; or, less grandly, align the local state of affairs with the conditions that will make that event inevitable. Causes, unlike laws, do not operate at the level of generality. Even so, we may be tempted into thinking that they do when we unpack the relationship between a particular cause and a particular effect and find laws "in operation". The laws, however, do not reach all the way down to singular events.

In the example just given, the laws in question are the laws of mechanics, not the laws of falling eggs. Question: Why did event A, a collision between object 1 (the egg) and object 2 (the floor) result in event B, object 1 changing its shape? Answer: Because a static, rigid object such as a floor will apply a force to an object that collides with it and the force will translate into acceleration of parts of the egg in accordance with the general law $F = ma$.

In other words, we are tempted to see particular cause–effect sequences – which unfold in accordance with the general laws of nature – as expressions of the *power* of the laws to make things happen and in a certain way. In short by mobilizing explanations that straddle singular events and general laws, as when we give a scientific account of the relationship between a cause and an effect, we find a justification for our sense that things are made to happen, rather than just happening, and so satisfy our need to see what happens as having sufficient reason.

This is, however, misleading. At the level of scientific, or even common-sense, explanation we connect not token individual events (this egg being dropped and this egg falling to the ground and being smashed) but types of event: causal *explanations* (as opposed to causal connections) are not token–token but type–type; it is this that makes them expressions of general laws. But, of course, classes of events do not have causal power. Putative causal powers are exerted through tokens: it requires a particular moment of carelessness to end up with a smashed egg. No actual smashed eggs result from the general propensity of eggs to get smashed by general falls to the ground. Classes of events – which are in the end only general descriptions awaiting instantiation – do not result in actual effects, actual happenings.

So the seeming rationale we get from the idea of causation is distant from the place the causal power is thought to operate. The laws refer to the broadest classes of events but the powers are, can only be, exerted through particular events. (It is tempting to think that we might unite the idea of causes as particular, singular powers and causes as explanations by describing causes as operating in a law-like way to increase the probability of their effects. However, we are still talking about *types* of causes and *types* of effects.) So the powers that causes seem to have to shape or guarantee what happens are ultimately merely the shadowy presence of the general laws we intuit behind particular sequences of events. We are left ultimately with general patterns of happening that express (or can be made to look like an expression of) general laws. The fact that lower-level laws gradually converge on more general laws in an ever more uni-fied scientific account of the world does not alter the situation that happenings happen merely because they happen. Relatively local laws (such as govern the fate of eggs) may seem to be explained by more general laws (such as $F = ma$ and the laws governing the effects of impacts on brittle objects) but ultimately we arrive at the most general possible laws, for example, the field equations of gen-eral relativity or the Schrödinger wave equation, where explanation gives way to manifestly pure – and phenomenologically empty – description.[7] Laws seem like explanations only to the lower-level laws looking up to them; but the explanatory satisfaction that the upward glance delivers is only the afterglow of our sense that events lit up by a viewpoint have particular explanations.

LOCALITIES, HAPPENING, AND THE APPARENT NEED FOR OOMPH: BREAKING AND RESTARTING THE CONTINUUM OF HAPPENING

Let us weave together the key strands of our discussion. Embodied subjects introduce viewpoints, localities, in the world, in which there are distinctions between: causes and effects; features of events that are causally relevant and features of events that are not; cause–effect pairs and the context and conditions in which causes may or may not lead to their effects; and these contexts and conditions and the rest of the universe.

All these distinct elements – locality, cause contexts and con-ditions, and so on – of course, have deep links with agency, since viewpoints are not merely spectator points. Perception is insepara-ble from the possibilities opened for that being – *Dasein* or human being – whose existential meaning is, as Martin Heidegger put it in *Being and Time*, "Care": for a being that locates its own being in a "there" that is offset against a background "there"; a disclosedness that reveals the world to itself – or a part of the universe to a part of itself (for more on this see Tallis 2002). As psychologists put it, they reveal objects as "affordances": possibilities for action. (This is the nugget of deep truth in the manipulation theory of agency: that reality of agency and the idea of causation have a shared origin in the irruption of locations in a location-less material world. The notion of agent causation is the *recto* to the *verso* of cause as agency.)

The opening up of locations – or worlds – around an embodied subject not only breaks up the seamless flow of happening into temporally and spatially discrete events – a coarse- or fine-grained granulation of that which is around the subject – but then requires that there shall be something that will restore the continuous flow of happening that, in reality, happens simply because it happens. Something additional appears to be required to explain, to give a hint of (sufficient) reason, why events take place; why the flow continues despite the "inter-ruption" of consciousness. Singled out events – which of course share the implicit contingency of all happening – are explicitly contingent; consequently, more explanation is sought. That further explanation is not provided by natural laws (irrespective of whether they are contingent) since, as we have discussed, they do not reach all the way down to the token events that are presented to conscious subjects. More seems to be required for them to happen: so causal powers are invoked. Hence the appeal to something that is imparted to events by their predecessors to make them happen; hence the idea that happening at time t_2 is mandated by happening at time t_1, through the combination of a quasi-inertial continuation of background conditions between t_1 and t_2 and the particular oomph that enables, within this background, certain events in t_1 to cause certain events in t_2.

There are accounts of causation that seem to occupy a middle ground between the continuum on the one hand and connections between distinct causes and effects. These include seeing causes and effects as being contiguous (no spatiotemporal gap) or being phases of a single underlying process, in which each phase causes the next phase. Under such circumstances the passage of oomph from cause to effect requires no material, but only a (descriptive) gap to be crossed and a flow of energy that passes through the cause and the effect or a continuation of the intrinsic momentum of a process.

As will be apparent, there is both complementarity and conflict between a cause-based and a law-based understanding of the physical world. Law-based explanations describe how things in general happen to happen, although they nonetheless seem to elevate the happening of individual events above brute contingency by describing them as regular instances of types, behaving just as all the members of their class behave. The law seems to say that what happened just now had to happen because it manifests a tendency that is apparent in all times and all places. The law – which is itself contingent – shelters the token event from the appearance of pure contingency. If things are happening as they usually happen, things are happening as they should happen: God may not be in his heaven but at least all is legal with the world. As we ascend to a view defined by laws of ever greater generality we eventually squeeze out locality, and causation is replaced by process and, finally, by frozen structures. At the level of, say, the field equations of general relativity, we have a manifold in which there is no sequence of events and therefore no need to invoke causes. Physics was destined to abandon causation because it progressively distances itself from the localities of everyday life in which token events occur in a particular order and require a local explanation to justify their occurrence.[8]

The appeal to laws of ever greater generality is another aspect of the idea that all token events (causes and their effects) have a common ancestry ultimately originating from (say) the Big Bang: simultaneous, non-interacting causal chains converge on a vanishing point where time and change began. As embodied subjects, however, our gaze – and our interests – fall far short of that backward glance. We therefore need the feeling of local powers at work to make events occur: and hence we see them as local effects of local causes. While causal chains can be in principle traced without limit up to causal ancestors and down to descendent effects, in practice causation is indexed to the locality of the embodied subject, a locality that privileges some causes or effects as immediate, near or relevant and the rest as mediated, distant and irrelevant. This, of course, reinforces the connection between manipulability and causation.

To understand the nature of causation, therefore, we have to see the ultimate background to our causal sense: the fact that we are localized subjects illuminating localities in a universe that, from the viewpoint of physical science, has no localities. It is these localities, not local causal forces, that are additional to the overall flow of happening that is the universe. The loss of causation when we ascend above localities is expressed very well by Woodward (2013). He asks us to consider this claim: "The state S_t of the entire universe at time t causes the state S_{t+d} of the entire universe at time $t + d$, where S_t and S_{t+d} are specifications in terms of some fundamental physical theory." And he quotes Judea Pearl who argues that "If you wish to include the whole universe in the model, causality disappears because interventions disappear – the manipulator and the manipulated lose their distinction" (2000: 350, quoted in Woodward 2013).

Woodward argues that "The systems of causal relationship that figure in common sense causal reasoning and in the biological, psychological, and social sciences" all have the character of belonging to "small worlds" located in a larger environment. By contrast, "fundamental physical theories do not, at least when their domain is taken to be the entire universe" (Woodward 2013). Pearl challenged the notion that we can think of the state of the universe at time t_2 as the effect of the state of the universe at time t_1: "If you wish to include the whole universe in the [scientific] model, causality disappears because interventions disappear – the manipulator and the manipulated lose their distinction" (2000: 350, quoted in Woodward 2013). In short, as locality is lost, so is causation.

While the account put forward in this essay locates the origin of causation in consciousness, it does not do so in either a Humean or Kantian way. It finds it in a place that is deeper than that in which mere habits of expectation are formed (Hume) but not as deep as the place where an undifferentiated noumenal reality gives rise to the phenomenal world of space, time, objects and so on (Kant). Our causal sense is rooted in the attempt to re-cement a world whose unfolding continuity has been broken up by a consciousness, a point of view that has irrupted into it. Seen in this way, universal causation is not of itself a constraint on agency but that in virtue of which there is agency. We should not speak of "a causally closed" world but of a world, opened up by consciousness, stitched together here and there by causal connectedness (for an extended discussion of this and its relationship to tensed time and freedom, see Tallis forthcoming).

No current idea of cause compatible with science – counterfactual, manipulation, and so on – does justice to, or retains, our primitive idea of sufficient reason for happenings to happen. This is because the viewpoint of science is remote from viewpoints: remote from the illuminated localities that irrupt into the flow of happening to give it a centre (and a periphery) and interrupt it to give it a now, with its local beginnings and local ends – its causes and its effects.

If there is no interruption, then there is no need to invoke quasimiraculous causation, a natural agency, as a universal restart button deflecting the course of events from mere general possibility to singular actuality. Happening is continuous and undivided. It is no coincidence that quantum mechanics that undermines the very idea of location also replaces causation with probability. The threat to location and to causation arose before quantum mechanics with the rise of fields and force fields and the convergence of mechanics and electrodynamics, but quantum field theory took this trend in scientific thinking to its natural limit.

The view of the world as a seamless unfolding process can dispense with causation altogether, except perhaps at a putative beginning. When an arrow is in flight, the successive phases of the trajectory are not caused by the preceding phases. The oomph is built in and the principle of inertia does not require anything to be transferred to the arrow. Keeping going is the default state. The world picture that does without causation would make processes all interconnected to the point where there are no connections as such, no bridges to be crossed, nothing to be transferred, no causal supplement required. Not only would the arrow's flight not be separated from other events in the world but the flight would not be separable from the movement of the bowstring that set it in flight. This would be an image of the world in which there are no localities; the origin would be a dimensionless point, prior to space, time and causation. It is an image familiar from science.

The most familiar part of this image is reflected in Newton's first law of motion (that every body remains in a state of rest or uniform motion in a straight line unless acted upon by a force) and more generally in the idea of inertia (whatever is going on will continue going on – and "going on" includes the stability of objects – unless it is stopped by an outside force). The power of continuation or repetition, of habit, is intrinsic to the universe. Neither dynamic states (such as an arrow in flight) nor static states (such as an unchanging pebble) requires anything to ensure that their successive states are the same as the preceding ones unless there is something acting on them to destabilize what is happening. This stability – expressed in laws of classical physics such as the conservation of mass-energy – is evident as the viewpoint withdraws to an ever greater distance, localities are lost and "outside" is pushed to the margins. Without the outside, there is nowhere from which causes may operate to disturb a system.

As the gaze ascends to absolute generality, not only is "outside" squeezed and the granulation of the unfolding of the universe into a network of discrete events is lost, but something else happens: phenomenal appearances or qualities disappear. At the most fundamental level, physical theories are about the world as mass-energy reduced to complex numerical relationships. As such, they are incomplete. As Richard Feynman has put it: "The next great awakening of human intellect may well produce a method of understanding the qualitative content of equations … Today we cannot see whether Schrödinger's equation contains frogs, musical composers, or morality – or whether it does not" (quoted in Gleick 1992: 436). I do not think it is possible for fundamental equations to have any qualitative content for the reasons just given. But Feynman's point is a key one. The ascent from viewpoints tethered to consciousness to laws of increasing generality is inescapably associated with the loss of qualities. The fact that the replacement of causation by probability is most explicit in quantum mechanics, where location, too, is under threat, should not distract us from the fact that delocalization (in space and time), loss of qualities and replacement of causes by laws reflecting the patterns or habits of the universe are present throughout science.

One further important consequence follows from these considerations. Those seeking to find the basis for what is thought of as the "directionality" of time in the material world often appeal to the irreversibility of the temporal ordering of cause and effect. We can now see that the so-called "arrow of causation" cannot confer directionality on the clock of the universe since the causal relation is the product of a viewpoint that is making a narrative, or more broadly existential, sense of the world. This late manifestation of the physical world can hardly be responsible for the difference between the beginning and the end of the universe. This, however, is a big story and beyond the scope of this essay (but see Tallis forthcoming).

AFTER-NOTE

In this essay, we started from the assumption that causes and effects are events. This is by no means universally accepted. For some philosophers, the world consists of states of affairs, so its unfolding is a succession of states of affairs. The causal relationships would be between state A at time t_1 and state B at time t_2. This is difficult because a state seem in a sense to be something that has come to rest, so the interruption in the continuous unfolding that causation is invoked to correct is more decisive. What is more, if a state of affairs acted as a whole, any causal influences would seem to be transmitted as block-to-block rather than the discrete events that we typically think of as the basis of cause. This model also seems to pre-empt any division into causes and background conditions; the distinctive platform from which causes operate and the platform that makes the world susceptible to their effects are lost.

Other writers have identified properties, objects and facts as causes. Properties do not seem to have the capacity to stand alone in order to bring things about. Objects seem to be the *site* of causes rather than causes in their own right, if only because they do not seem to be occurrents in the way that causes are. For D. H. Mellor, causes are facts. This is worth a closer look.

Mellor's argument is that causes "relate not particulars but the entities, if any, whose existence makes true the sentences 'C' and 'E' entailed by a true 'E because C'" (1995: 161, esp. ch. 13). These, he says, are facts. (To be precise, Mellor identifies *facta* – the immanent truth-makers for facts – as the basis for fact causation. In other words, he descends from facts to things on the surface of the earth in order to find causal efficacy.) This is linked to the other aspect of his account of causation: that causes raise the chances of effects. A particular event E does not have chances – it simply is. It is "*that* it happens" that has chances.

In order to get from event E to "that E happens", however, we have to take one or more steps back. The first is making E explicit as a discrete entity, cut out by a description. The second (another aspect of the first) is to see it as an example of a *class* of events of type E. And the third is to locate Es in a world of possible events and to compare the frequency of their occurrence in the presence or absence of events of type C.

All of this is clearly beyond anything available in the physical world and takes the notion of cause a long way away from the common-sense idea of causes as the intrinsic necessity, or at least inevitability, in the unfolding of the material world. More succinctly, what Mellor is doing is driving the causal relation from the material world and actual events into the world of discourse and possibilities that may or may not be realized.[9] However, causes-and-effects-as-facts do not have any of the characteristics that appear to link causes and effects as ordinarily understood; for example temporal order (facts do not *occur* at a particular time) and spatial contiguity (facts do not have physical locations). The Battle of Hastings occurred before the Battle of Waterloo but "The fact that there was a battle at

Hastings" does not take place before "The fact that there was a battle at Waterloo". Mellor's translation of causes into facts has the further disadvantage of allowing causes to include things that do not happen because these are just as much facts as things that do. As we have seen, however, such negatives borrow their apparent causal power from those things that happen: they are causal parasites.

ACKNOWLEDGEMENTS

I have strayed into the philosophy of causation mainly as a result of thinking about time (Tallis forthcoming). The topic is something of an away match for me, except in so far as it is related to the (I believe incorrect) notion of causation as the basis of the temporal arrow. I am therefore indebted to the guidance of four superb essays from the *Stanford Encyclopaedia of Philosophy*: "Kant and Hume on Causality" (De Pierris & Michael Friedman 2013); "Causal Processes" (Dowe 2008); "The Metaphysics of Causation" (Schaffer 2013); and "Causation and Manipulability" (Woodward 2013). The particular acknowledgements I have made to these beautifully constructed, lucid surveys of the current state of philosophical thought on these aspects of causation do not fully reflect the assistance I have received from them.

NOTES

1. While the general principle of causality was *a priori* , particular causal laws are not. Even so, "Although we learn many laws through experience, they are only special determinations of still higher laws, and the highest of these, under which the others all stand, issue *a priori* from the understanding itself" (A126). For Kant, it is necessary that an appearance at any given time should be determined by the previous state: "I render my subjective synthesis of apprehension objective only by reference to a rule in accordance with which the appearances in their succession, that is, as they happen, are determined by the preceding state. The experience of an event [*i.e.* of anything as *happening*] is itself possible only on this assumption" (A195/B240).
2. It is this model of causation that accounts for the initial resistance to the notion of fields of forces, and to so-called "action at a distance", exemplified in gravitational attraction, and the particular challenge presented to the mechanical world picture by electromagnetic fields. We are now used to thinking of more exotic causes operating in everyday life – for example, a lifting of the rules on credit resulting in a bank crash – but something of the fundamental intuition (but with a radically different balance between causes and conditions) survives, although the pushes and pressures are between abstractions and mediated by the community of minds and their actions and expectations. Hume points out that we imagine that "the communication of motion" is something with which we are so familiar that we imagine we could have anticipated it *a priori* before we had any experience: "Such is the

influence of custom, that, where it is strongest, it not only covers our natural ignorance, but even conceals itself, and seems to take place, merely because it is found in the highest degree" ([1748] 1975: 28–9). This is why for a while it was believed that a fully transparent account even of social causation would demonstrate that it boiled down the communication of motion by contact or impulse. The dream of becoming a Newton of the social world – and of a *Principia* encompassing social statics and social dynamics – has taken many forms over the past 250 years.

3. We can put it this way: the desired outcome, B (your waking up), can occur as a result of many events: for example (i) the sun rising and light coming in through the window; (ii) your full bladder contracting and sending arousing signals; (iii) my drawing the curtains and letting the light in; (iv) my clapping my hands. We may think of these as representing the set of conditions that could wake you up. However, (iii) and (iv) belong to a subset of events that I can influence: events that lie within my power to change. And, finally, (iv) is the actual event that I bring about in order to wake you up.

4. There is also the question of when we regard agency as coming into the universe. At what level of complexity of life does manipulation emerge? I am inclined to deny it to most organisms. Indeed, I am somewhat anthropocentric in this regard. And this is connected with the plausible case that humans alone have a causal sense. See Tallis (2005b).

5. The account of the function of causal explanations [or causal powers invoked as explanations] in this essay – that they bridge gaps opened up in a world that is seen as composed of discrete events rather than seamlessly unfolding – is not one that would be accepted by many philosophers. Wesley Salmon [1984], for example, argues that causality is a property of spatiotemporally continuous processes rather than a relationship between discrete events. This simply does not seem to reflect our causal talk at all, where we tend to think of (say) the lightning causing the thunder rather than the first slice of the thunder roll causing the second.

6. Lee Smolin observes how in physics that falls short of addressing the entire universe: "Most of what we know about nature has come from experiments in which we artificially mark off and isolate a phenomenon from the continual whirl of the universe" (2013: 38). He calls this "doing physics in a box". This box, it seems to me, is a halfway house between the parish of our consciousness and the putative view from nowhere corresponding to a complete theory of everything.

7. The ineliminable presence of seemingly contingent constants of nature – the gravitational constant, the energy state of the carbon nucleus – in the fundamental laws evident at this level underlines the passage from explanation to description. At the subatomic level, the ascent to the highest order of generality results in laws that correspond to quantitative descriptions of statistical probabilities based on what has already happened or, more precisely, been observed. A controlled randomness that results in a constant spread of observations reveals a universe that is probabilistic all the way down. Probability is constitutive, not merely an expression of our incomplete knowledge or our uncertainty as to what is going to happen next, or arising out of our incomplete access to what has happened already and our imperfect ability to interpret it, and hence extrapolate from it to the future.

8. An early manifestation of the ascent of physics to the view from nowhere of the theory of everything is the equation. Although most equations have the form in which the left and right side are linked by the equals sign (e.g. $F = ma$), some may connect the two sides with an arrow ($A \rightarrow B$) as in the case of chemical equations.

This may seem to suggest a causal relationship between a preceding and a succeeding state but this must not be confused with a causal link. First, the cause is outside the equation: it is whatever causes A to become B; and its effect is not B but $A \rightarrow B$. Second, the direction is at least in principle reversible. We can electrolyse water to produce hydrogen and oxygen and can combine hydrogen and oxygen to produce water. Third, as a consequence of this, and as we have already noted, it is a mistake to think of the two sides of the equation as representing a temporal sequence, although our reading it from left to right tempts us to do so. The point of an equation is to assert that, at one level, nothing has really changed: all that has happened is that the fundamental constituents have been rearranged.

9. In the standard terminology, events are immanent and facts are transcendent. The event of the assassination of Archduke Ferdinand is something that took place at a particular place and at a particular time. *The fact that* it happened is non-spatiotemporal, even abstract. This would seem to rule it out as something that could cause something else to happen: there is no literal contact between facts.

II

Tetchy Interludes

Friedrich Nietzsche observed that would-be disinterested, unworldly thinkers suffer from many "human, all-too-human" faults. Foremost among these is the danger of turning into a mere reacting machine and of being consumed by perpetual irritation. He wanted to correct the impression, given by philosophers' writings, that they are permanently exercised by the mystery of the world. There are few thinkers for whom wondering can be anything more than scattered arias intermittently relieving a sustained recitative of a prosaic, instrumental and, yes, not infrequently irritated, unenchanted understanding of the world. I am not, alas, one of those happy few. So, in the spirit of honesty – and of fun – I will share with you, the reader, some of my own tetchiness before assuming a celebratory tone of voice.

Chapter 9, "The Shocking Yawn: Art up its *Ars*" is a howl of rage against the second-hand, second-order and second-rate art passing itself off as a wake-up call. While the specific (and rather obvious) target of the essay is a well-known individual who has also been the *bête noir* of a newspaper by which my podex refuses to be absterged, I hope the spirit of philosophical inquiry is not entirely absent.

Chapter 10 derives in part from my acceptance speech for the 2013 *Philosophy Now* Award for Contributions to the Fight Against Stupidity. It is not enough to complain of others' stupidity without reminding oneself that the fight against stupidity, whose victories are only temporary, begins and ends at home. Scaling the higher reaches of stupidity, however, is rarely a solitary achievement. It seems unlikely that cliff-walking would have commended itself to a solitary lemming deprived of the benefits of group-think. Collective stupidity takes many forms but the most spectacular may be found in academic institutions meant to be devoted to promoting intelligent reflection on the world in which we find ourselves. Chapter 11, "Colonic Material of a Taurine Provenance" examines a forerunner to the current science cringe among some humanist intellectuals. Touched by the "strong contagion" of the white coat, those who professed so-called "theory" managed to combine ignorant dismissal of many aspects of science with equally ignorant use of its jargon and concepts.

In the trio of short essays that round off this section and make up Chapter 12, I explore, and lament, our limitless capacity for mission drift. The fact that our profoundest ideas, our greatest cultural achievements, are often subordinated to the most mundane of purposes is mostly, but not entirely, a grumble. I have a sneaking feeling that this capacity for shallowness is an indirect marker of our depths.

9

The Shocking Yawn
Art up its *Ars*

In the summer of 2012, Tate Modern hosted a major retrospective of the works of one of the most well-known contemporary British artists. Now that the exhibition has closed and the space has been liberated for more interesting items such as fresh air and daylight, it is appropriate that philosophers should reflect on the collective delusion that elevated this individual to the status of artist, indeed a Leading British Artist.

In discussing the case of Damien H, it may seem inadvisable to talk about his art. Hasn't everything – for and against – been said already? Those of us who are against will just have to wait patiently for the South Sea Bubble to burst and the credit default swaps to be called in. After all, to vary what was said of the British poetaster Edith Sitwell, he has more to do with the history of publicity than the history of art.

There is something to be said for this view but in Damien H's case "art versus publicity" is a distinction without a difference. While his true métier lies in his incomparable talent for self-promotion and his uncanny sense of what will open the wallets of the wealthy, his achievement as an artist in the traditional sense – slender in every respect except sheer quantity – needs to be examined precisely because it is the disproportion between the merit of the work and the attention it has attracted that makes him so worthy of examination. The art is therefore unavoidable.

And so too is the emblematic stuffed shark, which, after all, is not a bad place to begin, not only because it propelled H to international fame but also because it illustrates important features of the case. The item was supposed to shock in various ways: dead sharks are even more shocking than living ones (apparently); and a dead shark in a gallery is more shocking than one washed up on the shore. Of course, it is not shocking at all, any more than a pile of dead fish at a fishmonger is shocking. There was, however, another source of the rumour of shock: the *idea* of those who would be shocked or pronounce themselves shocked.

The cry "This is not art!" also helped. Hasn't *all* great art been execrated by the philistines? No, actually; but this error is sufficient to kick-start the faulty logic of his advocates:

Major Premise: All great artists have been despised by critics.

Minor Premise: This artist has been despised by some critics.

Conclusion: Therefore this artist is great.

The wider conclusion would be that not only the value but also the profundity of a stage play could be measured by the number of people who walk out of the theatre during the performance or (since timidity and politeness often rule on such occasions) declare afterwards that they were bored, baffled or voted with their consciousness and fell asleep.

Gallery spaces worldwide were well used to housing "found objects" and other (usually) pointless items. Nicholas Serota, the artistic conscience of the nation and director of the Tate, had already bought a can of *merde* (originating from the colon of the Italian artist Piero Manzoni) for the gallery for £22,350. Against such competition, how could a mere shark stand out? This is where

H's promotional genius came in, with the help of adman Charles Saatchi, who commissioned the piece. H gave his pickled piscine a portentous title: *The Physical Impossibility of Death in the Mind of Someone Living.* The title – which philosophers know could have been better illustrated by an empty space – had only a tangential relationship to the shark but everything to do with its success. This is not just art, folks: it is *metaphysical* art, addressing a fundamental existential angst, so we must overlook the fatuity of "physical" in "*physical* impossibility".

The objection that stuffed large fish – even sharks – are seen in many places (such as J. D. Electrical Supplies in Shoreditch, London) where they are not considered art, could easily be shrugged off. What Damien H had done was to "re-contextualize" the item by relocating it to a gallery. As a result (we are told) we saw: (a) the shark differently; (b) the gallery space differently; (c) art (especially Western, history of) differently; and (d) ourselves/our lives differently. That fish was therefore worth every penny of the £50,000 sale price: small fry, of course, compared to the hundreds of millions that Hirst has trousered in the after-shark.

The shark is, of course, shocking. It is shocking that anyone could claim to be shocked by it and coerce others into declaring themselves to be likewise shocked. It is shocking that anyone (artist, critic) could claim that it *ought* to shock people. It is shocking that the real horrors of the world are sufficiently forgotten – or that people are sufficiently sheltered from them – that it is assumed that a stuffed shark would be required to awaken us to the idea of death. It is, in short, shocking that there has been such a conspiracy of artists, critics, dealers and wealthy clients pretending that the item in question is a wake-up call to those who are insufficiently shocked.

So much for exhibit 1. The genius of the adman and would-be shock-artist was evident in the titles of subsequent works: *Two Fucking and Two Watching* (a rotting cow and a bull) and *Mother and Child Divided* (a cow and a calf divided). The latter is a favourite of Serota, who argues that "the disgust provoked by the work is part of its appeal". "Art is transgressive" because "Life is not all sweet"

(Serota 2000). Who knew? Not the visitors to the gallery, apparently, who required instruction in the tough truths of the real world.

Time for a digression on art and morality.

Aeschylus' saying "Call no man happy until he is dead" has seemed especially apt of late. Following the posthumous disgrace of Jimmy Savile, several septuagenarians and octogenarians have been drawn out of the comparative obscurity of their twilight years – when one could have been forgiven for thinking that the story of their lives had been to all intents and purposes already finalized – to face charges relating to sex crimes alleged to have taken place several decades ago. Among this ever lengthening parade was artist Graham Ovenden, once well-known and seemingly admired, but now notorious, for his nude portraits of young girls.

There is a revealing twist to this tale. After Ovenden was found guilty of indecent assaults against children, Serota's Tate gallery withdrew his works from their online collection and they will not be available for viewing even by appointment. Ovenden's conviction has, we are told, "shone a new light on his work" (Bowie-Sell 2013). It may seem odd that the gaze of the curator had to be supplemented by the spectacles of a county court prosecutor, one Mr Quaife, to reveal that Ovenden's canvasses betrayed that he was "sexually besotted with young girls". The episode does indeed shine "a new light": not on the paintings but on the rhetoric that surrounds much contemporary art.

Which brings us back to Serota, informing the philistine hordes that art is – or must be – "subversive", "transgressive" and "dangerous". The terms are mobilized to defend stuff that is to many people manifestly no good. "You are wrong", they are told. "This really *is* good because it subverts our expectation of what art is or should be. Is it not the *duty* of the artist to shock?" According to Serota, defending Hirst's *Mother and Child Divided* consisting of two brutally severed carcasses, "the undoubted shock, even disgust provoked by the work is part of its appeal" (2000). Interestingly, Hirst's best-known example of cack-handed butchery – the aforementioned *Two Fucking and Two Watching* – was banned from a New York gallery by health officials because it was feared that there might be an outbreak of vomiting among the visitors, although many, lured by the title, might feel cheated of an erotic, voyeuristic experience.

Hirst himself turns out to be a decent guy after all, when things get a little hot. He was one of a handful of cultural icons who responded to the horror of the 9/11 World Trade Center attacks with an appreciation of them as "a kind of artwork in its own right" for which "on one level they kind of need congratulating, which a lot of people shy away from". Public outrage prompted a statement issued through his company, in which he apologised "unreservedly for any upset I have caused, particularly to the families of the victims of the events on that terrible day" (BBC News 2002). You see, underneath the transgressive exterior he proves to be just as sensitive to the sorrows of others as you and me.

There seems to be a kind of inverted hypocrisy at work. We have comfortable, establishment figures – curators, critics, pillars of the art world – cheerleading for art that pretends to devalue conventional values. Now we discover that perhaps these are values that, after all, they secretly share. Or was sequestrating Ovenden's works after his conviction for paedophilia more a precautionary step than the result of moral revulsion at the artist? Even so, it is still revealing. Equally revealing is the risible episode when Tate Modern, home to much so-called "dangerous" art, cordoned off Ai Weiwei's *Sunflower Seeds* (100 million hand-painted porcelain seeds) because it had been warned of the risk of triggering asthma in visitors! (Those who arranged the exhibition did not pause to reflect on the health of the wretched people who had had to paint the seeds one at a time.)

It is absurd to judge works of art by the morality of the artist. We don't have to forgive Caravaggio's homicide of a rival before we can permit ourselves to be ravished by his work. But when the art is a direct expression of something truly evil in the artist, and invites collusion in that evil, then we have to ask whether we wish to value it. The founding thought of contemporary art criticism, from Oscar Wilde's *Dorian Grey*, was a corrective to the shallow, sentimental moralizing of the time: "There is no such thing as a moral or an

immoral book. Books are well written, or badly written. That is all."
That is, of course, not all.

The case of Ovenden should give pause to the prattlers of the art
world. Perhaps there may be a reality behind Serota's rhetoric and
some "transgressive", "subversive" art really is as objectionable as it
pretends to be. And perhaps some curators and critics should grow
up and recognize that a man who paints naked, suggestive portraits of
young children might actually be a paedophile. Or that art that is no
good cannot be redeemed by its claim to be transgressive – particularly when the talk of "transgressiveness" is mere posturing. Serota's
idea of transgression wouldn't hurt a fly, whatever it might do to the
odd calf or an innocent shark trafficked from the ocean to a gallery.

And so we return to H and art that may or may not be transgressive but is most certainly not particularly good, and to his heavy
reliance on portentous titles to assert creative ownership of found
items. This can occasionally get him into trouble. Which brings us
to exhibit 2.

In 2,000 H gave the cryptic title *Hymn* to a blown-up version of
a plastic anatomical toy of a male human being. (Hymn – him –
homonym – geddit?) Critics were enraptured. It was described as "a
masterpiece" and "the first key work of British art for the new century" (Dorment 2000). More importantly, it was bought by Charles
Saatchi for £1,000,000. Norman Emms, a commercial sculptor who
had made the original and discovered only by accident that his
work had been appropriated, was less impressed and sued successfully for compensation. The compensation he received was pitifully
small compared with the millions *Hymn* diverted into Hirst's pock-
ets: a truly shocking (as opposed to merely art-critically shocking)
reminder of the way the world works – that "Life is not all sweet".

The extent of H's appropriations (or "influences") – unbecom-
ing for an artist of such supposed originality – is astonishing. The
Carolina Biological Supply Company science catalogue (bisected
cow), H's one-time friend John LeKay (*Yin and Yang* is closer to
Hymn even than the work of Mr Emms), what used to be known as
The Spastics Society, and the artist Kerry Stewart (H's *Charity*) and

even the celebrity chef Marco Pierre White, have all been identified by his sworn enemies The Stuckists as involuntary grist to the Damien H mill.

And so to exhibit 3: spot and spin paintings. They are not original (thank you Thomas Downing, Walter Robinson, the *Blue Peter* children's television programme, and many others) – although the reach of H's publicity machine is such that he is known to many people who are ignorant of the history of art by which his originality (or more precisely lack of it) might be judged. Second, they are manufactured on an industrial scale (1,000 at the last count) and not, for the most part, by the Master Himself. Finally, they are utterly banal, if quite pretty. They have resonant titles, of course: the names of different brands of pills, which (according to Adrian Searle of the *Guardian*) "give them a slightly menacing, as well as a dangerously attractive, air" (2012). If you feel unmenaced and (dangerously or otherwise) unattracted by the name of a tablet, you are a philistine. Thus the way of coercive discourse.

So much for the art. But this book is dedicated to philosophy, so it is necessary not only to identify BS as what it is but also to dig a little deeper. Why has Damien H attracted so much adulation (as well as, of course, execration, although the latter mainly misses the mark) to the point where he was granted the apotheosis of a major retrospective at Tate Modern? What are the conditions that made his rise possible? A few powerful, impressionable characters with wobbly judgement like Sir Nicholas S and an adman such as Charles S, wealthy enough to shape the art market, are not sufficient explanation. More is needed. That more includes: Damien H himself; gullible billionaires entering an art market where things can be talked up and down without anyone looking particularly hard at the product; and the way art is discussed – the *theory* of the purpose it serves and of how it should be evaluated.

Damien H first. He is an adman's dream. He was the embodiment of the rebellious artist, from the wrong side of the tracks, out of his head on coke and alcohol, and thumbing his nose at an art world that was supposed to be dead (or complacent, or traditional – you choose your favourite cliché) before his arrival, and treated as an equal by pop stars. He was adored for his *chutzpah*. Notwithstanding the rotting animals, he made art glamorous, even sexy. And the art market, having found him marketable, marketed him (with the unstinting assistance of the artist) for all it was worth. Rising prices translated into rising value and rising value further boosted the prices. The wallet became elevated to the chief organ of taste.

And then there is the *theory*. The art market "loves theory", as sceptical art critic Jacky Wullschläger (2012) has observed, "because it spares the need for discrimination". I have mentioned the theory of art as shock therapy for those who are not sufficiently shocked ("Life is not all sweet", remember?) and the artist as shock therapist. There is also the theory of the artist as one who finds, rather than makes, his works, which dismisses all the traditional skills of the artist as irrelevant – very convenient for the unskilled. As Adrian Hamilton (2012) has said "Contemporary artists" – he meant *some* contemporary artists but that would have sounded less interesting – "have long since rejected concepts of personal creation for ideas of mass production, recycled imagery and synthetic materials". No one knows this better than poor Mr Emms the wronged toymaker, whose work was appropriated by H.

And then there is the issue of what Ernst Gombrich called "the beholder's share": what we bring to the work to complete the experience of it. Hirst's po-faced sharks and spot paintings demand more of the beholder. When we and a stuffed shark exchange blank stares, we may be at a loss to find any meaning in the latter. While the title assures us that there *is* meaning it doesn't tell us what that meaning is. There is a promise of meaning. We need help and, unfortunately, it is forthcoming. There are plenty of people willing and able to tell you what impact the work must have on you, and what it tells you about "modern society", "contemporary life", "the twenty-first century" or some such gigantic abstraction so you'll feel ashamed of the yawn that overtook you when you were supposed to be overwhelmed by shock. In short, you'll feel there is something wrong with *you* if Damien H's whimsies don't hit the spot.[1]

This is what much art – what the courageous and much reviled critic Julian Spalding has called "Con art" – has come to: an unilluminating critique of your failure to respond to it with amazement, shock or whatever emotion the critic thinks he or she should feel when walking around it in a gallery. Conceptual art is supposed to replace dumb "retinal" art with ideas. The trouble is that the ideas are third-hand: fragments of endless parroted chatter built out of clichés themselves constructed from unexamined abstractions. Even so, they are a magnifying lens through which the work is viewed; its nullity as art is concealed behind a fog of "significance".

This is worse than worthless; it does not merely add nothing – it takes away. Many of us have extraordinary experiences looking at, or reflecting on, ordinary objects. When such items are translated to a gallery and mounted on a plinth of portentous garbage there is a sense of loss. The con artist, far from enriching our everyday experiences, appropriates them for himself, and for those who regurgitate his arcane clichés, and sells them back to us on his own terms. One is reminded of the definition of a management consultant: someone who steals your watch and charges you for telling the time. At the very least, the con artist, buoyed up on his or her retinue of interpreters and promoters, is like someone who keeps on digging you in the ribs before treating you to an unsolicited, tedious, redundant commentary on what you are seeing.

Damien H's fortune was made before he was born: in 1917. That was the year Marcel Duchamp exhibited the famous urinal (*Fountain*) signed "R. Mutt" (an idea that may well have been stolen from a forgotten but considerably more original figure Baroness Elsa von Freytag-Loringhoven). He started a trend whereby works of art were judged less by the craft and vision that had gone into making them than by the theory upon which they were mounted. Duchamp's (slightly funny) joke has worn more than a little thin over the succeeding decades.

For nearly a century Duchampery has been taking the piss out of us. But piss is a fluid and it can flow both ways. Perhaps, as we approach the hundredth anniversary of the "scandal", we may cry

"We are no longer Mutt", refuse to be piss-taken any longer, and cases like those of Damien H will prove to be the last throes of a trend that has gone on too long. A little more attention will be freed up to celebrate those who are truly talented, truly original and truly liberating. It would be cheering to think that philosophy, with its power to detect bullshit, might hasten this process. But I'm not holding my breath – for fear of dying of anoxia.

NOTE

1. Hirst, of course, is not the only artist to provoke nonsense from art critics. You would not have to have much knowledge of physics (or common sense) to appreciate that this "authoritative" statement about twentieth-century art is garbage: "Just as cubism has unconsciously found a way of objectifying the dilated space and time of Einstein's universe, so Pollock's vision embodied the fissile indeterminacy of the quantum world" (Bray 2012: 45).

10

The Fight Against (e.g. My) Stupidity

Since about 1948 or thereabouts (when I was a tot in a cot) I have been Professor of Data-Lean Generalizations at the University of Me (this character made his first appearance, under his own name, in Tallis 2012a). There seems little chance that I shall retire from this post, which brings me great satisfaction, although I have several billion colleagues most of whom, *mutatis mutandis,* are equally well qualified for the title. The key qualification is to be able to punch above one's cognitive weight, making assertions that are either ill founded or entirely unfounded, usually in the belief that they are, or are probably, true "because I think so". The beliefs promulgated by a Professor of Data-Lean Generalizations encompass huge swathes of that boundless nexus of rumours called "The World Out There"; but, unfazed by the mismatch between the size of the universe and that of the human mind, I am prepared to defend some of them with considerable vigour.

If anything is likely to persuade me to retire, or at least partially retire, from this self-appointed post it is reading Kathryn Schulz's luminously intelligent and witty investigation of our propensity to error. In *Being Wrong: Adventures in the Margin of Error* (2010) she ranges widely and digs deep. Her inquiry is "built around stories of people screwing up" and involves "illusions, magicians, comedians, drug trips, love affairs, misadventures on the high seas, bizarre neurological phenomena, medical catastrophes, legal fiascos, some possible consequences of marrying a prostitute, the lamentable failure of the world to end, and Alan Greenspan" (*ibid.*: 17–18). Her thesis is that the propensity to error goes through our psyche like "Brighton Rock" through a stick of Brighton Rock. It is not "a hallmark of the lawless mind" but "our native condition", because the mind is not an unfoxed looking glass in which the intrinsic reality of things is replicated. We peer into the world through a succession of distorting lenses.

The first and most important is our body. While we are all familiar with visual illusions, mirages and the hallucinations that hover round the borders of sleep, we are unaware of the extent to which we may sometimes be deceived at this very basic level. "There is no form of knowledge, however central or unassailable it may seem, that cannot, under certain circumstances, fail us" (*ibid.*: 70). (She does not, I hasten to add, make the elementary philosophical error – that is to say an error available only to philosophers – of the argument from illusion; see Chapter 1, "Seeing and Believing".) Schulz recounts the case of Hannah, a woman who had had a stroke. Asked by her doctor to describe his face, she reported that he had short hair, was clean shaven, had a bit of a tan and was not wearing glasses. Unfortunately, his face was concealed behind a screen. Hannah was in fact blind but, being unaware of her blindness, she confabulated. She was suffering from Anton's syndrome, one of a group of similar neurological problems known as anosognosia, or the denial of disease. And such conditions are emblematic of the human condition: "To be blind without realising our blindness is, figuratively, the situation of all of us when we are in error" (*ibid.*: 68).

We are most likely to be in error where we are most confident, as is dramatically illustrated by a study of those so-called "flash-bulb" memories we have of surprising and traumatic events. We all know exactly where we were and what we were doing when President Kennedy was assassinated or when we learned of the death of Princess Diana. No we don't. Careful studies by psychologists such as Ulric Neisser have shown that an individual's successive accounts of such memories correlate very poorly with one another, although the memories remain just as "vivid". We find it difficult to set aside the notion that our experiences of the events have been "burned" into our brains. And it is easy to get healthy people to confabulate, as was demonstrated in a study in which two psychologists set up shop in a department store in Michigan. They asked their subjects to compare what they claimed were four different varieties of tights. In fact, the tights were all the same. Even so, shoppers not only declared a preference for one or the other but gave solid reasons for their preferences.

These are benign errors. Schulz's "Wrongology", however, visits some very dark places. Not long ago, Alan Greenspan was described as the "greatest banker in history". But his opposition to regulating the market for derivatives – to the point where he persuaded Congress to pass legislation actually forbidding the head of the Commodity Futures Trading Commission from taking any action – contributed to bringing about the crash that resulted in 40–45 per cent of global wealth evaporating in just over a year. Appalling miscarriages of justice, driven by the rock-like certainties of prosecuting authorities, may be impossible to overturn even in the face of new evidence, as reputations have been invested in being right – illustrating Nietzsche's observation that "convictions are greater enemies of truth than lies". Medical errors result in an annual death rate in the USA equivalent to a sold-out 747 crashing every three days, killing everyone on board. And Thabo Mbeki's confidence that he knew the cause of AIDS killed 300,000 of his fellow countrymen. The assumption that one is right can be very costly for others.

In many cases, we readily admit to our mistakes and take steps to avoid them in future. But some mistaken beliefs we cleave to with a passion. As Schulz says, with characteristic wit, once you are contradicted (particularly by your mother), a belief "can move from noncommittal to evangelical in a matter of milliseconds" (2010: 84–5). And this can be as true of beliefs about the recipe for a cake as about the origin of the universe. We take pride in being right;

indeed, the best way to be insufferable is always to be explicitly right about bloody everything. Being wrong is a source of embarrassment and shame, especially if our interlocutor treats it as a matter of life and death. Being insulted can turn us into sophists for whom victory is more important than truth. It will exacerbate our tendency to embrace the "Evil Assumption ... that people who disagree with us are not ignorant of the truth, and not unable to comprehend it, but have willfully turned their backs on it" (*ibid.*: 108).

It is difficult in the heat of the argument to remind oneself that dishonest victories are not only empty but are a small defeat for mankind – or at least the bit of mankind you are addressing. Or that a defeat in an argument may be a victory for truth, even if one acknowledges that the notion of truth has sometimes to be qualified: whose truth and from what point of view? Indeed, the kind of honesty that it implies – which includes the honesty of saying "I don't know, I can't make up my mind etc." – may occasionally be disabling as when we are faced with someone for whom victory is all. It is like choosing to be the one cyclist in the Tour de France who resists the temptation to take drugs. In the early 1980s I was a doctor in Liverpool, and local politics were dominated by a demagogue with a few simple ideas. With these very simple ideas and his stock phrases about capitalism and the working people of this country, he could run rings around anyone who had a more nuanced view, never mind someone who had subordinate clauses in their sentences. It was the Glasgow Kiss versus the Queensbury Rules. It took Liverpool at least two decades to recover from the effect of that man's rule.

So while we might remind ourselves there are worse things than losing an argument – there is winning an argument through over-simplification of the issues or dishonest mobilization of bad arguments or non-facts – it is still easy to get yourself into a position where you are prepared to go to the wall, or die in a ditch, for something that, in a cooler moment, you would acknowledge you weren't sure about.

We should be most on our guard when we think we have reached a secure position. There is a fundamental, and admirable, discipline of treating our own views with immense suspicion. Anyone who really wants to advance debate has to be prepared to be in constant war against himself or herself. We have, as Paul Valéry said in *The Evening With Monsieur Teste*, to learn to kill the puppet, the automaton, within. To paraphrase the poet W. B. Yeats, out of the quarrel with others we make rhetoric but out of the argument with ourselves we fashion true thought. But are we really prepared to change our mind in the light of further facts and further arguments? Or to consider whether there is actually something deeper – an unacknowledged principle or invisible frame of reference on which our position depends – that needs examination? Truly the political theorist and economist J. K. Galbraith spoke when he said: "Faced with the choice of changing one's mind and with proving there is no need to do so, almost everyone gets busy on the proof" (1971: 50).[1]

That is why the model of science is so attractive. It is, of course, a terrible mistake to think that the *methods* of science, particularly physical science, can be applied to understanding society and how we should order our affairs to promote our collective well-being. That is scientism, not science. But there is something that we can take from science and apply more generally: an ethos. It was beautifully captured by Richard Feynman in his famous commencement address to the students at Caltech, on "theories that don't work and science that isn't science". Here he is, talking about "integrity in science", a "leaning over backwards", as the principle of honesty: "If you are doing an experiment, you should report everything you think might make it invalid – not only what you think is right about it … You must put down all the facts that disagree with it, as well as those that agree with it" (1986: 341).

Attractive – but a counsel of perfection. The temptation to conscious or unconscious dishonesty in defending our beliefs is in part because, Schulz observes, our beliefs "are inextricable from our identities" (2010: 95). Our sense of our identity is itself bound up with the community to which, voluntarily or involuntarily, we belong. The pressure under certain circumstances to have the same beliefs as those with whom we identify can be irresistible, if only because dissent seems like betrayal. This is evident not only within religious communities, where apostasy is punished by vilification, excommunication or death, but in the kind of "groupthink" that gripped the Kennedy administration during the Bay of Pigs disaster, the Johnson administration in Vietnam and the Bush–Blair axis seeing non-existent WMDs in Iraq.

The existential investment is particularly profound in the case of beliefs about those with whom we are in love. The pain of discovering that there is more to the other person than was evident in the shared dream of the initial romance – even if it is just a matter of their having their own ideas about things – is a poignant reminder of something that all error tells us: that we are to some extent on our own; that we have world pictures that cannot be directly shared; that we are to a greater or lesser degree sealed up "each in his prison". Our resentment that the beloved should have a different take on reality is "in no small part, a resistance to being left alone with too few certainties and too many emotions" (*ibid.*: 199). At any rate, there is nothing to compare with falling in love for drawing "swift and sweeping conclusions based on scanty evidence" (*ibid.*: 263).

"Wrongology" threatens to be a dismal science, telling us unwelcome truths, but Schulz's sparkling introduction greatly mitigates the pain of the message with the pleasure-giving manner of its presentation. And, notwithstanding all that has gone before, Schulz ends on a rather cheerful note. There are, after all, many ways in which we can limit the damage caused by our inescapable tendency to err. And while there are individuals who continue to defend beliefs that have been refuted, with increasingly wild rationalizations, there are others who, at great personal cost recant their earlier creeds. One unlikely hero in *Being Wrong* is C. P. Ellis, an ex-Klansman (he was the head honcho of the Durham NC Klavern), who devoted the later part of his life to furthering the cause of justice for black people.

And while error itself is not a good thing, it is linked to other things that are good, such as our intelligence and our imagination. Without the inductive capacity that takes us beyond what the evidence truly delivers, we would not be able to find our way round the world; we would not enjoy the surprises, the defeated expectations, that comedy exploits; we would not have that hunger for knowledge and understanding, based upon our sense of our cognitive limitations, that drives us to the creation of art and the theorizing that underpins science. It is because we live in a domain of possibilities that we can imagine new realities and we are able to transform actuality as no other creature has. Mistakes, Schulz says, "enable not only our biological evolution but our social, emotional, and intellectual evolution as well" (*ibid.*: 336). So, perhaps I shouldn't require the Professor of Data-Lean Generalizations to retire yet. But, somewhat late in his career, he is on probation.

One thing I can be certain of is that (my and others') stupidity will survive this assault on its credentials. How could I think otherwise, knowing what I do of some of the thinkers whom I have most admired and whose thoughts have been my constant companions? Martin Heidegger, to whom I have devoted a monograph, was fooled long enough by the rhetoric of a mouth-foaming psychopath to give him (A. Hitler) a resounding endorsement. Another major philosophical influence, Jean-Paul Sartre, supported at various times Stalinism (20,000,000 deaths) and Maoism (70,000,000 deaths). Michel Foucault (good in parts, like the vicar's egg) continued to welcome the Iranian Revolution long after it was apparent to most people that Ayatollah Khomeini had created a theocracy thigh deep in a river of blood, where, incidentally, Foucault's own gay sexual orientation was punishable by death.

Blindness to reality among profound thinkers is not confined to philosophers. Valéry, not a philosopher in the conventional sense but a thinker I admire enormously, took the side of the anti-Semitic anti-Dreyfusards in the battle of ideas that divided France for several decades. Gottlob Frege – the father of analytical philosophy, inspiration to Wittgenstein and Russell – proved also (at least at the end of his life) to be an anti-Semite:

The diary shows Frege to have been a man of extreme right-wing political opinions, bitterly opposed to parliamentary systems, democrats, liberals, Catholics, the French, and, above all, Jews, whom he thought ought to be deprived of political rights and, preferably, expelled from Germany.

(Dummett 1973: xii)

This, of course, goes beyond stupidity to something considerably more sinister; but a certain kind of stupidity would have assisted him to his views J. M. E. McTaggart, a great metaphysician of the first quarter of the century, was "a bloodthirsty patriot" who led the group that expelled Bertrand Russell from his lectureship in Trinity College for his pacifism. His profound questioning of the nature of reality (in particular the reality of time) seemed to sit comfortably, apparently, with an unquestioning allegiance to the cause of killing Germans in the First World War. And, finally, Giuseppe Ungaretti who provides one of the two epigraphs for this book, was an ardent supporter of Mussolini and the Fascist cause.

It may be that philosophers, with their propensity to look past particular details to the most general ideas about the world in which they live, are particularly at risk from a certain sort of stupidity: that of not seeing what is in front of their own noses. But this is precisely the kind of generalization that anyone who is on guard against himself should pounce on.

The spectacle of other people's stupidity is more enjoyable than awareness of your own and moral indignation is more fun than shame. What is more, others' stupidity is more readily visible. And even acknowledging your own past stupidities might lead to the wrong conclusion: that you have left stupidity behind in a progression towards ever more intelligence and wisdom. Such Whiggishness is no more justified in relation to oneself than it is in relation to the history of nations.

It may seem paradoxical to try to see aright our universal, inveterate tendency to be wrong, but Schulz succeeds brilliantly. I am tempted to say that *Being Wrong* is one of the most important books published for many years, but this judgement would presuppose that I had checked all the other millions of books for their comparative

138

importance. Even so, this sobering and yet liberating inquiry could make a major dent on the stupidity of the world, including even mine. But, having read this book, I know I may well be mistaken. I hope I am not. The tot in the cot is a little chastened.

NOTE

1. How frequently, or how easily, you should change your mind is a delicate issue. We have all met individuals who seem to bear the impress of the last person who leant on them. I like to think that the tough time I give myself arguing in solitude would prevent me from being such a character. I would say that, wouldn't I?

11

Colonic Material of a
Taurine Provenance

PRELIMINARY NOTE

In 1996, Alan Sokal, a professor of physics at New York University, submitted an article to *Social Text*, a leading academic journal devoted to postmodern cultural studies. The article "Transgressing the Boundaries: Towards a Transformative Hermeneutics of Quantum Gravity" was "a pastiche of left-wing cant, fawning references, grandiose quotations, and outright nonsense" (Harrell 1996: 1133–3) "structured around the silliest quotations [by postmodernist academics] I could find about mathematics and physics" (Sokal 1998: 11). It was accepted without being sent out for peer review: most tellingly, without the editors seeking the advice of a physicist or anyone qualified to judge the assertions made about physics in the article. The fallout was spectacular. The cry of "Gotcha!" echoed round the world.

This looked like the beginning of the end of postmodernist waffle. That, at least, was what some people (including myself) thought at the time, although things have not turned out that way. The conclusion of this essay that follows – published in 1999 – reflects that optimism, although the gravity of the intellectual disease it describes should have warned against hope of a complete, even less a rapid, cure.

* * *

When I was a boy, I was friendly with a lad who lived a few doors away. We used to take bicycle rides together and have gunfights on the wasteland and light fires and play scratch cricket. Our ways parted as our interests evolved in different directions. There were no hard feelings and, indeed, much residual good will. William (this is not his true name, which I shall withhold for the sake of his family) did not share any of my own developing intellectual interests and I felt none of his love for sailing. I was surprised, therefore, when one evening my mother came across an interview with William in the *Liverpool Echo* in which he declared that his real passion was "cybernetics". I felt that I had misjudged him and wondered whether, after all, we did have more in common than I had thought. The next time I ran into William, I asked him about his interest in cybernetics; more particularly, I asked him what "cybernetics" was. My ignorance was genuine, rather than assumed. To our embarrassment, we both discovered that William, too, was ignorant about the nature of cybernetics. For him, it was just a word. It had something to do with science and technology and the future and seemed rather glamorous and was much talked about then. It was clearly just the thing to impress the readers of a provincial newspaper. I didn't pursue the matter and we saw little of each other subsequently. The last I heard of him, he was doing well as a solicitor. Poor William could not have expected that his comments about "cybernetics" would have been taken up ("interrogated", "problematized") by a reader of the *Liverpool Echo*. This was hard luck. Even more unjustly, he was not awarded a tenure-track post in humanities on the strength of his allusion to cybernetics, or a Chair in the Systems of Thought at the University of Paris.

I was reminded of William when I read *Intellectual Impostures* (1998) by Alan Sokal and Jean Bricmont (henceforth S&B). Like William, other characters they have examined, including Julia Kristeva and Jacques Lacan, have the habit of using terms of which they have not the faintest understanding, in order to impress the impressionable. Unlike William, they did not grow out of it and, also unlike William, they were rewarded not with obscurity but with international fame and the adulation of seemingly intelligent academics the world over.

For many years, Kristeva, Lacan *et al.* got away with murder, confident that their readers would have only the slightest acquaintance with the areas of knowledge they expropriated to prop up their ideas and their reputation for scholarship, indeed for omniscience. Few, if any, real historians took note of Michel Foucault's divisions of history into periods separated by abrupt changes in the *épistème*; with few exceptions, analytic philosophers did not think of Jacques Derrida as someone to engage in a debate about the contemporary significance of J. L. Austin and speech act theory; and for every ten thousand students who learned about Jean-Jacques Rousseau's ideas via the wilfully eccentric expositions by Derrida, there was hardly one who had read, and reflected upon, Rousseau's writings for herself.

Eventually postmodern theorists attracted the attention of a few experts in the disciplines into which they had strayed. Linguists looked at their linguistics and found it littered with elementary errors. Derrida, for example, repeatedly confused the sign of a whole with the signifier and so have his many hundreds of thousands of obedient disciples (for a non-expert view of Derrida's and others' confusion over Saussure, see Tallis 1995a). This error is one of the cornerstones of his work. Other linguists (e.g. Harris 2003) were amused by the Derrideans' ignorance of linguistics outside Saussure, this ignorance perhaps strengthening their confidence in their ability to pronounce on the whole of language. Historians have examined Foucault's egregious versions of the history of thought and have discovered that even the relatively small and (according to taste) original or eccentric empirical base upon which his broad sweep theories are poised is not infrequently at variance with the documentary evidence (see Merquior 1985). Indeed, one does not have to be much of a scholar to demonstrate that Foucault's *épistèmes* and the so-called *ruptures epistemologiques* separating them – the central notions of the book that brought him his international fame (*The Order of Things*) – are, to say the least, tendentious. Names that should fit into one of his periods are awkwardly active in others and disciplines that transcend his periods prove to be more numerous than he had thought. (One or two people did try to point this out to him while he was alive but you can't tell a Professor of the History of Systems of Thought at the Collège de France anything.) Perhaps Foucault was speaking autobiographically when he described discourse as the violence we do to things.

Some of the most detailed critical examinations have been carried out on postmodern theorists' misrepresentations of philosophical ideas and of the history of philosophical thought. Inspection of what some postmodernists say about major figures such as Plato, Descartes, Husserl and Peirce in support of their own theories – in which, not infrequently, isolated comments have been made to stand for huge chunks of "Western thought" – have revealed an iniquitous mixture of genuine misunderstanding and strategic misquotation.

Surely, then, the game should have been up a long time ago. This has been suggested by Terry Eagleton. In a review of M. J. Devaney's (1997) devastating critique of some of the philosophical assumptions underpinning postmodernist "thought" (*"Since at Least Plato ..." and Other Postmodernist Myths*), he commented wryly on the danger of critics "muscling in" on areas about which they know nothing. For a critic "muscling in on philosophy", there is, he pointed out:

> The alarming possibility that a real philosopher might weigh in on your arguments, rather as you might seek to impress someone at a party with your smattering of knowledge about the Dead Sea scrolls, only to discover later that he is a New Testament scholar. (1998: 2)

And he adds of Devaney that she "brings to aspects of postmodern thought the grossly unfair advantage of a knowledge of the history of philosophy to postmodernism" (*ibid.*). At any rate, it is true that there is always a risk that somewhere there might be a reader of the

Liverpool Echo who will take notice and ask you what cybernetics is or question your credentials for talking about it.

So *is* the game up? The appalling truth is that all the damaging revelations about the incompetence of the postmodern theorists seem to cause little or no damage to the major players or, indeed, to the industry itself. The reasons for this are spelled out by Eagleton: "there is too much spiritual and material capital now invested in the postmodernist industry for its executive directors to be able to afford to listen" (*ibid.*). The continued dissemination of postmodern theory in the face of decisive criticism is extraordinary; there are few liberal arts students who do not encounter theory in their courses and for many of them, such as those studying literature, it lies like an incubus over the entire curriculum. How can this be possible?

The protection built into theory and its web of affiliated schools, weatherproofing it against criticism, is very thick indeed: it is composed of layer on layer of ignorance. The hundreds of thousands of first-year students in English studies who are given an encapsulation of Western philosophy as "logocentric" by their teachers will, for the most part, not themselves have read a page of Plato, Descartes or Heidegger – key thinkers cited in the argument. Nor, in many cases, will their teachers or the teachers who taught them. The bibliographies that are dished out to support the postmodernist history of philosophy will often exclude the actual works of Plato, Descartes or even Heidegger. Instead, they will list Derrida, Lacan, Foucault and so on; or, more likely, popularizations of Derrida, Lacan, Foucault and so on, and the work of their intellectual descendants. Both teachers and texts, in other words, will be several orders removed from engagement with, knowledge of, reflection upon, the thinkers whose thoughts are incorporated into the postmodernists' global systems of understanding that students have to accept on trust. For every student who has read Plato, ten thousand will have been subjected to Derrida's error-ridden account of the *Phaedrus*, which was one of the foundation stones of his famous theories about logocentricity as "the pattern that will dominate all of Western philosophy" (see Devaney 1997: esp. 26–35).[1]

Those (and I include myself among them) who imagined that demonstrating the factual errors, empirical inadequacy, logical inconsistency and explanatory failures of postmodern theory would be sufficient to raze the card castle to the ground had not taken account of this multi-layered insulation of the theorists. We made the same mistake as General Haig before the Battle of the Somme when he anticipated that, after a week of continuous bombardment and a million shells, the Germans would allow the British soldiers simply to walk over the lines. And like Haig's infantry, we found ourselves in no-man's-land, weighted down with sixty-pound packs (in our case loaded with useless things like facts and arguments), waving our rifles at undislodged machine guns behind ten-foot-high barbed-wire entanglements. The Germans had had only two years to dig in before the Somme; the postmodern theorists have been building their trenches and tunnels and bunkers for thirty years.

Nor had we reckoned with another tactic: silence. One can minimize the impact of valid dissent by denying it the publicity involved in rebuttal. Or with a third tactic: *argumentum ad hominem* of such ferocity as to deter others from popping their heads over the parapet. (My own experience in this respect, although very irritating, was relatively mild. See Tallis [1995c]. At least my livelihood was not at stake.) Those who criticized theory were diagnosed, classified, stereotyped, mocked, and sent away to lick their wounds. Derrida's contemptuous treatment of John Searle – who showed how, at the heart of Derrida's careless pyrotechnics, was a simple misreading, in this case of the philosopher J. K. Austin – typified the kind of deliberate refusal to engage scholars in real debate that kept critical, and knowledgeable, minds at bay (see Searle 1983b). Derrida took *argumentum ad hominem* a step further towards the playground by focusing on Searle's name: *argumentum ad nominem* that mocks him as "Sarl" (Derrida 1988). (Derrida plays with Searle's name, calling him 'Sarl' [*Société a responsabilité Limitée*, Society with Limited Liability]. This is *premier cru* Derrida: laboured puns passing for jokes intended to illuminate the ambiguities of the world, statements of huge scope, and the passionate pursuit of incoherence.)

The additional advantage of this pugilistic approach was that debate was obscured in a smokescreen of scandal; in the ensuing darkness all arguments, good and bad, looked pretty much the same and the whole thing could be presented as a punch-up between the revolutionaries and the conservatives, or between the old fogeys and the Young Turks.

Nor, finally, had we reckoned with the sheer volume and size of the industry; for every book questioning Derrida's use of Saussure, there are many hundreds taking it for granted and expounding its significance for students who have to learn to speak fluent Theorrhoea if they are to survive their end-of-year assessments. Derrida is on a thousand curricula; critical examinations of his work do not figure in a handful. Those who teach theory are not foolish enough to draw attention to critiques of theory: no place on the reading lists for them. Only academics committed to truly critical thought and the disinterested pursuit of truth (that superannuated category) and careless of career prospects would be foolish enough to shoot themselves through the foot by drawing attention to dissenting voices.

For all these reasons, the publication of *Intellectual Impostures* is an event of first importance for the future of the humanities. Apart from its very great intrinsic merits, it has, on the back of Sokal's brilliant hoax, attracted enormous publicity both within and beyond academe. Moreover, S&B have set new standards for the criticism of postmodern theory and they bring new hope that the Castle of Untruth might at last be stormed successfully. Never before has a critique of the lords (and ladies) of intellectual misrule been carried out so thoroughly or with such magisterial authority.

S&B are careful to state at the outset that they do not pretend to undermine the whole of postmodern theory, or that they have discredited the entire *oeuvre* of its founders. And yet their patient, quiet examination has implications, and will have effects, that go far beyond their specific remit. It may even be that students, made aware at last of a universe of discourse outside the dogma of their theory-besotted teachers, will give the dissenting voices a fair hearing, and the game will truly be up.

S&B define (academic) postmodernism as "an intellectual current characterised by the more-or-less explicit rejection of the rationalist tradition of the Enlightenment, by theoretical discourses disconnected from any empirical test, and by a cognitive and cultural relativism that regards science as nothing more than a 'narration' a 'myth' or a social construction among many others" (Sokal & Bricmont 1998: 1). They investigate with scrupulous care the way that *eminences grises* such Lacan, Luce Irigaray, Kristeva, Bruno Latour, Jean Baudrillard, Gilles Deleuze, Félix Guattari, Paul Virilio and others have used mathematics and the physical sciences in their writings about language, literature, the human psyche, feminism and contemporary culture. S&B have discovered that these luminaries are Williams, every man and woman of them. Their writings are littered with, and the apparent force of their arguments is heavily dependent upon, terms and concepts of which they have not the faintest understanding. Because their audiences are slightly more sophisticated (although no less gullible) than the readers of the *Liverpool Echo*, the terms they borrow have to be more recherché than "cybernetics". So Kristeva uses items lifted from mathematical logic and set theory, Lacan mobilizes mathematical logic and topology, Irigaray broods on solid and fluid mechanics, Deleuze and Guattari plunder differential and integral calculus and quantum mechanics, Baudrillard invokes Euclidean and non-Euclidean geometries, and so on. But the appearance of erudition is, for the great part, just that: an appearance.

Consider, for example, the project that established Kristeva's reputation: her investigation of what constitutes a poetic language.

For us poetic language is not a code encompassing the others, but a class A that has the same power as the function $\varphi(x_1 \ldots x_n)$ of the infinity of the linguistic code (see the existence theorem, …), and all the "other languages" (the "usual" language, the "meta-languages", etc.) are quotients of A over more restricted extents … (limited by the rules of subject-predicate construction, for example, as being the basis of formal logic), and disguising, because of this limitation, the morphology of the function $\varphi(x_1 \ldots x_n)$. (Sokal & Bricmont 1998: 41)

Me neither. And this is only a beginning. Many of her pages are littered with axioms, such as the following (the axiom of choice),

$$(\exists A)\left\{Un(A)\cdot(x)\left[\sim Em(x)\cdot \supset \cdot(\exists y)\left[y \in x \cdot \langle yx \rangle \in A\right]\right]\right\},$$

which are familiar to mathematicians schooled in set theory but for the majority of her readers (including myself) utterly opaque. This formula, she claimed, "is applicable in our universe E (sic) of the *pl*" (*ibid.*: 42).

Roland Barthes saluted her work as "entirely new and precise". And a commentator has asserted that:

What is most striking about Kristeva's work ... is the competence with which it is presented, the intense single-mindedness with which it is pursued, and finally, its intricate rigour. No resources are spared: existing theories of logic are invoked and, at one point, quantum mechanics. (Lechte 1990: 109)

The rest of us might have some reservations – particularly about the use of quantum mechanics. Lacking the knowledge to check the validity of the terminology and its incorporation into the argument, and out of something between modesty and pusillanimity, however, we would hesitate to classify it as CMTP (colonic material of a taurine provenance).

It is only now, thanks to the authors of *Intellectual Impostures*, that we can say that our instincts were justified. For S&B are two very remarkable people: not only are they theoretical physicists for whom set theory, matrix algebra, topology and their application to quantum mechanics and non-linear systems are the basis of their daily labour – so they are neither fazed nor impressed by it, they just do it – but they also have a deep understanding of wider cultural and philosophical issues. For the first time, scholars with the necessary credentials to judge the claims of Kristeva – and others like her who mobilize advanced mathematics and cutting-edge physics (or the outer surface of it) to back up their global assertions about language, literature, the self, and so on – have looked at what she has written and have subjected her use, or invocation, of science and mathematics in her writings to a minute examination. And what they have found is that her concept-dropping (cf. name-dropping) is totally inappropriate and betrays what are, to them, elementary confusions and embarrassing misunderstandings.

S&B have shown that Kristeva's account of "*pl*" (in "E (sic) of the *pl*", *vide supra*) is strictly meaningless, as are numerous other passages that they quote and analyse at length. For instance, the use of the axiom of choice has no relevance whatsoever in linguistics and cannot help to elucidate poetic language. The introduction of this axiom in mathematical set theory is motivated by the study of infinite sets, or of infinite collections of sets.

> Where does one find such sets in poetry? To say that the axiom of choice "makes precise how every sequence contains the message of the book" is ludicrous – we're unsure whether this assertion does more violence to mathematics or to literature.
> (Sokal & Bricmont 1998: 42)

It is worth noting, in passing, that one of the very many virtues of S&B is the length and number of the quotations; many of the excerpts they analyse are a page or more long, not sound-bites taken out of context. Their criticism, moreover, is linked to a luminously clear explanation of terms that are misused, or at least the more fundamental concepts from transfinite set theory and mathematical logic. Their explanatory notes are an intellectual feast and make one hungry to be in the company of real mathematicians.

Among the numerous (and to them elementary) errors that S&B expose in Kristeva's text are (a) her belief that Kurt Gödel asserted the opposite of what he actually did assert in his famous incompleteness theorems; (b) her misunderstanding that the axiom of choice implies a notion of constructability; and (c) her mistranscription of a definition of the set of functions $C_0(R^3)$ in a way that would hit in the eye anyone who knew about the necessary field. None of her audience would have spotted this; most of them – and most of the readers of this book, I suspect – like me untrained in advanced mathematics, would not have understood a word of what she said and would have to take her arguments – and their relevance to poetic language (say the distinctive character of "Shall I compare thee to a summer's day" as opposed to "If you touch my car I shall bash your head in") – on trust. Nevertheless, it was this kind of junk that earned her a chair in linguistics at the University of Paris VII eight years after she astonished *toute Paris* (including the all-powerful Roland Barthes) with her "new and precise" work.

A betrayal of trust seems an egregious way to a chair, but they order things differently in the postmodern world, where truth is a superannuated concept. It would be interesting to know who was on her appointment committee and how much they understood of set theory and mathematical logic. The defence that this all took place a long time ago (early 1970s) and Professor Kristeva has moved on to other things (even setting herself up as a psychoanalyst of sorts) won't, of course, wash. If it was shown that I had arrived at the chair I occupied between 1988 and 2006 on the basis of what, in my own sphere of clinical medicine, would be regarded as fraud, I should feel obliged to resign, however many years ago the work was done. Besides, Kristeva has hardly redeemed herself by moving out of her brand of quasi-mathematical poetics only to embrace the work of an out-and-out fraud, Jacques Lacan.

Lacan, whose dogma on the Symbolic, the Imaginary and the Real (for a critique see Tallis 1995b) Kristeva has advocated with uncritical passion over the past twenty years, also borrowed concepts and terms from disciplines of which he had no real knowledge or understanding.

For over a decade before his death, he was obsessed by the notion that certain topological figures might cast light on psychiatric illness and the human mind. He believed, for example, that the torus was "exactly the structure of the neurotic". (The ghastly details are set out in Roudinesco [1997], which is all the more compelling for being written by an adoring, non-judgemental disciple. The ludicrous "exactly" beautifully exemplifies the way intensifiers are used whenever counter-intuitive notions of huge scope and nearly zero comprehensibility are being asserted without argument, fact or illustration.) His disciples, too, therefore, believed in the torus: in the ever-deferred hope, perhaps, that belief might bring understanding. (*Credo ut intelligam.*) At any rate, they listened in awe to his day-long seminars on such things as the Borromean knot and continued to do so even when, in his tragic final years, as a result of multiple strokes, his speech was mangled by dysphasia and his cognitive functions were somewhat intermittent. By then even his silences, as dysphasia gave way to aphasia and his mind emptied, were attended to and subjected to lavish deferential interpretation.

Now S&B have shown what no one has hitherto been knowledgeable enough to demonstrate: *precisely* (the term is used appropriately on this occasion) what was wrong with Lacan's use of mathematics. It is not only empty glitter but also internally flawed. Lacan's writings, in addition to supporting his bad, ethically dubious psychiatric practice (see Tallis 2000: 284–9), are also lousy mathematics. Lacan makes advanced errors – muddling the very specific technical meanings of certain terms from topology (such as "compactness") and so on – that only serious mathematicians could spot. But he also makes elementary ones, as when he confuses irrational and imaginary numbers or the universal and the existential quantifier, the latter the kind of mistake a first-week student in mathematical logic would not perpetrate.

With the help of his pseudo-mathematics, Lacan could gibber for hours, while his disciples listened in silence:

I will posit here the term "compactness." Nothing is more compact than a fault, assuming that the intersection of everything that is closed therein is accepted as existing over an infinite number of sets, the result being that the intersection implies this infinite number. That is the very definition of compactness... (Quoted in Sokal & Bricmont 1998: 21)

The confusion here – pointed out by S&B – of the topological notion of compactness with other notions outside topology would have entirely escaped the attention of his unmathematically schooled audience. What did they think as they listened to this stuff for hours? Many of them were in love with him, or with the idea of him, or with the idea of their own election to his inner circle. And others perhaps were simply awestruck, like the villagers in Oliver Goldsmith's poem *The Deserted Village*:

And still they gazed, and still the wonder grew.
That one small head could carry all he knew.

A wonder that would have been greater had anyone among the psychoanalysts and other quasi-medical hangers on at his seminars noted the all-too-obvious and tragic fact that the head in question was, in his last few years, afflicted with a progressive dementia.

S&B are not distracted by the Mixmaster prose (in which all sorts of glamorous terms are poured into the pot and spun round at 500 rpm) from the particular uses to which individual terms are being put. So when Lacan argues:

Structure is the aspherical concealed in the articulation of language.

It is clear that, as far as meaning is concerned, this "takes hold of it" of the sub-sentence – pseudo-modal – reverberates from the object itself which it wraps, as verb, in its grammatical subject, and that there is a false effect of meaning, a resonance of the imaginary induced by the topology, according to whether the effect of the subject makes a whirlwind of asphere (*sic*) or the subjective of this effect "reflects" itself from it.

(Quoted in Sokal & Bricmont 1998: 20)

S&B coolly observe that Lacan has failed to clarify what he means by structure: even if one assumes the term to be confined to a strict mathematical usage, topology provides but one interpretation of structure. There are many others: order structure, vector-space structure, manifold structure, and so on. Since Lacan has not clarified which sense of "structure" he means, his argument, such as it is, is empty.

In their discussion of Kristeva, S&B point out that "she makes no effort to justify the *relevance* of the mathematical concepts to the fields they are purporting to study – linguistics, literary criticism, political philosophy, psychoanalysis" (*ibid.*: 47). And the lack of relevance of the flaunted erudition is a constant finding in *Intellectual Impostures*: it is there merely to impress and terrorize the uninitiated. The surface appearance of relevance is sometimes sustained by treating metaphors as if they were literal truths. This is particularly evident in the writings of the feminist philosopher Luce Irigaray.

Irigaray, like Kristeva and Lacan, betrays a thorough misunderstanding of the science she exploits in her writings. She evinces a particular interest in hydrodynamics and is fond of technical terms such as "laminated planes", "solenoid movements" and "springpoints". But S&B's main concern is with the way she uses hydrodynamics to underpin some pretty large assertions about sexual politics and the oppressed and marginalized situation of women. Her conclusions are, to put it mildly, somewhat underdetermined by the science she invokes.

Among Irigaray's claims to fame is her argument that science is sexist; for example $E = mc^2$ is "a sexed equation". The reasons she gives for believing this are tenuous to say the least. The equation "privileges the speed of light over other speeds that are vitally necessary to us. What seems to me to indicate the possibly sexed nature of the equation is not directly its uses by nuclear weapons, rather its having privileged what goes faster" (quoted in *ibid.*: 100). The muddle here is so dense that it is probably not worth unpicking it. Suffice it to say, as do S&B, that Einstein's equation has been verified to a high degree of precision. Whatever Irigaray might feel about privileging the speed of light over "other speeds that are vitally necessary to us", the equation would not be valid if the speed of light c were replaced by another speed: by, for example, the average speed of a woman running after an escaping toddler in a supermarket. To put this another way, if the equation is sexist, so is nature; if scientists are sexist in respect of this equation, it is because matter is. And if matter is sexist, so are women, who are made of matter just as men are (although on that there is more to be said, as we shall see).

The sexism of science, Irigaray argues, explains why fluid mechanics is not as well developed as solid mechanics. The inability of (masculinist) science to deal with turbulent flow is explained by the association of fluidity with femininity: whereas men have sex organs that protrude and become rigid, women have openings that leak menstrual blood and vaginal fluids. Hence male science cannot cope with fluid dynamics. This seems somewhat to overlook that men, like women, are 90 per cent water; that, like women, they have 5.5 litres of blood circulating round their bodies; and that they bleed, salivate and, yes, take a leak – just like women. Notwithstanding these inconvenient facts, this is Irigaray's explanation of why women are erased from masculinist theories, and fluids have been erased from science.

There is, of course, a huge literature on fluid dynamics and turbulence. It has been one of the key areas investigated over the past few decades using the new analytical tools derived from chaos theory. A full definition of the conditions under which flow will become turbulent still eludes scientists; but there are also incompletely solved problems in *solid* mechanics, and, indeed, throughout physics (see e.g. Smolin 2006).

One would think that misrepresenting the facts, misusing specialized terminology (Irigaray is even worse on mathematical logic than she is on fluid dynamics), and using metaphors that are tendentious to the point of lunacy would be a high price for an intellectual to pay. One is curious to know what end would justify these desperate means. Astonishingly, Irigaray's goal is to support conclusions that no male chauvinist pig would dare shout out in his sleep:

But every stage in this development [of the female sexual economy] has its own temporality, which is possibly cyclic and linked to cosmic rhythms. If women have felt so terribly threatened by the accident at Chernobyl, that is because of the irreducible relation of their bodies to the universe.

(Quoted in Sokal & Bricmont 1998: 113–14)

This is not an isolated episode of essentialist redneckery. Elsewhere, Irigaray links rationality and objectivity with masculinity and emotion and subjectivity with the female. To "reduce women to their sexuality, their menstrual cycles and rhythms (cosmic or not)" is, as S&B point out, "to attack everything the feminist movement has fought for during the last three decades. Simone de Beauvoir must be turning in her grave" (*ibid*.: 113). There is a bitter irony in the deployment of so much mystification and intellectual dishonesty to *bien-pensant* ends only to discover an unexpected commonality of view with the rednecks. The reason that Irigaray has not attracted the anger of ordinary oppressed women is the obscurity in which the works that have brought her international fame among academics are wrapped.

Interestingly, the snobbish misuse of science in postmodern thought sits side by side with hostility to science itself: to its claims to be useful or true. S&B deal particularly effectively with the epistemic relativizers such as Bruno Latour, who assert that science is "social through and through" and scientific "facts" are social constructs. (Bruno Latour's [2004] thoughtful modification of his idea that scientific facts are mere social constructions was prompted by his worry that people were taking his ideas too seriously – to the point of denying man-made global warming as an objective reality.) None of those who relativize scientific knowledge to the authority of discursive communities can explain the three most important things about science: that it makes stunningly accurate predictions; that it produces technology that works; and that that technology is as effective in Blackburn as in Soweto – so that antibiotics for a gravely ill old man in Blackburn do the trick as for a gravely ill young woman in Soweto.

It is interesting to reflect on the irony that the fraudulent use of scientific jargon has been a prime means of winning over the herd to postmodernist discourse, while true science is treated with disdain by postmodernists. How perverse that so many humanist intellectuals can be utterly enslaved by the evidence-free, opaque pseudo-science of someone like Lacan, while true sciences, such as physics or pharmacology, are objects of suspicion. Or that science can be relativized, while the mangled representations of science in the addled brains of amateurs like Irigaray are treated as truths to be accepted without question. There is an analogy here with the postmodern theorists' attitude to facts. We are told that there are no facts, only discursive communities and their interpretations; so postmodernists require us to support only those facts (usually wrong and/or highly selective) that they mobilize to support their vast empirical assertions about the course of history, the nature of society or the politics of the self.

S&B wrote *Intellectual Impostures* above all because they felt that postmodern theory – notwithstanding its rhetoric of subversion, its much-protested support of the marginalized, the dispossessed, the oppressed – was undermining genuinely progressive thought. Reflecting on his hoax, Sokal emphasized that his main concern was not "to defend science from the barbarian hordes of lit. crit. 'we'll do just fine, thank you'", but "to combat a currently fashionable post-modernist/poststructuralist-social-constructivist discourse – and more generally a penchant for subjectivism – which is, I believe, inimical to the values and future of the Left" (Sokal & Bricmont 1998: 249). The last thing that those who seek social justice need is the anti-scientific, anti-empirical, relativizing, obscurantism of writers like Irigaray. If one discards the notion of objective truth, based upon facts outside human discourse, and sneers at the notion of "empirical reality", then one plays into the hands of the powerful, for whom denial of certain facts at least is extremely convenient: the path from asserting that "$E = mc^2$ is a sexist equation" and that it has everything to do with male domination and nothing to do with nature itself to Jean Baudrillard's assertion that "the Gulf War never happened" (see

Norris 1992; it was merely the sum of its media representations), to the denial of the massacres in East Timor or of the reality of the Holocaust, is short and straight.

Needless to say, S&B have caused widespread outrage by pointing this out. The announcement for a conference at the University of California-Santa Cruz (quoted by Sokal & Bricmont 1998: 196–7) spoke of "a spectre haunting U.S. intellectual life: the spectre of Left Conservatism". S&B and others of their kind were criticized for their opposition to "antifoundationalist theoretical work" and "for an attempt at consensus-building ... founded on notions of the real". S&B were portrayed "as socially conservative Marxists trying to marginalize feminist, gay and racial-justice politics and as sharing the values of the American right-wing commentator Rush Limbaugh" (*ibid.*). The conflation of a belief in objective reality (the default position of all conscious beings) with subscription to the poisonous beliefs of a bigoted shock jock is an interesting measure of the level of thought, understanding and judgement that the postmodern ideology fosters.

The difficult position of those who are concerned about social justice, but who also abhor the confusions and dishonesty of postmodernist theory, has been succinctly expressed by Wendell Harris in a recent review of John Ellis's *Literature Lost*:

It is easy for an American with even a rudimentary social conscience to find multiple evils in American economic, cultural, and social systems and in Western culture generally. Only wilful blindness can fail to recognize continuing racial inequality and sexual discrimination, the increasing gulf between the rich and the poor, the existence of millions who lack access to adequate medical care, and a court system that has less to do with justice than with the cleverness of the lawyers one can afford. That the shrill chorus of condemnation flowing from the cultural critics currently dominating university humanities programs can point to real evils makes it difficult to challenge these critics' equally real confusions and excesses. Effective response is made doubly difficult by the multitude of political and religious conservatives whose response to all attempts to achieve equality is the cry "freedom being trampled by political correctness" – one does not care to be mistaken for one of their number. (1998: 497)

The difficulty of conveying and sustaining what are not very difficult distinctions – between, say, opposition to oppression and opposition to dishonest and ineffectual ways of opposing oppression – is itself a measure of the degree to which postmodern theory has debased, coarsened, confused and corrupted academic discussion.

This, above all, is why the publication of *Intellectual Impostures* is an event of the utmost importance in the humanities. It also accounts for the determined attempts of what Eagleton (1998: 2) describes as the executive directors of the postmodernist industry have made to avoid engaging it on its own terms, or indeed, any terms at all. Unsurprisingly, Kristeva dismissed the book as "an intellectually and politically insignificant act" (quoted on the back cover of the paperback edition of *Intellectual Impostures*). Well, she would say that wouldn't she? After a brilliant thirty-year career founded upon CMTP she is not going to abandon a winning formula and start cultivating intellectual transparency. And her *sangfroid* was to be justified. In 2004, a few years after S&B's exposé, she was awarded the huge Holberg International Memorial Prize. The irony of this is especially bitter, given that Ludvig Holberg, after whom the prize was named, was instrumental in bringing enlightenment to Nordic countries. (And Kristeva was joined by Bruno Latour as a Holberg Prize winner in 2013.)

She was, moreover, being perhaps unwittingly overmodest: an exposé of the nullity of her *oeuvre* is – or should be – a matter of the first importance. For Kristeva's writing is of the greatest significance, less (as will by now be evident) because of any intrinsic merits (who knows whether it has any?) than because of the attention it has attracted and the man- and woman-hours (indeed person-centuries) that have been squandered in reading, recycling, worshipping, citing, quoting and expounding her gnomic thoughts. And also for the immensely influential bad example that she and a handful of others have set, showing that not only can you get away with murder but that you can tough out well-founded criticism by simply ignoring it.

Derrida – who always ignores criticism (as has been repeatedly pointed out) – responded to S&B with a characteristic haughty sneer: *"Le pauvre Sokal"*. This was echoed by John Sturrock (1998) in a laidback review that made clear that intellectual integrity was not something to get overexcited about and that worrying about factual truth is the kind of pedantry one should despise. Sturrock concedes that "the imposters [Kristeva, Lacan *et al.*] are abusing concepts that they don't know enough about to call acceptably in evidence" but then, astonishingly, argues (in defence of Irigaray!) that while her "invocations of the sciences concerned may be worse than dodgy", nevertheless, "in that libertarian province of the intellectual world in which she functions, far better wild and con-tentious theses of this sort than the stultifying rigour so inappro-priately demanded by Sokal and Bricmont" (*ibid.*). In other words, better uncheckable opaque junk that excites the ignorant with the illusion of near-understanding than the rigorous sciences that S&B profess (sciences, incidentally, that are not only rigorous but also beautiful, imaginative, exciting and – as a bonus – in many cases quite close to the truth and consequently useful in the world out-side the text).

The attitude of influential literary journalists like Sturrock only underlines the significance of *Intellectual Impostures*. But it also shows how its impact might be blunted. This book should bypass the "executive directors" and reach out to the students. It must not, therefore, be trivialized by the scandal it has caused. Its critique of postmodernism should not be sidelined as simply part of a lit-tle war within academe, an obscure spat between "insular Anglo-Saxons" and the "Latest Foreign Fraud" (which is how Sturrock tries to present it). For this reason, it is worth spelling out in a little more detail just why S&B's book is important.

First, although S&B modestly refuse to claim that their examination of Kristeva *et al.*'s way with scientific jargon invalidates the rest of their work, on which they suspend judgement, there is much independent evidence that the dishonesty S&B have uncovered is part of the wider culture of charlatanry in postmodern theory. The various habits that S&B list in their Introduction – (a) "holding forth at length on theories about which one has, at best an exceedingly hazy idea"; (b) "importing concepts from the natural sciences into the humanities or social sciences without giving the slightest conceptual or empirical justification"; (c) "displaying a superficial erudition by shamelessly throwing around technical terms in a context where they are completely irrelevant"; and (d) "manipulating phrases and sentences that are in fact meaningless" (*ibid.*: 4) – are the immemorial vices of the academic charlatan. Never, however, have they been so prevalent, so well funded and so well rewarded.

These vices have flourished with the rise of so-called "interdisciplinary" studies, which have assisted a decline in standards of rigour and honesty in certain quarters in the humanities. They are not, of course, truly interdisciplinary. When Kristeva impresses an audience of literary critics with her grasp of set theory and when Lacan talks to a mathematically and medically ignorant audience about advanced topology and psychiatry, they are relying on the absence of experts from the disciplines whose terminology they have pinched: people who can tell fake jewellery from the real thing. Even where such individuals may be present in the audience, they will be in the minority and, in the heated and partisan atmosphere that surrounds the Great Postmodernists and their thousands of disciples, are unlikely to be able to dent the charlatan's reputation. It was not for nothing that John Bayley once described "interdisciplinary studies" as giving cunning and opportunistic academics the "chance to rise between two stools".

I saw this process in action recently, at one of only two non-medical conferences I have attended. The speaker was arguing *à la* Irigaray that twentieth-century microphysics, with its emphasis on energy rather than matter, and its notion of an atom that was composed mainly of nothing, should allow women a more female relationship to their own bodies. I took the opportunity in question time to point out that (a) this "female" physics had been created overwhelmingly by men (Max not Maxine Planck and Albert, not Albertine Einstein); (b) that the new physics applied not only to female bodies but also to male bodies – as well as to pebbles, scorpions, vomit and dog-dirt; and (c) that Susan Stebbing had long ago shown up the fallacy of feeding back the discoveries and concepts of microphysics into the macroscopic world of bodies visible to the naked eye – her target had been Arthur Eddington. (While the billiard-ball world of the atom is no longer in place, the billiard-ball world of the billiard ball most certainly is; see Stebbing [1958].) The speaker did not deal with this question very well but I was prevented by the chair – who was clearly shocked by my interjection – from questioning the speaker further, as (she said censoriously) there are other people who want to have their say. These other people were full of praise for "a rich contribution" and stimulating presentation and offered the speaker a good deal of underarm bowling. Afterwards, the speaker (a tenured academic at a very prestigious university) came up to me and said that, had she known that there was to be an expert in the audience, she would have been more cautious in her arguments! I am not an expert, equipped only with A-level physics and a certain amount of unbewitched common sense. This response was at least contaminated with the residue of honesty and even shame.

The correlative of contempt for the truth is contempt for one's audience. The most direct expression of this is the infamous duration of the lectures given by many of the *maîtres à penser*. It was not unusual for Derrida to talk for four or more hours. And Lacan would, as noted, go on for an entire weekend. (Whether comfort breaks were allowed is not noted by his hagiographers.) This kind of harassment bears an eerie resemblance to Castro's four-hour harangues of his cowed populace sweating in the sun, or Brezhnev's and Mao's addresses to the congresses of their respective parties. The Great

Postmodernist Thinkers and their representatives make no concessions to their auditors or readers. Even if the passages from Kristeva, Irigaray and others cited by S&B did not turn out to be nonsense scientifically, it would still be obvious that they were never intended as acts of communication, any more than the demented and aphasic mumblings of Lacan in old age, listened to with respect and awe by his anguished disciples, were genuine acts of communication. Communication requires not only that one knows what one wants to say but also that one has an idea where one's audience is at and how best one can reach them. Kristeva, whose aim was not to communicate but to show off, to impress, to terrorize, knew very well that her audience would be unable to understand the pseudo-mathematical garbage she was imposing on them.

The notion of an audience of academics willing to listen respectfully to at best unproven, at worst meaningless, assertions of enormous scope, opens up deeply worrying questions about the impact of postmodernist theory on the institutions that support contemporary humanities. We have known for a long time that once someone is elevated to the status of *maître à penser* he or she is unassailable: his or her views cannot be challenged. But this immunity must now apply to a much wider number of teachers: to all those many thousands who parrot the *obiter dicta* and world-encompassing assertions made by the *maîtres*. This implies a huge constituency of students, graduates, post-docs, lecturers, readers, professors and so on willing to remain silent while the dogma, couched in a bituminous prose, is intoned. I am not talking about a few besotted groupies enthralled by a charismatic figure like Lacan. I am talking about a fair slice of the humanist intellectual community. I am talking about herd behaviour and I am talking about a huge herd.

The deceitful use of scientific and other jargon by individuals who have no wish or intention to be understood is bad enough when it is addressed to a handful of disciples. When it is poured into the minds of teenagers who have it foisted upon them as part of a compulsory curriculum and have scarcely enough time to remember it, never mind to think critically about it, the abuse of trust shades into something more serious: indoctrination. It is usually unsuccessful because of the saving indifference of most young people to abstract ideas and the lack of sanctions other than failure in examinations. But it is sickening, nonetheless; even more so when one thinks that this deference to the *maîtres à penser* and their intellectual descendants sits side by side with the postmodern theorists' constant talk of revolt, rebellion and subversion, and when one reflects that rhetoric about overthrowing established power structures is combined with uncritical and childlike acceptance of whatever opaque utterance pops into the *maître's* head.

The profound significance of S&B's lucid, deeply passionate and authentically erudite book, is that, by shining real light on the fake jewellery of the leading postmodernist theorists, it has shown what has happened to academic humanities in the final decades of the twentieth century under the influence of individuals like Kristeva, for whom intellectual legerdemain has become a way of life. It is an important moral act, although S&B would, I suspect, distance themselves from that kind of portentousness, judging that it should be reserved for those who believe that they are subverting the power structures of Western civilization by offering a new Lacanian reading of a popular film.

At any rate, S&B have made a decisive contribution to the dispiriting task of uncovering the extent to which fraud, as James Drake (personal communication) has pointed out, has become institutionalized in the humanities. Science fraud is more common than was once thought, but still rare enough to be news; humanities fraud, being structural, rather than episodic, is never news; indeed, it is hardly visible. The brilliance of Sokal's famous hoax (given as an appendix in Sokal & Bricmont [1998] and also available on the internet) was that it was fraudulent to exactly the degree that the works it was parodying were fraudulent. No wonder the editors of *Social Text* felt badly treated; the article that had made them a laughing stock of the academic world was no worse than hundreds of similar boluses of garbage published month in, month out in dozens of similar journals. Its global assertions, its lack of factual evidence, its incoherent logic, its errors in the use of science, its superficial erudition unsupported by real knowledge or understanding: all these are endemic in the world of postmodern academe. And it is so easy to get away with murder. As Katha Pollitt noted, "the comedy of the Sokal incident is that it suggests even the postmodernists don't really understand one another's writing and make their way through the text by moving from one familiar name or notion to the next like a frog jumping across a murky pond by way of lily pads" (quoted in *ibid.*: 194).

S&B's Epilogue contains many interesting and important reflections on the fraudulent expropriation of the natural sciences by postmodern theory. They wonder "how we got here". They single out (a) the neglect of the empirical, (b) scientism in the social sciences, (c) as a correlative of this, the prestige of the natural sciences, (d) the social sciences' "natural" relativism, and (e) the traditional philosophical and literary training, which ill equips individuals to deal with scientific texts. Most usefully, recognizing that "interdisciplinarity is the order of the day", and acknowledging the advantages that might come from the incorporation of science into the humanities, they list some of the lessons that might be drawn from their investigation (*ibid.*: 176–9). They should be pinned on the wall of every humanities department where postmodern theory is taught and there are resident worshippers of individuals like Kristeva:

1. It's a good idea to know what one is talking about.
2. Not all that is obscure is necessarily profound.
3. Science is not a "text".
4. Don't ape the natural sciences.
5. Be wary of argument from authority.
6. Specific scepticism should not be confused with radical scepticism.
7. Ambiguity may be a subterfuge.

To these one might add: do not lie to yourself or to anyone else; or – do not betray the trust of your students, your peers, your readers and the intellectual community at large. Precisely because it is so easy to mislead your students and even your peers in the field of cultural criticism and the humanities and even easier in the field of interdisciplinary studies, one should be aware of it as a permanent temptation to be guarded against.

Academics intending to continue as postmodern theorists in the interdisciplinary humanities after S&B should first read *Intellectual Impostures* and ask themselves whether adding to the quantity of confusion and untruth in the world is a good use of the gift of life or an ethical way to earn a living. After S&B, they may feel less comfortable with the glamorous careers that can be forged in the wake of the founding charlatans of postmodern theory.

Alternatively, they might follow my friend William into the law, although they should check out in advance that they are up to the moral rigours of such a profession. At any rate, being a lawyer might be a little more comfortable than being a postmodernist for the next few years. For, after S&B, a spectre will be haunting the exponents of theory: the Truth. Poor old Truth that the giants of postmodern theory have so thoroughly trashed. It's set to make a comeback. So watch out.

AFTERWORD

This essay was published nearly a decade and a half ago and, as signalled in my prefatory note, its conclusion has proved far too optimistic. The habit described by S&B of "importing concepts from the natural sciences into the humanities or social sciences without giving the slightest conceptual or empirical justification" has proved hard to kick. The remorseless rise of the idea that humans can be understood in *biological* terms – that men (and women) are essentially beasts or (if that sounds too judgemental) that they are organisms acting out a biologically prescribed agenda rather than conscious agents – has been reflected in the development of new disciplines that try to re-badge humanities as "animalities". Neuro-aesthetics, evolutionary literary criticism, neuro-musicology, neuro-poetics, evolutionary art theory: these are some of the fruits of the endeavour to dress up academic humanities in the clothes of biological science (see Tallis 2011). By the markers of inputs (grants, new posts) and outputs (academic papers, journals to publish them in, and conferences) they are flourishing. As S&B taught us, colonic material of a taurine provenance has fertilized the ground in which the weeds of false scholarship may grow in abundance.

The fight continues.

NOTE

1. Derria's interpretation of Plato's *Phaedrus* is demolished by Vishwa Adluri (2011: esp. 112–14). Adluri's careful reading exposes the tendentiousness of Derrida's subordination of Plato's text to his own preconceptions.

12

Mission Drift

THE *LOGOS* OF LISTMAS: BOXING DAY REFLECTIONS ON THE
GOSPEL ACCORDING TO JOHN 1:1 AND 1:14

The more I think about my own species, the more I am astonished
at our infinite capacity for mission drift. This is the other side of our
miraculous ability to take the fundamental givens of our lives and
turn them into something else. Breathing is appropriated for flute-
playing, reciting 500-year-old sonnets or cracking dirty jokes. The
feeding necessary to maintain thermodynamic equilibrium, elaborated into dining, spawns a thousand customs, rules and ceremo-
nies, from the killing of the fatted calf to the annual ritual of buying
Nigella Lawson's latest recipe book.

We should not, therefore, be at all surprised at the metamorphoses undergone by the December Festival. Its original significance is so thickly encrusted with secondary meanings that the
joke "they're even dragging religion into Christmas nowadays" can
be misunderstood as a serious complaint. Not that "they", whoever
they are, are making much headway. Even the brushes with religion
are often mere trimmings: the congregations at carol services are

there mainly for the tunes and the nostalgia rather than to praise the Only Begotten.

How we get from A to B is a matter for cultural and intellectual historians and anthropologists. Here, on this slightly hung over Boxing Day morning, I just want to *measure* the distance from point A to point B. Point A was a story, back-storied by some heavy theology: approximately 2,000 years ago, according to John 1:14, "the Word was made flesh, and dwelt among us". And Point B? 2,000 years later, we witness the flesh celebrating this in a bonfire of consumption. I bet those "feet in ancient times" didn't expect to kick-start turbo-capitalism.

Of this, too much has already been said; and no one, being preached to by their own dyspeptic body this Boxing Day morning, needs an additional sermon. Anyway, some of us have grown wiser over the years. Gone are the hepato-toxic misadventures of our youth, when the journey home in the early hours of Christmas morning was along streets that had set out to sea, equipped with rubber pavements and lamp-posts that responded sarcastically to polite requests for directions and in something like Welsh.

But even those who manage to sidestep the mandated excesses are still caught up in the frenzy. For there is another aspect to Christmas, less easy to escape than pigging out. To explore this, let us return to Point A: "In the beginning was the Word" (John 1:1). What happened to the Word? Well, after a few forays into large- and small-scale nastiness – wars, oppression, physical and psychological torture, and the rest – it multiplied and formed up into ... *lists*. *Logos* became logistics. Christmas, as an irritated senior doctor told me when I, a medical student, turned up late for a dinner, "is a matter of *organization*". Thus we arrive at Point B.

Raymond Briggs, inventor of the grumpy Santa, a little while ago admitted that, while he supported "the principle of a day of feasting and presents", he was anxious about the arrangements (Duncan 2012). His anxiety, he confessed, began in October. This is a late start. For me, Christmas 2012 first announced itself in August. My wife and I, cheering ourselves up on the night of our return from sunny Greece to fifty shades of Mancunian grey, had a meal in a local pub. A meretriciously decorated Christmas tree propped up the announcement that bookings were open for Christmas dinner. "Hurry, hurry! It's later than you think!" The months that followed witnessed a gradual quickening of pace and a network of logistics growing ever more dense.

The logistics of Listmas are a long way from an event that may or may not have happened over 2,000 years ago. That event was the fulfilment of a promise made in the distant past of the distant past. This signified, we are told, a new covenant between the universe that man had found himself in and the God that some men had thought had placed him there. It seems remote from a long and possibly unsuccessful search for the address of someone who was thoughtful enough to send you a card but not thoughtful enough to realize you might have forgotten their address; or from the mystery of the Incarnation to puzzling over what to buy for an otherwise forgotten relative, as you fight your way through a tide of others similarly preoccupied, while a pop version of "Silent Night" is bellowed out at the volume that neuro-economists have determined will maximize the will to buy. Or, to switch testaments for a moment, there is an impressive chasm between contemplating God saying "Let there be light, and there was light" and watching (for the twentieth year in succession) the Christmas lights refusing to light up even when, as a last resort, you plug them in.

So it's not the excess that marks how far we have drifted from the revelation of God's presence on earth, it's the complexity. More particularly, the wrong kind of complexity. Think of the line manager in the department store reminding himself to vary the Sellotape order in (say) November from "plain", to the "holly and robin" pattern. Or of the journeys to and fro for the right-sized batteries. Or of the unwanted pullovers knitted lovingly by aunts with arthritic hands. These are, admittedly, better ways of honouring the idea of a loving God than the bloodbath of confessional wars or physical or psychological abuse that Christ's followers have sometimes inflicted on those who don't love the right God or in the right way. But they do seem spectacularly beside the original point.

What's more, the opportunity–cost starts to weigh on your mind. The four-hour search for that missing postal address to which to send a merely reactive card could have been used for doing good – for example, fighting the Coalition government's Health and Social Care Act 2012, which will bring death to some, suffering to many and possibly financial ruin to many others – instead of fretting that there is someone out there thinking badly of your discourtesy. Anyway, next year, I am going to be properly organized. Start the shopping the day after Boxing Day, leave the decorations and the Christmas tree up, and use the time thus freed to think about – well, what? Perhaps about how we spend our time – or our time is spent – and how we are always looking past the present to a future we never quite reach, past experiences to an idea of experience that eludes us, and, how, preparing so hard for Christmas, we find, when all the arrangements are in place, it is Boxing Day and next Christmas is already coming towards us with its lists of things to do.

JOHANN SEBASTIAN PHONEHOLD
OR BAROQUE AROUND THE CLOCK

But it is Bach, making music in the Castle of Heaven, who gives us the voice of God – in human form. He is the one who blazes a trail, showing us how to overcome our imperfections, through the perfection of his music: to make divine things human and human things divine.   (Gardiner 2013: 558)

Cultural history has many cunning passages but few can be more cunning than those that link the work of the great Johann Sebastian Bach with this moment of impatience as I wait, on hold, after a sequence of wrong and irrelevant numbers, for the person I am trying to contact. My waiting is serenaded by a reassurance to sheep that they may safely graze. I tap out my anger in time with the rhythm of the reassurance: Da, da, der, dada, der, dada, dada ...

To lessen the chance of an explosion when I do get through – as a self-feeding irritation draws added sustenance from any attentive hearing it may get – I shall focus on a few of the connections. (This is called distancing and it is the secular equivalent of trying to see things *sub specie aeternitatis* and it rarely works; my tried patience reminds itself that it is being tried.)

Here, then, are three paths from JSB (Johann Sebastian Bach) to JSP (Johann Sebastian Phonehold): (a) the history of my trying to make this phone call and why; (b) the history of the telephone and of phone behaviour; and (c) the history of music and its dissemination.

The frustrations of the obscure

Why was I trying to make this phone call? That answer will already be hinted at when I say that I was an unpublished author trying to get through to the editor of a literary magazine. I wanted to make my name as a writer and there was a rumour that the magazine in question was the place to get published, following which the chances of becoming well known might fall from 1:10,000 to 1:1,000. Whether this is on the strength of its contents I don't know. I suppose I should know, given that would-be contributors are "advised to study the magazine carefully before submission". Sound advice, but not everyone has the time to do a day's work, write and revise stories, post manuscripts (a matter of getting stamps, envelopes, addresses and Sellotape in unnatural proximity) *and* study the numerous magazines that may be an outlet for his work.

Two months after I had posted the story, I did take a look at the magazine. Dull stuff, nicely printed, and nothing to make me feel that I was knocking at the wrong address. A month after this, I rang the magazine and had my first dose of frustration and my first fix of reassurances to sheep that they might safely graze. I was also offered a reassurance as, with beginner's luck (which, in common with all beginners, I believed was the order of things), I got through to someone who appeared to be at the cognitive and executive heart of the operation and seemed almost to remember my manuscript. She would get back to me. This was, indeed, reassuring. The signal of my story "A Quartet for the End of Time" was not, after all, lost among the competing noise of rival signals sent out by a thousand more or less illiterate and more or less uninspired wannabes who also will have not studied the magazine but also wish to be famous.

The morning passed and I was not got back to. The evening came and I was not got back to. Many other things happened in my life and so it was another week before I realized I had not been got back to. I was not yet wealthy and famous so I had to be patient. It is the ancient prerogative of the powerful to keep the less powerful waiting (see Chapter 13, "Anteroom: On Waiting"). I was still counted among the less powerful and must accept being kept waiting, a strange condition that does and does not exist in which you do and do not exist for the one who keeps you waiting. In the end, I attempted to put a term to waiting. I rang.

The switchboard answered less promptly this time. I had, it seemed, already used up one of my tickets. I blame my garbled story – the one I spoke, not the one lying in manuscript form in an office whose author-drowning chaos I could envisage with ever more clarity – on the fact that I was first put through to the marketing department after a second dose of reassurances to sheep. No, I did not wish to buy advertising space in the magazine. Nor did I wish to subscribe to it. I wished only to help ensure it was worth subscribing to. Eventually, after a third helping of JSP, broken off in mid-chord, I got through to someone whose main concern was the name of the person to whom I had spoken before. Unfortunately, I had taken no names. "In that case I don't think I can help you now. Tell you what, I'll have a look through what we've got in the office ... There's an awful lot of stuff about." And in response to my protest (I could feel a dangerous heating in places that usually felt cool – for example, the tips of my ears), said she would look into it as a matter of priority because (she agreed with me) I should certainly have received some kind of decision after three months. And then my other phone rang and I had to terminate the conversation: I was being summoned by the same day job as prevents contributors like me from studying the magazine in question with sufficient care.

I started spending more time in the virtual anteroom of the magazine, in the company of different individuals with expensive voices who seemed to promise an end to waiting but were merely devices for structuring the waiting, punctuating an otherwise seamless flow of angry monologue with myself, excerpts from which spilt from time to time into phone calls to the magazine. Unluckily for these individuals, I typically reached them after an exasperating detour through marketing, through a broken connection, through a switchboard that could not be re-engaged through being engaged. I was therefore more brittle than was pleasant for either of us. Some of my more detailed speeches were too long – after all, my listeners, too, had a job of work to do – and were, besides, too impassioned and (frankly) at times too personal.

As when, for example, I explained what a small part the story had in my overall life plan and what a disproportionate amount of my (precious) time chasing its whereabouts was taking. I pointed out that being prevented from getting through to the right person to find out about the fate of the story was to be stuck in a digression from a digression. The superordinate goal was fame, and possibly wealth with the concomitant freedom to think without the unwelcome interruption of salaried labour that neither appealed to my appetites nor played to my strengths. In support of this seemingly receding goal, I had not only written the story but also got together stamps and envelopes and addresses and Sellotape and then remembered, in the face of a torrent of distractions, to post it. (The experience I am speaking of is set in an analogue age, long before the invention of email.) Even if the piece were accepted, there would still be proofs to wait for and correct, publication day to be got to, and the long silence after that as it was ignored by those who could not tell Stork from butter, wheat from chaff, signal from noise, until it was joined in the public consciousness by more and more stories from my pen and my name at last cut the skyline. So many steps, and I was stuck on one of them – a moss-covered step in the basement of everything – talking fast to the wrong person because I was running out of change to feed into the public call box! It was as if (I said, varying the metaphor, as I could detect waning interest) my life had got caught up in a thousand self-embedded subroutines or I had ten thousand left-hand brackets without right-hand closure, like a draw full of odd socks. It was as if, I said, each of the thousand paces that separated my study from the postbox had to be planned, even negotiated, separately. It was like a thousand-mile journey down a motorway in first gear.

I was still talking long after my increasingly silent interlocutor had gone, back to her own life, acting out its own version of the pursuit of happiness. When I attempted to resume the conversation, or at least to reconnect with her consciousness, I encountered: silent payphones that pocketed my money but did nothing else; accidental misdiallings that reached people who were sometimes grumpy, often puzzled, occasionally understanding, and always irrelevant; and calls abandoned on hold because the train was about to leave or there was pressing business. Such was the anteroom of the anteroom that I accessed with ever more difficulty. Increasingly, I seemed to be put on divert, on hold or, as now, on phonehold, thinking of those early reassurances. As sheep should know, such reassurances are not worth the air they are bleated into.

The miracle of technology

I dealt with my temptation to smash whatever phone I was talking into by trying to appreciate the pyramid of technological miracles upon which it sat. The history of the telephone has been written elsewhere with doubtless more authority than I can muster but, if thinking over a few highlights makes it easier to control my rage, then it may be worth visiting them.

The steps leading up to the means by which we are able to throw our voices many millions of times further than our unaided throats can manage, and are able to target those voices to one pair of ears only, are numerous. By that I mean they encompass nearly all our understanding of the physical world and hundreds of thousands of patented ingenuities. When you are shouting angrily down the phone – as I was – you are holding the product of much of the collective brainpower of humanity in your sweating, white-knuckled hand.

The telephone brings together many forces of nature, and nearly every branch of physics, in the service of the transmission of human meaning – sorrow, delight, love, hate, consumer disaffection, greed – and phonehold music, which contains all or none of these meanings. At the heart of the telephone is the microphone: a vibrating diaphragm that matches the vibrations that pat the air when we speak and correspond to the human voice. To see the voice as a sound like any other is chillingly clear-sighted. To see sound as vibrations in the air that may be replicated by a vibrating object other than that of their primary source is an insight of genius.

The exploration of the connection between vibration and sound began with music. The transcription of sounds into waveforms and generalizing those waveforms into the harmonies that govern the universe was the project that first made Pythagoras tingle and has made humans so powerful. Bowstrings, sand patterns, early music: and, suddenly, a vision of the universe, the Pythagorean dream realized 2,500 years later, beyond the wildest.

Digressions, digressions, I need digressions! How does the vibrating diaphragm come to replicate the vibrations of the voice box of the man enquiring of the whereabouts of the fate of his manuscript, and with such fidelity that the rising octaves marking the transition from polite wondering to angry demand are deafeningly obvious? Enter electromagnetism. The speaking voice makes a diaphragm vibrate and this moves a magnet attached to the diaphragm in such a way that its field is cut by a wire. Thanks to the observations of Mr Faraday, this was predicted to create a varying electrical current, which can then be transmitted down the wire linking the furious author to the "person at the other end" (that, alas, is the nearest she gets to an official title – a handle to refer to her within the scornful and scorn-filled anecdote of the scorned author). Amazingly, the prediction turns out to be true. More amazingly still, the varying current, when it reaches the other end of the wire, causes a varying magnetic field that attracts another magnet attached to the diaphragm at the receiver, with forces that fluctuate more rapidly than the feelings of a lover or an author, and causes it to vibrate, too. Together, electricity, magnetism, acoustics and mechanics bring my voice to hers and her voice to mine.

As we have become less astonished at the phone – think of those early calls when callers were moved by the sound of distant loved ones separated from their bodies and when they talked against the sound of frying silence, feeling their distance as well as their closeness! – it has become more objectively miraculous. Radio waves connect us and my mailbox in the sky – one of many billions – can be opened at once, and still we get cross. And still I am cross.

We are cross because we are kept waiting. Because we are powerless. Because we are supplicants. And so we must be soothed. Hence those repeated visits by the operator circling the waiting impatiences like a nurse doing a ward round, "I'm still trying to connect you", and by the electronic politeness "We are sorry to keep you waiting. You are in a queue and your enquiry will be dealt with as soon as possible."

The uses of sacred art

Enter Johann Sebastian Phonehold, soother in chief.

Is this a suitable job for a man whose music summarized all that had preceded him and influenced all that followed him? The "jowly, bewigged" genius who was one of the greatest cultural events in the past 1,000 years? Thus do I come to my third theme: the history of music and its dissemination. Of course, that's far too big a topic.

What about the history of the dissemination of music? That'll do, so long as we keep it snappy. Just a few asides will suffice. This is, after all, phonehold thinking.

Music, unlike painting, or literature, has always been liable to spill out of the places where it is made. People have to come to paintings (or did until recently) and books have to be disseminated by effortful printing. Music spreads out: it has no natural boundaries. Who knows where those Neolithic campfire chants ended up? What pricked ears marked their boundaries in the cold, unpopulated air? Music is not only heard but overheard. Even so, it was, until recently, relatively confined. Church music took place in churches. Madrigals were sung in drawing rooms. Trios performed in salons. *Tafelmusik* was played in coffee houses. And then came concerts in concert halls and brass bands in bandstands and music in public for the public. Even so, the ratio between the hearers and the overhearers, between the listeners and the inflicted upon, still favoured the former, until the genius that made phones possible also made possible those radio waves that James Clerk Maxwell (awestruck at how the mathematical truths about electricity and magnetism converged with those about light) predicted: a dark light that would carry intelligence just as richly as bright light does but, unlike bright light, would be able to slip through the opacities of our opaque and lumpy world. Because everything was glass to this new form of radiation, it could carry information from everywhere to everywhere. Suddenly music, which to the mathematical stare of the physicist and engineer is mere information, a sequence of waveforms (just as Pythagoras said the universe was and so set in motion the earlier noted dream that was a gradual awakening to the nature of things), was everywhere. The concert in a hall for 500 is heard by 2,000,000 listeners and overheard by 10,000,000 who have no desire to listen. John Dunstable, hardly heard outside England after the century in which he had a European reputation (and the only English composer to do so until Purcell) was played simultaneously in Chicago and Calcutta.

Our lives became a more dense bombardment of stimuli. Our brains were force-fed. Our pauses, our silences, fewer. Waiting made us more restless. Impatient. Violent, even. Waiting needed to be sweetened: hence the sublime creations of Johann Sebastian Bach being doled out in phonehold fragments.

Thus is the fate of masterpieces and insights and visions in the world. The products of genius are rehearsed by ill-tempered conductors; paintings are glazed with weary eyes made wearier by theory; Shakespeare is an exam hurdle, work for a tenure-track academic, a night out for those unlucky enough not to be able to get tickets for a decent West End show. *Rigoletto* becomes Ring-Tone-Oletto. Edvard Munch's *The Scream* is painted on pub signs and the howling misery of its protagonist is warped by the cultivated pectorals underlying the tee shirt on which it is printed. Pages torn from a volume of verse are used to stabilize a table with uneven legs. And so on.

So my thoughts grow into global grumbles but, despite them, my innards remain gripped in the fist of my local anger. I know that the claim that my call is being dealt with has the same truth-value as the reassurance to the sheep that their grazing will be safe.

The story of my story, like that of the sheep, will not have a happy ending.

SURREALISM: LOVE, LAUGHTER AND STALINISM

At the heart of surrealism was something entirely admirable and irresistible to a philosopher trying to wake up out of ordinary wakefulness. The surrealists were electrified by the lost or buried magic of the commonplace, of ordinary artefacts, of nightly sleep, of the intricacy of streets, of the chance meeting of disparate things: most famously of an umbrella and a sewing machine on a dissecting table. They were in love with the world. And yet their project ended in acrimony and recrimination, and excused, *en route* to the ruination of their original vision, some deeply unattractive postures, creeds and actions.

There are many reasons why things went so badly off the rails. The most important was a tendency towards a spiritual tyranny, most pronounced in the founding father André Breton, aptly named the

Pope of Surrealism. His style of leadership, his unsleeping obsession with controlling the movement, defining what was allowed to take place under its name, the psychological terrorism that placed the surrealists under his rigid and often gratuitously cruel authority, destroyed the spirit of the movement. The flowers of the surrealist imagination withered under the defoliant of a lidless papal gaze in which, to a greater or lesser extent, its practitioners felt caught.[1]

There were other reasons for the demise of surrealism. The voluntary subordination of many of its leading figures, notably Louis Aragon, to Soviet communism was one. This was an act of astonishing self-betrayal and it arose from a hatred of the *bourgeoisie* – people like you and me – who seemed to be smug, asleep, small-minded, tight-fisted of soul, exploitative, dominating, and so on. But it also grew out of something more admirable: a mistaken desire to be of use to the world and to find some practical purpose for the movement. The surrealists, it seemed, lacked the courage of their lack of convictions. As a result, a movement devoted to unfettered freedom of thought, imagination and action placed itself at the disposal of totalitarian regimes. They sacrificed their project on the altar of an ideology that dismissed human freedom as an illusion and made belief in it a heresy to be punished. The ghastly artistic results of this *trahaison* are discussed in Tallis (1998: 104–9).

Surrealism was also disfigured by striking acts of cruelty, forays into imaginary and real violence, a nauseating sentimentality (a not infrequent accompaniment of cruelty and violence) and a shallow silliness that came from an excessive preoccupation with the stale, adolescent aim of *épater la bourgeoisie* and consequently with the secondary, trivial activity of cocking snooks. This seems even more tiresome nearly a century on, where there is hardly a snook left uncocked (see Chapter 9, "The Shocking Yawn"). In the end, hatred – an easy, self-fuelling, emotion – conquered love and laughter; and Breton's desire "to escape the human species" cancelled any sense of wonder at human consciousness. Surrealism killed itself.

To what extent this was deliberate and to what extent inadvertent is difficult to say. The movement's self-destruction may have been

the logical outcome of a pervasive silliness that had many manifestations: notably, a preoccupation with dreams that did not serve the
function of waking us out of wakefulness; flirting with cut-price mysticism, such as astrology, séances, Tarot cards; and a pointless obsession with coincidences and the ill-named "objective chance". In its
attempts to break into a dubious invisible world, surrealism missed
its vocation and betrayed a failure of true imagination that grasps
how the visible world is more amazing than any number of invisible worlds. Those accidental coincidences that were made to carry
such a heavy weight of symbolism could never be as profoundly significant and deeply mysterious as the contrived coincidences of an
average planned meeting between two people who transport themselves over huge distances in order to fulfil a shared intention to be
together. And when it comes to coincidences, nothing can compare
with the radiant coincidence of a sunlit primrose with itself: or with
self-coincidence of things that have come to pass, of things in their
being present before us, in their declaration that they are "There!"

Rejecting the occult, and stale, off-the-shelf, joss-stick mysticism
does not necessarily condemn you to myopic, literal-minded, slum-
berous common sense. There is a valid form of magic realism that
delights in what simply, indubitably, is. It is sufficiently astonished
at thoughts – and the way they draw light from so many different
quarters – as not to have to claim them as the voice of occult forces,
dress them in tutus made of petals, kit them out with gossamer
wings, put them in flight and call them "fairies".

The surrealists (dimly) knew this but the increasing difficulty
they experienced in finding inspiration in the (wrong) places they
searched in (with wrong eyes) frustrated them. This may have contributed to their propensity to violence, to jeering at individuals
whom they placed under stale and (in certain parts of the world)
lethal categories (such as "the bourgeoisie" badged as "class enemies"), and to dishonest pretence (such as that the products of automatic writing, sleep games and hypnotism were in the slightest bit
interesting to anyone except their authors and those who wanted to
promote them for their own purposes).

The surrealists should perhaps have allowed fewer drugs[2] and more music into their lives. Unlike drugs, music does not close you off from the life you have brought to the experience. Indeed music may bathe the actual world in a lovely light: a light of memory perfected by a perfected emotion. (Breton was tone-deaf and impervious to music. "Let the curtain fall on the orchestra", he said [quoted in Caws 1997: 10]). And a greater ratio of actual love to the idea of it might have helped as well. Love, rooted in deep, enduring companionship, as well as physical closeness, may transilluminate lives with the light that is truly their own. And the intuitions of the immensity of the light upon which the present moment draws may be granted at any time, even though it is often difficult to know how to accommodate it in an everyday life of practical responsibility.

At any rate, by the late 1930s surrealism and its practitioners had lost their way and, with some notable and wonderful exceptions, had earned their ghastly posthumous fate: namely, to become the darlings of the advertising industry. Yet there was in their original vision, in its nascent intuitions, something fundamentally worthwhile, a sense of possibility not to be lightly given up, and a feeling for the mysterious interconnectedness of disparate aspects of our multifarious world – evoked for me a few years ago by the sight of an Egyptian doctor, a delegate at an international meeting at which we were both speaking, on a boat trip to Capri, wearing a baseball cap marked COMO and bearing a motif of a Churchillian bulldog itself wearing a baseball cap.

So we should not be discouraged from trying to revisit the delight, the extended sense of possibility, the "love and laughter" with which the movement began. The surrealists' interrupted adventure needs to be taken up again. Let celebration begin.

NOTES

1. Breton's role in the demise of surrealism was not fully apparent to me until I read Ruth Brandon's utterly absorbing *Surreal Lives* (1999), which also gives him full credit for establishing surrealism as a movement. The fatal flaw in surrealism – the

path that opens on to a dozen modes of dishonesty, flummery, fraud, fakery, and so on – is signalled in Breton's famous assertion that "lucidity is the chief enemy of revelation" (quoted in *ibid.*: 219). Enter, stage left, a herd of bulls with laden intestines.

2. The fact that so much surrealist activity was fuelled by drugs is another sign of the collective failure of the imaginative will. It is (just about) worth asking whether the present Epimethean project could be helped along by drugs or even achieved through drugs alone. I think not. The problem with major mind-altering drugs, aside from their frequent long-term destructive effects on the body and sometimes the mind, is that an attempt to enhance awareness of the depth and meaning and richness of everyday life by a means, a chemical substance, that is in itself depthless, meaningless and impoverished, is profoundly self- contradictory. While drugs may temporarily help users to expand into, mentally occupy, the world that they live in and live out, they also take them away from it. The episodic nature of trips, and the disconnection between the context of the trip and the rest of the drug-taker's life (there is, for example, no particular connection between heroin and the user or between amphetamines and the things it makes the user excited over), eventually results in him or her being closed off from, rather than opened up to, the world.

Drug-induced delight is analogous to sexual experience uprooted from love or even companionship: eventually, it is reduced to a series of worldless or world-impoverished operations. This would be undesirable even if the universe of the drug user didn't progressively constrict to a cycle of need, pursuit of drugs and the wherewithal to purchase them, satisfaction of the need, and "coming down" from satisfaction; even if every moment of enhanced awareness were not countered by succeeding moments of diminished awareness; even if the abysmal lows did not mock the increasingly banal deliverances of the highs. In the life of the drug-taker, nothing is built; there is no enduring extension of awareness or understanding. (This, by the way, is not a reason for maintaining the present pernicious policy of criminalizing the possession and sale of drugs. "The war against drugs" has killed more people and wrecked more lives than drugs. Peace must be declared.)

III

Celebrations

In the essays that follow I endeavour to display the complexity of our consciousness by picking up glints on its surface and diving here and there into its multidimensional depths. The appearance of patchiness, randomness, is not deceptive. There is no systematic way of celebrating what is celebrated here.

The anteroom of "Celebrations" is occupied by waiting: that seemingly emptiest of all activities, but redeemed in retrospect by the dizzying multiplicity of its modes, occasions and scales. I then listen to the buzz of sound beyond the anteroom, meditating on words, voices, phrases – those "airy nothings" by means of which we gather up parts of world, make straight or mocking sense of them, and give familiar shape to the oceanic reality in which we are immersed.

Where I have looked through the telescope of individual words, the ones I have chosen are not the usual suspects – the Good, the Beautiful and the True – but the humble linguistic "crannyware": near-grunts and banalities that pepper our speech. No one is going to be distracted from what "Oops!" or "Aaarh" tell us about the folded nature of our communications by arguments over their fundamental meaning or the existence or non-existence of their referents.

After words and voices I exhibit a few artefacts randomly chosen from those that are stacked wall-to-wall in our lives and form the landscape in which we pass our days. The examples, again, are humble, this time in the sense of being ancient, or universal, or commonplace or, as in the case of the wheel, all three. Even so, these *bonnes à penser* reveal a chasm between human beings and the natural world that gave birth to them.

Art, religion at its most inspired or fervid, scientific inquiry, outstandingly altruistic behaviour and so on are frequently invoked as evidence that we are not simply "naked apes". While such capacities are indeed impressive evidence of our superiority to chimps, okapis and frogs, the routines and furniture of daily human life provide more compelling proof of our collective distance from the rest of creation. Concentrating on the outstanding achievements or exemplary behaviour of a minority of ethically or cognitively gifted individuals may give the incorrect impression that what is special about humans is to be found only or most typically in the special attainments of a few outstanding people.

It is more to my present purpose to focus not on individual genius – which, after all, puts out only a little from the mainland of the collective wisdom, brilliance, competence and creativity of mankind over the millennia – but on the genius built into ordinariness: on what is embedded in the everyday artefacts, ordinary institutions, ordinary perceptions, ordinary phrases that make up daily life; on the joint work of uncounted millions of anonymous men and women, rather than the personal achievements of named individuals, although their names should be honoured as well. The furniture of our daily world is more brilliant than the finest moments of individual consciousness, for all their sophistication; artefacts – linguistic and non-linguistic – are the crystallized intelligence of the race; the pooled capabilities woven into machines exceed those of individual bodies animated by individual thoughts.

This is, moreover, the best way of making visible the gifts we have received from our collective past and the gigantic efforts – of construction, of precision, of power, of imagination – that have gone into making our not infrequently civilized everyday life. We tend to forget how far humans have journeyed from our original wretched state, how much this journey cost our predecessors and how little inevitability there was about it. We need to correct a reprehensibly ungrateful "presentism" in our thinking about humanity that looks straight past the millions of stories of sacrifice, of struggle, of courage, of vision, of tenacity, of amazing ingenuity, that underlie our present comfortable state. We need a historiography of gratitude not one solely of cynicism and suspicion.

To say this is perhaps to raise higher expectations of what follows than is on offer. Time, therefore, to draw the reader's attention to the book's second epigraph: "M'illumino / d'immenso" ("Mattina" [1919], in Ungaretti 2003). This is an entire poem by Giuseppe Ungaretti, founder of "Ermetismo" (hermeticism) an early-twentieth-century movement in Italian poetry.[1] This ordinary moment, it says, the here and now in which I am writing this or in which you are reading it, sips light from the distant corners of the world, gathers significance and sense from great stretches of time near to, and far from, the present. The daylight in which our hours are steeped is composed of many lights, blending senses drawn from myriads of disparate sources. Its moments presuppose much that has been lost in the vast darkness of individual and shared human consciousness. What I am doing at any given time, what I am hoping and thinking, draws on many layers of absence, is nourished by invisible frameworks of understanding whose roots reach into many remote places; it is, in short, illuminated by an *immenso*. If the pieces that follow have a common agenda, it is to gloss – to touch on here and there – this fact about daily life: to make visible the immensities that illuminate our quick instants; to recover a little of the light by which we are lit in every moment of our lives.[2]

NOTES

1. To pre-empt misunderstanding: the hermetic notion that the cosmos is a unity is only partly true. The vulgar astrology that sees our fate in the stars – or our small hopes and fears mapped onto and influenced by the way some favoured stars seemed to be arranged to the untutored eye – is an example of just how wrong it is.

2. This is a scarcely a project without precedents and not to acknowledge them would be to fall into a variant of that ungrateful presentism to which I have just alluded. There will be some writers I have read and forgotten and others by whom I have been more consciously, if indirectly, influenced. For me the most important is James Joyce. *Ulysses* combines a fascination for the bric-a-brac of modern life, a "caressing of the details" (as Nabokov would say) of urban life, and, above all, an intense sense of the interconnectedness of things – lives, minds, groups – with a profound awareness of the miracle that keeps a semi-ordered intersubjective world afloat despite the near delirium of subjects who sustain it and for whom it exists as *their* world.

13

Anteroom
On Waiting (Queuing and Milling)

They also serve who only stand and wait.
(John Milton, "On His Blindness")

The eponymous hero of T. S. Eliot's anti-heroic *Sweeney Agonistes* has this to say about human life:

> Birth, copulation, and death.
> That's all the facts when you come to brass tacks:
> Birth, copulation, and death.
> ("Fragment of an Agon", in Eliot 1963: 131)

This seems to leave an awful lot out. There is rather more to life than this alphabetically and chronologically ordered trio of biological events; more to our patch of living daylight than the beginning, the end and a few intervening highlights designed to satisfy life's longing for more of itself. Tying one's shoelaces, handing over a heavy object, challenging the zeitgeist, winding people up, worrying about a cousin's health, making soup, effing and/or blinding, setting up a business, putting aside money for a grandson's university fees, pausing for breath, envisaging the consequences of a new policy strategy and simulating amusement are just a few of the non-copulatory things that populate the nano-thin slice of light between the darkness before and the darkness after.

This occurs to me as I am waiting for a train, and (multitasking being the order of the day) thinking about our infinitely varied lives. The list grows – trying to remember a joke, peering into the dark, running an outpatient clinic, practising a knowing look, crossing Antarctica on foot, campaigning against cuts in public services and so on – until I come upon the thing I'm doing at this very moment. No, not thinking – that's had more than its share of airtime in philosophy – but *waiting*.

The more I think about it, the bigger waiting appears. It fills so much of our lives: certainly more than copulation, even in the life of a dedicated seducer such as Don Giovanni. It comes in a thousand shapes and sizes and modes. A few examples will have to stand for a trillion instances: waiting for someone to finish a sentence; for a friend to catch up on a walk; for the bathwater to run warm; for the traffic lights to change; for the message on the computer screen to pass from "connecting" to "connected"; for a fever to abate; for the music to reach a climax; for the wind to drop so you can fold a newspaper; for a child to grow up; for a response to a letter; for a blood test result, an outcome, or news; for one's turn to bat; for someone to cheer up, admit they were wrong, or say they love you; for spring, for Christmas, for finals; for the end of a prison sentence; for The Second Coming (steady work, as Christopher Hitchens [2008: 172] said); for a long-awaited heir; for fame or wealth or peace; for retirement; for the end.

Waiting reflects our helplessness, our inability to control the pace as well as the course of events. We may wait singly or collectively, privately or publicly. We may have to wait because others are ahead of us, acknowledging our subordination to the "General Other": bowing to those social constraints that, as the sociologist Émile Durkheim pointed out, are as real as physical forces. Taking our place in the queue, we surrender our position at the centre of the universe, accepting, in a gathering of "anyones", a place determined solely by the time of joining. The intensity of our resentment of queue-jumpers reflects the depth of this aspect of the social contract. Permitted queue-jumping is a privilege accorded members of the aristocracy, the *nomenklatura*, the rich: those whose private self-importance is externalized to show they are of greater importance than others whom they have leapfrogged. As for the rest of us, we plan to arrive early, before the crush; or we borrow someone else's time and body to represent us in a queue. The ultimate proxy in a queue is our name, which makes its snail-like progress up a list of names towards the moment when we are called for our elective operation or admitted to membership of the golf club.

Waiting transforms time into delay and we bear delay with less equanimity if we think it avoidable. Waiting for a late train, we mill about, alert for the announcement that boarding is to start. At the signal, the milling of the crowd is transformed into a swarming until a broad river of intentions is shaped into something like a queue as it slows to pass through human and mechanical barriers and onto the platform.

We may wait patiently or impatiently. Waiting for someone to finish the sentence, we want to shout "Spit it out, man!" We may betray our impatience by pacing up and down, drumming on the table, or sighing. Or we may use the same usually involuntary events deliberately to signify our impatience and coerce the thoughtless, or sluggish, or merely incompetent, into speeding up. We resent being kept waiting even when the alternative is not in the slightest bit attractive. This is beautifully captured in a famous short poem by Berthold Brecht, "Der Radwechsel" (Wheel change):

> ... I do not like the place I am coming from.
> I do not like the place I am going to.
> Why do I watch [the driver] changing the wheel
> With impatience?
>
> (In Hamburger & Middleton 1962: 236)

Waiting – patient, impatient, agitated – has many allotropes. Our lingering may look like skulking or loitering, and then we experience ourselves as objects of potential suspicion. Because we have no particular business to transact at the place where we are detained, we fear others will deem that we have no business being there. We look at our watch repeatedly, perhaps even manufacture a sigh or two, signifying that we are up to neither good nor bad.

To be kept waiting is to be designated as comparatively unimportant. As Roland Barthes said, to keep others waiting is "the constant prerogative of all power" (1978: 40). The one who is loved arrives late, and the one who loves tries not to arrive early. Dysfunctional states and oppressive regimes make their citizens wait for goods, services, papers and justice. But even those who wish to serve others find they may cause their clients to wait. There is no profession that does not have its waiting rooms, where the asynchrony between the lives of client and provider is played out.

Slavery and paid employment both entrain much waiting: all jobs makes us waiters. We await the next customer in the shop, bar or restaurant; the next patient; the next client. We have to stay at our post, keeping the shop open and the service running. We are on call, or at least on beck, more-or-less tethered to a larger or a smaller spot, waiting for the phone to ring, the pager to bleep, the customer to make the doorbell ping, the next item on the production line that requires our attention. Payment by the hour obliges us to hang about in clock-freezing attendance, for a fixed period of time, even when there is nothing to keep us productive.

A supreme expression of the power of the job over the person is the life of a squaddie reduced to a mere atom of military capability and obliged to wait *to attention*. Pending further instructions, his limbs rigid, his expression frozen, his gaze straight ahead, he is not permitted to move without explicit command. Imprisonment goes one further: prisoners are detained precisely to prevent them from engaging in activities – criminal or innocent – that they want to do. And prison sentences are defined primarily by their duration: inmates "do time".

Of course, waiting may be intermittent rather than continuous, and it may impose no evident constraints. My waiting for promotion, for fame or for retirement does not prescribe the spot in which I have to stand or even what I shall do at a particular moment. Many things over which I have no control – the arrival of the Big Day, for example – require nothing of me, except that I do not get myself in a position that will prevent me from collecting my reward. And some waiting, far from being burdensome, may be actively cultivated. We enjoy the journey to our goal, and its million steps, for their own sake. As waiters, we are sometimes in conflict with ourselves, as when we listen to a story, aching to find out how things turn out, but not wanting anyone to spoil the ending. Don't – do – keep me in suspense.

We can sometimes anticipate being kept waiting, and take steps to mitigate the feeling of helplessness at our time being wasted. We take a newspaper to the doctor's surgery, or use the spare five minutes in the ticket queue to make that postponed phone call, hoping that the recipient is unavailable so that we can leave a message and secure the tick in its box, or we check our diaries while awaiting our spouse's return from the loo. This rarely works out as well as hoped; you never know when you are going to be interrupted. Hardly has "connecting" changed to "connected" on the laptop screen than your name is called and you find you are keeping others waiting as Windows tidies up before it puts out the lights. Or you endlessly interrupt yourself, repeatedly looking up for your plane to be flagged on the screen and "Wait in lounge" to jump straight to "Last call for flight". Never an idle moment! (Unless our idleness is voluntary rather than imposed, when we are tourists, spectators or cultivating mindfulness.)

Our lives are absolutely riddled with many different modes of waiting. Even those things we have waited for – pastimes, events, successes, completions – are themselves shot through with waiting. A long anticipated game of cricket is filled with micro-waits embedded in its very substance. Enjoying music, we listen out for the next note, or that lovely motif that is gone as soon as it is complete. So many pleasures take the form of waiting for their end, perhaps so we can be on to the next thing. The habit of looking forwards is hard to escape.

The narrative of our lives sometimes seems like a densely woven network of "not yets". "Now" is simultaneously fattened and hollowed out by the future to which it points, and which, with the input of the past, makes sense of it. Indeed, it is only because the present is both impregnated by and eaten away by a past that makes you someone who waits, and also shapes the future for which you wait, that "now" is more than an uninhabitable instant. If the mouthful of soup were not seasoned by the anticipation of its successors, and the soup course by the *entrée*, it would not be possible to enjoy something as big as "a meal".

The world is a waiting room. When all the waiting is over, so will be your life. You won't cease cooling your heels until your soul has lost its warm body. Whether it survives this loss and goes to a place where there is no more waiting is not something I can discuss now because my long-awaited train has arrived. I swarm, queue and sit down, waiting for the station to slip away: just one of the day's many waits my journey is taking me to. Time, before I turn to the day's tasks, for a final reflection. The myriad modes of waiting – and the boredom that sometimes attends them – are the other side of the richness of our lives. Whether that was a conclusion worth waiting for, or a conclusion at all, is not something I shall wait to find out.

14

Words

Naming Airy Nothings

> ... the poet's pen
> ... gives to airy nothing
> A local habitation and a name.
> (Shakespeare, *A Midsummer Night's Dream*, 5.1)

Daniel Dennett is one of those thinkers who make you glad to be alive and philosophizing. He writes beautifully, using language in a rich and inventive way, and he sets out his positions lucidly and wittily. Added to which, he is – or so I believe – exhilaratingly wrong about some very important matters.

He subscribes to a version of the mind–brain identity theory that sees the mind–brain in computational terms. This requires him to deny the existence of some basic constituents of consciousness such as qualia and to reduce the self to a mere construct analogous to a "centre of gravity". He also espouses a form of what I have called "Darwinitis": the belief that Darwin's mighty theory explains not only the genesis of the organism *Homo sapiens* (which, of course, it does) but is also the key to understanding the nature of human persons. He fills the yawning gap between our biological roots and our cultural leaves with memes: units of cultural transmission that are supposed to be analogous to genes that are units of biological transmission.

There are other areas of disagreement between us. For example, he seems to believe that language is necessary for consciousness, although it seems more likely that we need to be at least conscious in order to produce the meant meanings that characterize human language. Another of his theses is that propositional attitudes such as my beliefs exist only in so far as they are ascribed by others endeavouring to make sense of my behaviour, although this leaves the status of his own belief about beliefs rather problematic.

I could go on, but to summarize Dennett's thinking – elaborated over several decades – in this way is to do an injustice to a subtly argued, coherent body of work. Indeed, he has accused myself and others like myself who do not share his views about the conscious mind, the human person and other key concepts of caricaturing his thought rather than addressing it. So I would strongly advise you to immerse yourself in his classic *Consciousness Explained* (1991) and more recent works such as *Freedom Evolves* (2003). After that you should read his bruising exchange with John Searle in 1995 in the *New York Review of Books* (collected in *The Mystery of Consciousness* [Searle 1997]) to see why he leaves consciousness *un*explained. If you are a glutton for punishment, my *Aping Mankind* (2011) will enable you to discover why (in different ways) *both* Dennett and Searle are wrong.

All of which is by way of introduction to something close to my heart and on which I think Dennett and I are in agreement. In a wonderful essay, "Sakes and Dints" (2012), Dennett reflects on the task of philosophy. In part, he argues, it should mediate between the scientific image of the world and what the American philosopher Wilfrid Sellars (1962) called "the manifest image": how things appear to us, how we seem to experience them, when we are untutored by physics. In the world according to the manifest image, the sun moves around the sky; the differences between up and down, between movement and the state of being at rest, and the past and future, are absolute; objects such as chairs are solid throughout; and everything there is exists in a definite state and at a defined location. Five hundred years of science, we are told, has taught us that this is all nonsense, although it is difficult to see directly that it is.

For Dennett, philosophy should, of course, be on the side of science and help to cure us of the folk psychology, the unreformed common sense that is difficult to shake off when we address problems such as the nature of the conscious mind and its relationship with the brain. I am not convinced that philosophy should be as subservient to science, but I entirely agree with his concern to find a way of mediating between the manifest and scientific image of the world and that this should be connected with the project of capturing the ontology (the study of what kinds of things there are) of everyday life.

Dennett argues that we should pay attention to "the riotous assembly of candidate *things* we find in the manifest image" (2013: 100). In doing so, he is consciously going against a tendency to reduce the world to a handful of kinds of things described in the most general terms. In some respects, the ambitions of the reductive philosophy he opposes parallel that of science, which prepares "the disheveled cornucopia for scientific accounting, with everything put ultimately in terms of atoms and the void, space-time points, or (by somewhat different reductive trajectories) substances and universals, events and properties and relations" (*ibid.*).

Philosophy that aims to simplify the world in this way always runs into problems, because some of these fundamental categories prove difficult to define in an illuminating manner and relate rather awkwardly to each other and also because their claim to inclusiveness looks somewhat shaky. The ontology of everyday life contains items, as W. V. Quine (1960) pointed out, such as "sakes" and "miles" that frustrate the minimalist endeavours of the metaphysicians eager to rise above their cognitive niche (defined by individual cultures, eras, languages, disciplines, and so on), to a synoptic view that renders the universe, or at least everything they know of it, mind-portable. Cahoots, smithereens and haircuts, to take three of Dennett's examples, may seem unworthy of ontological attention and perhaps they can be ignored; but awkward items such as "holes" prove impossible to dispense with. For abstract objects, holes have a surprising tendency to turn up in actual, local places, and present careless walkers with real and present dangers. Nobody fell down a mere concept or the shadow of a word.

Behind Dennett's delightful explorations is the deep philosophical question of how far we should ascribe thinghood, picked out by count nouns, beyond those items that the philosopher J. L. Austin wryly referred to as "moderate-sized specimens of dry goods" (1962: 8); or how far we should extend "stuffhood", picked out by mass nouns, beyond materials such as "earth", "water" or "air". There are many items that do not fit comfortably into our standard ontologies. Sensations and thoughts, as Wittgenstein pointed out, are not things but they are not nothing either. And time is neither a thing nor a stuff, but attempts to describe our world without it have proved unsatisfactory (to put it mildly), notwithstanding some of the wilder claims of advanced physics.This should not inhibit us from contemplating – and rejoicing in – the luxuriant ontologies of everyday life. Some philosophers, of course, like Shakespeare's poets, are very partial to adding to them, giving "airy nothings" a name, and then finding a habitation for them. I am particularly fond of "ness-monsters": items that seem to be thickened into something like real existence by the addition of "ness". My favourite is "Nothingness", one of the eponymous pair in Jean-Paul Sartre's masterpiece *Being and Nothingness* ([1943] 2003). Without Nothingness, Being would not be *for-itself* (as conscious beings are) or – by contrast – *in-itself*, as in the case of material objects encountered by conscious beings. Nothingness opens up distances in the plenum of Being, that enable conscious beings like you and me to act within Being, in a world opened up as *our* world.

If that seems a lot of work for Nothing to take on, think of the quantum vacuum whose instabilities, we are told, tipped the world over from Nothing into Something, and which betrays an interesting double standard operating in certain philosophical traditions. Analytic philosophers mocked the existentialists' reification of Nothing. Rudolf Carnap (1959) assembled some of the things that Martin Heidegger said about Nothing in "What is Metaphysics?" (1978; culminating in "The Nothing itself nothings") and mocked them. The Nothing endorsed by advanced physics, however, gets a more respectful hearing.

There are some terms – some nouns and noun phrases – that clearly have no pretence to correspond to things. They are what we might call "linguistic crannyware": designed to fill in the cracks between the territories carved out by different phrases. Among these are placeholders, which mark a place that seems poised halfway between language and the extra-linguistic world. The inventory of the contents of my house would never include "thingumabobs" and it would be difficult to sell "gubbins" or "bits" (with and without "bobs") on eBay. But we couldn't do without them.

Western philosophy has been preoccupied by universals that designate qualities that do seem to be in the outside world but are incapable of entirely independent existence. Consider, for example, warmth or the colour green. We may see these items as ontologically deficient or, on the contrary, regard universals, as Plato did, as being too good – perhaps too ethereal as a result of being close to our eternal unchanging intellect – to live in the bog-standard reality of the world of stand-alone bump-into-ables. Other items are clearly intra-linguistic, incapable of life outside sentences; for example, the referents of noun phrases such as "economic trends" and "the evolving concept of charity in Western thought". Many words, like lexical cut-outs carving up bits of a multidimensional semantic space, seem in danger of proving to be breath-filled nothings, even when they are set down in relatively stable threads unpacked from drops of ink.

Philosophers are haunted by the spectre of "reification", of the mistake of thinking that words always stand for things: that even abstractions have a smidgeon of the thinginess, share the ontological heft, of the kinds of things we can sit down on or throw out of the window. Reification has caused many to frown but nowhere have the furrows been deeper than in the forehead of the Polish engineer, mathematician and philosopher Alfred Korzybski, for whom this was an obsession.

Korzybski argued that our knowledge of the world is limited not only by our nervous systems (a truism that is not the whole truth, otherwise we would be unable to transcend our nervous systems to see the limitations they impose on us) but also by the structure of language. The world seen through the lens of language is a mosaic of abstractions. Our tendency to confuse these abstractions with reality itself – a failure to recognize that "the map is not the territory" – was, he said, the cause of "endemic un-sanity". The educational movement of general semantics was devoted to combating this peculiarly modern scourge.

Korzybski saw the power of airy nothings to shape the way we think about the world and consequently how we act upon it and each other. They are the agents of those social forces that the sociologist Émile Durkheim identified as being as potent in human lives as physical forces are in the natural world. The ability to classify the contents of the world enables us to look further at the cost of *overlooking* more, forcing upon singular realities general categories that lift them above the material world and yet imprison them in a sociolinguistic one. In speaking about the world we inevitably simplify it (not least by calling it "the world" and referring to it as something that can be spoken of).

I have strayed a long way from Dennett but my point is that there is only one pleasure greater than disagreeing with a philosopher one admires. It is to discover an area of agreement. In our different ways we are both in love with the richness and complexity of the world and value the noble effort to ascend to a summarizing vision without simplifying it. And perhaps that agreement goes deeper than our disagreement.

15

Voices

I

Now and then we sensed the afternoon's immense silence cupped between the mountains. When we climbed out of the car, the same silence leant on our ears, its almost palpable presence the other side of the air's freshness and delicious fragrance. Later, as we paused halfway up a steep hillside, it could be heard through the steamed-up windows of our panted talk. And just now, near the end of the day – a late winter afternoon already tinged with night – we catch it again as we stop to look back at the monumental beauty of the mountain from whose top we have just descended.

This time I am determined to take notice of the silence; to listen into its spaciousness; into its recesses, now far chambers of the dusk, where the sounds we hear at a distance acquire their timbre of distance. This is our last chance before we are enclosed once again in the small spaces of our lives, before our minds are swallowed up in our own talk and gloved in engine noise, as we mine our way through country darkness and the sodium-tinted glooms of the town towards tea-making and plans for evening: our last chance to give ourselves up to the fresh evening spaces into which expand the bleating of those sheep filing around the carnassial of rock, the barking of the dog scampering after them down the steep turfed fell-side, and the cawing of those rooks in the wooded hillock close to us; such sounds as give form – edge and magnitude – to silence, making it The Silence; rather as the faint wood-smoke and grassy scents and the chill feel of a slight breeze make mere air into The Air.

We look and listen, awaiting selves that will be opened by and open to the beauty of what we see and The Silence encircling what we hear with the greatness of great spaces: waiting to be gathered in the calm luminous trance that we intuit at its heart. Our friends, who do not pause, slowly recede from us. Their talk lingers behind them: even a hundred metres away we can almost hear what they are saying. Their laughter peels untaxed across space as if the air itself were party to the joke. Their voices seems so close that it is surprising to see their bodies diminished by distance: it is as if those voices were untethered to their mouths.

Because we cannot catch what is being said, it is the unravelling of sound, rather than words, that we hear, and in this great quiet they are not the familiar voices of individual known people but examples merely of the human voice: the voice of a man, the voice of a woman. The woman's voice, especially, strikes me in this way. Overlying the sounds there is a continuous upper surface of youth and femininity. It is dew-silvered in the cold evening air: glints of music sparkle on the peace through which it widens. If, as Paul Valéry said, a poem "is a prolonged hesitation between sound and sense" (1960: 637), her voice was inchoate poetry. And yet, as it continues to unravel into this spacious quiet palmed in the mountain's massiveness, it assumes a place among other animal cries – the bleating and the cawing – that have widened towards us through the air. And these sounds in turn seem to belong with other natural sounds: with the rush of the wind through the trees; and with the clunk of stone falling on stone, older even than the wind and the trees.

You walk on and I stay for a little while longer, listening to the air talking to itself. There was a past when listening humans would hear no words, no ideas, not even the idea of one's place in the universe. And then the wind became laden with gods. Gods were contaminated with priests. And in the interstices of the spaces occupied by priests, the poets, who listened to the wind and heard lines of verse, planted their flowers. Leaning against this boulder, I want to listen into the mouthless, earless air talking to itself before even the trees gave it a thousand tongues.

Failing to achieve wordlessness, I recite Gottfried Benn: "In Tibet it was the wind, in the jungle the insects, here it's the vowels" (Benn [1961] 1971: 74). And before that? What answer to what question could our ears, reaching into the silence beyond the vowels, beyond the cries, beneath the unheard sound of rockfalls, possibly hope to receive?

They are now far away and you, too, are distant. Space has damped the voices. They are recalled to the diminutive distant persons from which they have emanated. The stillness of the air re-collects, rather as the sea in the wake of the ship's wake smoothes itself. The silence seems on the verge of breaking into ur-meaning.

But, just as I seemed to be on the edge of slipping to one side of myself, I am restored to my habitual person by a cold breeze. The meaning of the broken silence haunts my thoughts like a secret placed beyond their reach, swept away by the fluency that our togetherness provokes: it seems, as I catch up with you and we turn to one another, that we have let that meaning elude us too easily. (Although the gathering darkness, too, seems to tell us that the light had a secret and we let *that* go also without finding out what it was. Yet what choice had we but to let it go?)

Our friends have reached the car and are wondering where we are. One of the voices calls to us. These are sounds that insist that they are not simply the mechanical consequence of object striking object; that they are not the self-opaque cries of animals without inner mirrors; that they are human utterances. How far these sounds are from the elder recesses of the silence we had strained towards! It seems, unexpectedly, that the elusive meaning, like a bloom on the silence, had lain, after all, in the strange many-layered distance between it and the voices that had wiped the bloom away.

The sense of this distance persists as something lost to our imagination. And then our talk and our engine noise, our tea-making and our plans for evening, thaw the nag of its half-presence and we acquiesce in forgetfulness.

II

They were too far away for us to hear what they were saying; so we heard not statements and questions and commands expecting some response, but voices simply. Distance lent fragrance to the sounds, as if they were sprinkled with dew absorbed from the air through which they had travelled: the lovely air of those hills, native element of ravens, buzzards and other masters of altitude and space. In a thickened bloom on its sound, the mystery of the voice was made explicit.

Strange, this power of the voice to weave, unpick, construct and destroy differentiations of the human presence; to set before a listener some half-realized idea of the human essence.

From one flesh stem, opaque to all the others, strings of sounded sense issue into the world to be consumed by other sense-seeking stems of flesh. The formless intuition inhering in one flesh, the "what it is like to be" that flesh, is manipulated into chosen impressions.

Voice, showman of the human essence, of the possibility of promise. "I think ...", "I feel ...", "I ... I ... I ... I ...", the invariant hero of a million voices, capital of million worlds, the mover of a million mouths.

So long as there is someone who does not know the speaker or cannot reach her through intuitions that bypass her words, her voice has residual power. And who is entirely without those who do not yet see or see through her? Who has fallen so low as to be surrounded solely by others who no longer see him but only see through him; who no longer hear him but only their own thoughts about him? Outside of a prison camp, does any voice ever surrender, ever allow others entirely to expropriate the impression he makes, turning it against him into a judgement before which he is helpless?

Voice, folded enfolder of mindlight. Voice, weaver of presence. Voice, fabulator of essence.

This is how it goes. Out of bodies come words; and through those words the bodies meet in touches-at-a-distance that flesh cannot emulate. Fistless blows, weightless caresses, carried on threads of sound. In dialogue, there is an interweaving of senses without collision of bodies: persons meet on surfaces unknown to retina and epidermis; new modes of visibility and tangibility, of sight and tact, are created. The voices construct and dissolve interfaces that belong neither to bodies nor to the places that environ them but to persons who belong partly to both and wholly to neither.

Actions liberated from place; objects freed from inertial mass and the thrall of gravity; occurrence in time discharged from servitude to position in space. Speaking unpacks presences emancipated from the outlines of the arms and waist and face: a surface unmapped by geography; outside the edged infinities of geometry; beyond heaviness and extensity; beyond the threats and promises of size and distance; in a different plane from eye-born and limb-born blows and caresses.

The acts of speech are neither actual deeds nor merely potential deeds; are at once only acoustic shells, delineating by some mysterious alchemy the outlines of actions, mere programmes for doing, and yet acts, doings, in their own right; cheques drawn from accounts way off the gold standard, the hard currency, of action, and yet currency in themselves. Their equivocal status is rooted in the nature of that which they express; for they are, or aspire to be, the materialization of consciousness itself, through providing a place for the sense that the world makes to a conscious being. In them the evanescence of presences is thickened and slowed into slightly less evanescent sounds.

Consciousness, the sense of things, is here and yet not here: I am an edged body that is right here and also an edgeless reaching backwards and forwards in time and space, whose limits are invisible and have no location in time or space. I am a self-world, which means that I am elsewhere as well as here, never entirely here and never entirely elsewhere. Threads of sound express this by being both edgeless and occurrent, here and nowhere.

Being here and not entirely here: this is the knot tied at the roots of consciousness, where the voice awakens out of silence. And so the voice, which gives material form and local occasion to consciousness that is neither actual nor merely potential, is composed of acts that are neither deeds nor merely potential deeds. This, then, is the voice: the body boundless beyond its touched and touching boundaries.

Strange – convoluted, crenellated, ghostly – surfaces beyond sight and touch, patched out of the meanings of words.

III

Je dis: une fleur! et, hors de l'oubli où ma voix relègue aucun contour, en tant que quelque chose d'autre que les calices sus, musicalement se lève, idée rieuse ou altère, l'absent de tous bouquets.

I say: a flower! And, out of the oblivion where my voice banishes no contour, what rises up musically (as something other than the lilies I have known) is this laughing or perverse idea: the absent thing of all bouquets.

(Mallarmé 1886: 6; quoted in Bergeron 2010: 138)

We say of assertions or descriptions that they "put something into words". It is not things but the sense of things that is put into words. In words, things are refined – or impoverished – to a particular sense they make for us in a certain context: this sense is separated from the things in which they are, pre-verbally, embodied. A sense hitherto embedded in, or misted over, space-occupying particulars is now sounded in words. Verbal meaning is the shimmering significance of things lifted off and stabilized. Whereas the sense of an object can fluctuate from moment to moment, that of a word is relatively fixed; at any rate, any variation within its significance is constrained within the filter of signification.

And therein lies the difference between the lived or perceived world, on the one hand, and the spoken or written world, on the other: between things described and their descriptions; between events that give rise to stories and the stories they give rise to. Reference (upon which all else that is enacted in speech depends) sets the two worlds at a distance, in virtue of this difference between the significance of an object, which is situation-dependent, and the signification of a word, which is relatively fixed. The significance of a stone varies according to whether it is merely there to be noticed *en passant* or has to be thrown and varies some more before and after it is thrown; the signification of "stone", on the other hand, remains unchanged. More or less.

We sometimes overestimate the extent to which physical objects, the material fabric of the world, have their meanings fixed by their material properties, forgetting that a brick may also be a weapon as well as a building block, an obstruction to vision as well as part of a shelter, a work of art as well as something heavy to fill one's ruck-sack on a training exercise, part of the mess the builders have left as well as evidence of progress. We correspondingly underestimate the extent to which our conversations – whose words typically present objects through just one of their meanings, thereby reducing their presence to the presence of a particular meaning – stabilize and purify the meanings of states of affairs that are described.

We must not infer from this that descriptions, stories and so on are all false: that every voice, in so far as it makes assertions about the world, is a fountain of lies. That the ungraspable essence implicit in the voice in the fresh mountain air, in any voice, is thousand-folded mendacity. The language that makes the world explicit is not "a mobile army of metaphors", as Nietzsche (1954: 46) said, but a mobile army of metonyms, as he said in the same sentence. Part of an object (one slice of its aura of significance, a sliver of its 360°-solid-angle nimbus of possibility) stands for the whole. Metonymy is not falsification, any more than to grasp a cup by a handle is to fail to grasp a cup.

Verbal reference is not of itself a lie-maker. How could it be when reference is the necessary precondition – the existence condition – of *both* truth and falsehood? Reference opens up the possibility of truth values ("true", "false") but it is not of itself falsifying any more than it is truth-guaranteeing. We have no more grounds for concluding from the fact that all utterance involves reference that it is always false than we have for concluding that it is always true. The boring meta-truth is that some utterances are false and some are true. The metonymy of utterance, however, liberates us from the weightiness of the world; it enables us to fly over great tracts of what is there. We can capture the universe in mouthfuls of air. (The universe, undiminished, remains unimpressed.)

These, then, are some of the ways that the flower in the meadow differs from the flower in the spoken voice or on the printed page, the lilies in the field from the lilies in the semantic field. The separation of meaning from its usual material substrate makes possible the generation of ever more elaborate immaterial meanings. Speech frees us to create sense, to materialize the possible, and senses that would be impossible in the material world: to create novel modes and surfaces of consciousness – massively general, unbreathably abstract – underivable from pure perception and untransformed sense experience.

IV

Although, to the distracted, talk often seems mere chatter, the self's exile from its own depths, language is never a superficial, a mere adventitious, feature of human consciousness. The language that stains the surface of our awareness, in those places where we meet with ourselves and others in our least-considered everydayness, is also entwined with our deepest roots and our most exquisitely attuned antennae. There is no solitude in which a human being is so alone as to be entirely outside language, so remote that she does not become present to herself through the mediation of discourse conducted in signs and symbols that belong to a collective. To be without speech or any speech-derived system of communication or self-communion is to be an outward-facing consciousness utterly without image or even sense of self.

In language, surfaces and depths have their home: in speech alone does human depth acquire material substance of its own; and in speech also depths are swallowed up and the plains of triviality become established between the uplands of happiness and delight and the abysses of fear and pain. In discourse we may lose ourselves or come uniquely into self-possession: be dissipated or gather to the most intense modes of ourself.

The trivial – that most improbable of all the productions of human consciousness – is that which engages our attention without touching on nerves of pain, fear, desire or delight: that which detains consciousness without engaging it wholly; which spreads awareness without enabling it to turn back on itself in order to catch a glimpse of its own inexpressible particularity outlined against the featureless generality of some imagined eternity. Under the trivial we include whatever contributes to multiplicity without enrichment, to expansion without growth, to extension without intensification. To it belongs whatever pushes consciousness of stale centuries of habituation away from those states of wonder, doubt or rejoicing that centuries of civilization have freed men and women to define as their proper states of being. The judgement that some activity or concern or statement is trivial (or is trivializing – what a verb!) owes its possibility to modes of consciousness brewed in centuries of ever more reflexive talk. Language itself has made possible the distinctive, pervasive feeling that the consciousness shaped by, or steeped in, it is unsatisfactory through being superficial, through being trivial.

Deliberate silence may not help us to pass from the surface of language to the depths, from dissipation through gassing to true self-presence, if only because, as soon as we cultivate silence with a conscious purpose, we cease to be innocent enough to be entered and refreshed by it: as saints and mystics know, who have wrestled with their self-presence in their endeavours to give themselves over to God, silence shrinks from an eagerly awaiting attention; or it becomes a mere negative of talk, a ragged hole in the continuum of chatter. No such bubble of silence could carry us down from the surface to the ocean bed. Only within speech can we overcome the power of speech to trivialize that which is spoken of.

The depths of the world are materialized not outside but within language. In speech the sea of the world of sense experience pausing on the threshold of factual knowledge first found shorelines within itself and consciousness had the means to map the universe in which it was hitherto dissolved. What the world meant to conscious beings found a home of its own in the world: places for meaning were staked out in the nexus of meaningful places, and consciousness increasingly encountered its own image as selves, groups, civilizations. In speech, aspects of reality were distilled to seeming essences of themselves in words that at once exaggerated and fell short of, at once degraded and perfected, glorified and lampooned, the actual. In stories, the glowing ash of experience in memory became the material out of which there could be constructed new heavens and hells of consciousness unrealizable in experience.

How profound, therefore, must be the shallows of language to drown such depths and create the category of the trivial! How rich the soil around the commonplaces of speech, nourished by the skulls of so many discarded gods, by the shed skins of so many dreams that generations of speakers have passed through in the endless awakening to greater explicitness! If we have moved far from first things, from the first-order things of the childhood of human consciousness, how deep must be the world into which we have moved and the talk which is at home in that world and holds its fragments together.

V

Is it her singing that enchants us or is it not rather the solemn stillness enclosing her frail little voice.

(Kafka, "Josephine, the Singer", in Kafka 1995)

208

The voices return as I awaken out of a half sleep distant from those voices to record how half sleep remembers them.

Words that have meaning mean something other than themselves: their material presence is effaced so that they might materialize the senses of the objects they refer to. And yet those voices – belonging to a lost day many days ago – have echoes: they unfurl into an agony of distance and loss that clutches at my waking thoughts. The sounds of their voices in those fresh evening spaces were incompletely sacrificed to their meanings: I could *hear* them when, precisely because they were too far away, I could no longer understand them. A rim of particularity clung to the generality of "voices": the form that exhausted their content left intact the thin peel of tone and timbre which now reverberate in my mind.

From this narrow room, I remember that voice in the open air as almost sparkling on the silence: the very presence of a presence cutting a silhouette in the evening, boundless between the mountains; a gentle fountaining of humanity as the cooling day darkened into night. Remembered thus, those words that reached our following silence seem from this distant half sleep to take up a place in a river of words running alongside our life, as we pass from sentience to sentences and from sentences to silence. A river running out of childhood into youth; out of youth into middle age; through old age to death's edge.

A few at random:

"Dadda!"

"It's not fair. Peter always has the chocolate one."

"And then he said he loved me but I still did not know whether it was right or not."

"They said I would be promoted."

"The children have been getting on my nerves recently."

"The wedding reminded me of our special day."

"I saw a photograph of my little granddaughter last week."

"My back seems to have got worse since my husband died."

"Nurse …!"

Sentence-spinning stem of flesh! Sentence succeeds sentence as the flesh-stem grows, blossoms, fruits, withers and dies. The voice whose tissues are those acts through which consciousness gives itself a place in the material universe, evaporates as it is spoken: "we/ breathe ourselves out and away" (Rilke, Duino Elegies, "Second Elegy", ll. 19–20, in Rilke 1967: 228). Each of its sentences marches into silence and creates no enduring furrow.

And your voice will give place to a silence other voices will fill.

16

Two Fragments of Sculpted Air
Aaarh and Oops!

AAARH

At the time of the events in question, one of my sons was a student at a northern university some forty or fifty miles away from the place where I habitually live. That is why, a few years ago, I had to take a train in order to see him with my own eyes and to hear his voice unmediated by telecommunication systems that, for all their virtues, filter out those paralinguistic elements that make a conversation a conversation rather than merely a verbal exchange.

I was missing him. His going to university had seemed the culmination of a succession of ever lengthening farewells by stealth, the climax of a loss that had come upon us gradually until we suddenly realized that our child's childhood – and consequently a large segment of our own lives – had passed away. The night before my visit I had had an unpleasant dream. It was dominated by an image of my son on a slope, in some woods, not exactly walking away, simply turned away and "awaying". He was "over there" rather than "over here" and he would be ever more over there. I could feel his independence in the circle of his preoccupations, needs and duties and hopes, his separate path: my little lad now his own man. It seemed as if I had passed through my life – his birthdays and Christmases the landmarks of his childhood – without touching the sides, as if I had never been entirely there and consequently had never fully experienced the experience of our being together. The panicky sadness that pervaded the dream was a tributary of a wider feeling that, although human lives seem to be together, that togetherness is placed over separate aloneness; and we always leave the brightly lit places of our shared conversations to walk alone in moonless thickets of private night.

I was, it may be inferred, in quite an advanced state of the emptying nest syndrome.

Well, we met and, after I had admired his flat and been introduced to his flatmate, the three of us went out to the pub. At some stage during the conversation, my son and his flatmate fleetingly adopted an accent that was meant to signify an individual hailing from the West Country. This was reassuring; it meant that everyone was relaxed. At any rate, I was not an awkward presence, a ghost from his pre-student past, imprisoning him in expectations and habits of reaction that had not kept pace with the changes that, under the impact of higher education and much lager-enriched socializing, my son had undergone.

Of less direct personal importance, but of more Epimethean significance, was the dim realm underneath the quick deed of a repeated speech act that figured in their conversation – "Aaarh" – whose lineaments I would now like briefly to trace.

In common with many other countries, England is unimaginably large compared, say, with the size of the bodies of its inhabitants: the reported distance between (say) Lands End and Carlisle is by many factors greater than the interval between any head and any foot. It is also populous and has been so for some time. The combination of physical extendedness and a population running into millions permits a striking variety in the demeanour of its inhabitants. This is reflected in the variations that are seen – more properly, heard – in the crafting of spoken words. For many centuries, humankind had access neither to rapid transport nor to mass communication. Consequently, exchanges with similar-voiced friends and relations far outnumbered conversations with different-voiced strangers from distant parts. Given that we tend to drift towards the way of speaking of those with whom we most frequently speak, this mild but ubiquitous incest of oral intercourse reinforced local intonations. Individual variation, relatively undisturbed by influxes of various sorts, was subordinated to group variations lassoed by isolingual lines. This gave these variations in speaking style the time and space to differentiate and stabilize into distinct dialects.

Thus the origin and durability of *regional accents* as a consequence of which you betray your provenance and seem, whenever you speak, involuntarily to say as much about yourself as about the matter in hand (every spoken word is a shibboleth). One's alterity (as English literature graduates would call it) to others is uttered involuntarily alongside one's voluntary utterances. The otherness of others is not only a menace; it is also, as we shall see, a source of fun.[1]

One of the features of student life, often bound up with the long, lecture-free, book-free, care-free hours of drinking and networking outside the library and the study, is a certain jokiness of conversational style. Sometimes you could be forgiven for thinking that students meet just to be jokey. (Here, as is so often the case in human affairs, appearances are deceptive.) The jokiness of the intelligent young less often takes the form of denumerable set-piece jokes than of humorous allusions to a wide variety of the manifestations of the human world:[2] the humour, that is to say, is adjectival rather than nominal, a matter of colour rather than content. Often those allusions become funnier by dint of repetition; in particular, certain phrases take on the status of "catchphrases". They are intended to capture the consciousness or demeanour of certain people and reciting the catchphrases is a perfect form of jokiness because it constitutes a way of telling that tells nothing except a way of telling.

One would have to be very stupid to imagine that this is an empty exercise. Repeating a catchphrase – particularly with a certain mimic mastery – binds the group together in acknowledgement of a common way of seeing the world (finding the same things funny) and a common past (finding the same things funny as they did last time: a repetition that says "us" just as memory says "me"). Group solidarity, little hooks of social coordination: you name it, catch-phrases may well provide it. Certain phrases may be repeated so often that they may define the banter of an entire term and, even more remarkably, come to stand for that period of time.[3] The catch-phrase of autumn 1999 may be more evocative than that season's falling leaves, for all that the latter filled young, and one assumes impressionable, nostrils with the odour of their martyrdom.

As a matter of fact, the object of our present interest – "Aaarh", uttered first by my son and then by his flatmate – is not a limited cir-culation atom of jokiness, confined to the evanescent oligolect, bind-ing a loose chapter of chaps, but something a little more enduring. For "Aaarh" belongs not to a small circle that draws circles around itself (defining and asserting its identity as the experts would say) by means of shared laughter but to a vastly wider community whose edges are as ill defined as a rural fog or the spatiotemporal scope of a warning that is in place about such a fog. If it seems fanciful to suggest that the community of "Aaarh" has boundaries as elusive as those defining the edges of a fog warning, and the territory where it is in force, consider this: the community of "Aaarh" encompasses several centuries of jokiness, indulged in by persons of many classes, instantiating a wide range of ages, intelligence quotients and life chances. To cut to the chase: stand-up comedians, toffs, barrow boys and students all enjoy assuming rural accents. Over this time, and for these people, in these hugely varied circumstances, "Aaarh" does a fantastic, even miraculous, job of work.

Most remarkably, this one utterance, in the anteroom of language, is mobilized to invoke an entire way of speaking. Uttered in a growly, back-of-the-throat tone it invokes – with dazzling metonymic power – an entire dialect and, through this, a wide slice of humanity and its associated way of life. The dialect is (very roughly) "deep rural", supposedly spoken in remote parts whose paradigm is "Wessex" and, beyond this, Somerset and Devon: in short, the West Country, where the digital world has less complete penetration and those second-class natives, the horney-handed sons of analogue toil, are still to be found. Those who cite "Aaarh" assume what Thomas Hardy's Angel Clare deplored as "the pitiable dummy known as Hodge" "personified in the newspaper-press"; for the distance of jokiness (and jokiness frequently consumes the world from a distance – more precisely, one part of the world from the distance of another) is beyond that at which Hodge is differentiated. And the way of life, like the dialect, is also "deep rural". "Deep" here is an intensifier, reflecting the sense that the rurality invoked is an advanced, even severe, form. The depths in question are pre-consciously elaborated in spatial remoteness, concealed from view, coombs in which the hidden is hidden, and narrow lanes sunk between high walls, where exuberant, untrimmed vegetation and lack of repair blur boundaries.

The actual meaning of the vocalization – and it is a vocalization rather than a word in the conventional sense – is very unclear. Its function encompasses: a greeting or encounter-mark or appellation – as in "Aaarh, Jim lad!"; an affirmation or agreement ("Yaarh" or "Yeah" is the equivalent several socioeconomic classes up); and interstitial material, the pointing applied between phrases that carry more specific meaning, which helps to maintain continuity of verbal presence when there is possibly a slight patchiness of communicable sense – "linguistic crannyware". In this last aspect, "Aaarh" may be made to stand for the notion that rural speech is closer to breathing than the hurried patter of the city, as country life is closer to the earth and country footwear is more clogged with the soil and rumpled-tiled country kitchens closer to clay and more invaded by fields.

This last is (need one say?) rather fanciful but it does capture something of the way the urban imagination "yokelizes" folk and their places of residence remote from the metropolis. (The notion of such stuff should be treated with the utmost suspicion. Urbanity is the correlative of undifferentiated rurality. The concepts are like two leaning arches permitting each other to stand.) The received idea is that the rural is slower than the metropolitan in respect of both vehicular transport and mental processing: the pace of life and the pace of thought (as reflected in the pace of speech) are less driven. I suppose I should have worried over these assumptions; more to the point, being by many decades the senior member at the pub table, should have challenged this stereotyping of a marginalized group of people. The professors of otherness, the readers in alterity and the senior lecturers in "ism" in the humanities department in my university would have disapproved.

I didn't, for several reasons. The most reason-like reason was that the conjuring of stereotypical hayseeds was utterly harmless and without malice: as inconsequential as Bill Brewer and Tom Cobley's cider-inflamed mocking of city toffs like my son, his friend and myself. Less like a reason, and more like a cause, was the delight the exchange gave me. Two pints into the evening (and there was such brilliant sunlight pouring through the pub window after a rainy day), and happy to be here, I was in receipt of a special kind of glimpse that I shall resist calling a vision.

The "Aaarh" opened an elevated window on to a landscape triangulated by disparate things that nevertheless sat comfortably in the semantic field (or meadow) of "Wessex" and the "Southwest". The capital of that landscape was an inn antipodal to this northern pub, populated with grog-blossomed faces, gap-toothed merriment, bare boards and slanting sunlight, all afloat in a cidrous dream the colour of evening. (The inn was of course an Inne and "Olde Worlde". This gave me additional pleasure to think that when old itself gets old, it reacquires the final letter – e – that it had in the old(e) days.) These second- or tenth-hand images did not seem at that moment even slightly shop-soiled. The burr instantiated in "Aaarh" was mind honey, gathered from mossed apple trees and thatches above Cotswold stone, distilled from layers of accumulated time reaching back to smocked ancients living out their lives in lucky, unhurried places. This vision created in a Sheffield pub full of students cast a slanting light across the depths of the world that we – my son, his friend and I – *shared*. In this harmless gathering up of great swathes of a reality ninety-nine per cent imagined, was hinted a shared delight in the unfathomable world we shared.[4]

This sharing, rather than any particular transaction, was in part why I had crossed the Pennines to see him. I returned across that mountain range not only well oiled but – despite a further epidemic of mobile phone calls – also well pleased, in love with my life, the world and, of course, my son.

OOPS!

I want to approach this little item in a state of relative innocence, with no sense of anything being settled in advance, or of a defined goal. In order to keep the Owl of Minerva caged until dusk, I shall consult the *Oxford English Dictionary* (OED) only after I have thought myself empty on this subject. I fear that the OED, by far the greatest book in the English language, the most comprehensive account of the boundless collective genius that is our mother tongue – an endless comb whose every cell is loaded with the honey of past time and lived thought – may fail me in a rather subtle way.

The OED will, of course, tell me what part of speech we are dealing with – interjection, I suspect – and then what it signifies. It will give instances of its use and trace its origin out of the undifferentiated murmur of history and follow its metamorphoses in the mouths and under the pens of all those who avail themselves of this public resource. All very fine, but I fear that the precision of its account will be at odds with the requisite delicacy. "Oops" will be handled too roughly and may, by dint of rough handling, curdle to something more solid than it essentially is. "Rough handling" is perhaps an unfair way to describe its being taken seriously as a fully paid-up word and being given the kind of job description and accoutrements of office that go along with being an entry in a dictionary, irrespective of whether the word in question is "oops", "the", "brick", "simple", "iron" or "classroom", "good", "beautiful" or "true".

I won't do any better than the OED, of course: the soft membrane that defines the territory of "oops" will opacify and thicken under my handling. The metalanguage through which I try to talk about this pert little item, this delightful little bubble of sense, will prove as clumsy as tongs picking up tatters of fog or, come to that, grasping a bubble. The blunders, however, will be my own and the clumsy thoughts carry the odour of my own mind. A bit of my world will therefore be captured, although the word itself may be lost in the process.

To cut to the chase: the core business of "oops" is with minor upsets: "oopsets", we might say. Its territory is that of the unexpected and unwanted slip, slide or fall. It encompasses many kinds of lapse, which may be (very crudely) categorized or dichotomized as "mechanical" (especially gravitational) and "social".

Mechanical occasions for "oops" include falls arising from a misjudgement of the coefficient of friction of the walking surface (ice, banana skin, new shoes) or of the local pattern of irregularity on the rumpled surface of the earth (unseen obstacle, unseen hole). Other mechanical mishaps we are prone to while alive include: *banging into* (persons, natural objects, artefacts) with or without *knocking over*; *dropping* (artefacts, contents); and (where that which is dropped is liquid or sufficiently fine-grained, like sugar, to behave like liquid) *spilling*. These are all consequences of our being embodied subjects rather than Kantian logical subjects or Cartesian ghosts.

Social lapses are less easily catalogued but they will include (to select a handful at random): *crass comments* (jokes about death in the hearing of the recently bereaved or about obesity next to someone whose movements from Place A to Place B require local authority planning permission); *infringements* of dress codes; *straying into* areas from which one is excluded on account of gender, age or some other disqualification; *making noises* (talking, clapping, sweet-paper rustling, breaking upper or lower gastrointestinal wind) when one should be silent; *moving* (out of rank, etc.) when one should be still; betraying to others something of oneself that one has kept hidden.

While mechanical lapses typically end with a sore behind, social ones characteristically deliver a red face. There is, of course, considerable overlap. Mechanical lapses may redden the face as well as bruise the bottom: we feel foolish when we fall. As we fall, we descend not only from one physical level to another, lower one, but also descend from one condition of being to another. The mechanical fall partakes of the fall from grace in the onto-theological sense, something that exercised the philosopher Henri Bergson in his po-faced endeavours to explain laughter. When we miss a step on a staircase we are momentarily reduced to a physical object acted upon by physical forces. We abruptly regress through the links in the Great Chain of Being and are reminded of our lowly beginnings (and our ultimate ends). Falling reminds us that we are fallen creatures for whom eventually *gravitas* must give way irredeemably to gravity.

The possible numbers and kinds of gaffe are limitless: the price of non-embarrassment is eternal vigilance. Such vigilance cannot be sustained when we are doing, and remembering, so many things at once. How can I be expected to notice the ice on the pavement when I am so busy disagreeing with what I heard on the radio about the right way to bring up children or thinking to myself about the ends and aims of medicine? How can I enter a room full of acquaintances and acquit myself in the banter that will make my presence a welcome addition while still remembering sufficient of everyone's life course to avoid observations or allusions that will be deemed insensitive? No cause for surprise, then, that "oops" is so frequently required to acknowledge the seepage of accident through the tightly drawn mesh of control in which we attempt to contain our lives: the perpetual invasion of unwilled happening in the card castles, erected by our will, we endeavour to stay within.

"Oops", then, is busy; but what is it busy about? When I say "Oops" in response to one of my own lapses, I comment, like an in-house Greek chorus, on my own fall. It is an attempt, perhaps, to reclaim a small accident for my will. This is a long way, however, from full-blown magic thinking; I recognize its limited potency, as is evident from the fact that I omit it in the case of large accidents. I don't fall down a cliff shouting "Oops", as if "oops" were a self-unravelling rope I might grab before I hit the ground. "Oops" may quite appropriately acknowledge a splash of milk on starched linen from faulty pouring but not a stream of boiling water on the thigh of one's hostess. And if I say "Oops" of a social gaffe, I am more liable to do so offstage to an uninjured third party than to the recipient of my insensitivity. "Oops", after all, may be accompanied by a laugh to make light of the event. It is fine to jest at wounds received but not at those accidentally dealt. Laughing (worse, giggly) "Oops" would turn a large stain on a tablecloth into a large stain on one's character.

Others observing my unfortunate performance from the sidelines may say "oops" to third-, fourth- and higher-order parties. "Oops" may also be an ironic understatement reflecting others' pleasure in my *lapsus*; or it may italicize the fall; or even assert, through this understated annotation, the observer's superiority. A knowing smile may finish this job off nicely. Under such circumstances, "Oops" is a kind of citation. That is why I feel that it is ripe at some time to become a jokey saying; even a catch phrase (*vide* "Aaarh" *supra*). Perhaps it has done this already and a comedian has built a fortune on it.

What most fascinates me about "oops" is that it is so standardized; that there should be conventionalization, formalization, of the sound you make when you experience the eruption of the unintended through the trellis of intention that weaves our waking hours; that we should have words not only for everything but also for things that are not quite things. Truly is it amazing that (to transplant a phrase from Robert Frost's disturbing poem "Design") "design govern in a thing so small". Perhaps I am (for not very clear reasons) thinking that accidents should be signalled by accidental – and hence highly variable – vocalizations, not by something so standardized as to have a spelling. The formalization of the most spontaneous vocalization is a striking tribute to our appetite for precision and precise communication.

Not so amazing, perhaps, if we recall that random footsteps bequeath paths and paths become stabilized through the additional use they attract, and that they lay the route for future roads and motorways. There is, therefore, always a tendency towards standardization in language. Besides, there are some permitted variations.

The most important of these is "whoops", which, in virtue of lasting longer, more precisely mimics the very sliding process that it deplores. It is amenable to indefinite extension: when a slip grows into a slide, "whoops" may take on board as many vowels as necessary – "whooooops" – and so provide a running (or sliding) commentary on the passage from the first intuition of instability to the buffers of the final bump.

The period when one is most prone to lapses is, of course, childhood, although old age with its falls and its cognitive challenges runs it a close second. I can recall how our younger son – now well into his relatively "oops"-free years of maturity in which the upright position is a less explicit achievement – was so prone to falls when he was a toddler that we tried to ration them, allowing him one every quarter of an hour. (Now that *is* magic thinking.) By late morning he had already reached and used up the 4.15pm fall. "Oops" seemed insufficient response to his mechanical lapses, particularly as the mouth-drying, heart-stopping nature of the falls became, on repetition, somewhat irritating. (This reflects a fundamental property of the nervous system – indeed, of all excitable tissue – for which there are many pretty names: recruitment, facilitation, kindling, wind-up are a few.) "Oops", therefore, had to be augmented and quilted. Hence "Oops-a-daisy", where the bald ejaculation is served with a low-cost bouquet of flowers. Thus do parents comfort themselves against the little disasters that sweat in through the cracks of childhood even more copiously than they do through the cracks of adult life. "Oops-a- daisy" is, of course, a sitting verbal target. When Roald Dahl had a character who repeatedly said "Oops-a-blooming-buttercup" – and thereby brought much pleasure to my lapse-prone toddler (or toppler) – I had a sense of inevitability rather than surprise.

There is, as ever, much more to be said. The relationship between "oops" and "oo", "ooh" and "oh" would repay attention. The winded surprise of "ooh" (that seems to grow out of the solar plexus) seems a particularly close cousin. And one would like to be able to delineate exactly the kinship between "oops" and the aforementioned "whoops". "Whoops" seems more masculine, perhaps because it is closed off at both ends (I see its openness wrapped in an outer coat of consonants) and so rather more robust than "oops", which seems to be a floating bubble rather than merely belonging in one. But I suspect I have not only strayed into politically incorrect essentialist notions of gender but also gone on too long and exhibited precisely that precision – or rigour that may seem pedantry to some while to others it is the expression of love – that I had kept the OED closed to avoid.

I hasten therefore to the OED for the last word on "oops". To my astonishment, I find only its absence between oophoritis and ourali. For once, I have discovered linguistic treasure overlooked by Oxford. To add insult to injury, "oops" is there in Webster, which records that it is an "interj.": "Typically mild apology, surprise or dismay (as when one drops an object or makes a *faux pas*". I couldn't have put it better myself.

As for poor, OED what can one say but "Oops!"

NOTES

1. Nobody knows where to draw the boundary between appropriate political correctness and a sense of humour but everyone has a view or feels that they ought to have one. Many graduates in alterity studies have learnt that making fun is a way of dealing with the Menace of the Other. Fun is not merely made but poked. The story is, of course, more complex.

2. Retailing set-piece jokes is often seen as the last refuge of the humourless. Quotation and mimicry are more important. I realized how decisively my son had left childhood behind when he mimicked the way people place things in quotes by waggling the index and big fingers of his hands like antennae.

3. And even the *leitmotif* or visiting card of a particular individual. For over a decade now, I have counted among my familiars an American acquaintance of my son who used repeatedly to say "Good luck with that one". I have never met him, or heard of him in other ways, but he lives on in our imagination, a free-floating fragment of irony.

4. My thoughts could not have been further from Marlow's sentiments as expressed in Joseph Conrad's *Lord Jim*: "It is when we try to grapple with another man's intimate need that we perceive how incomprehensible, wavering, and misty are the beings that share with us the sight of the stars and the warmth of the sun. It is as if loneliness were a hard and absolute condition of existence; the envelope of flesh and blood on which our eyes are fixed melts before the outstretched hand, and there remains only the capricious, unconsolable, and elusive spirit that no eye can follow, no hand can grasp" (quoted in Hamilton 2001: 67).

17

Lexical Snacks

Of: attributes, exacts, abstracts, assigns; touches origins, forges attachments; pins predication, tacks ascription, posts the writ of possession, transmits links of lineage (genitive and genital); and confirms apostrophic succession.

So much for the semantics.

And the phonetics, the deep phonotactics, the morphophonemics? – Large words landing on a slim diliteral that speech-in-a-hurry pops to a half-airborne comma splashed with the cowlick of an ess. It sounds as "ov", needing a twin "eff", in order that its eff might sound entirely effable.

But not, alas, affable, as evinced by those labials, that pout as they pat those effs to the ear. The lip thrusts move to the postures of "from". The heartsunk listener starts to make "off".

Semantics again.

Concerning "off", note only that the unvoiced eff, conjuring white absences, flake-falls muffling the v-hard "f" of "ov", bandaging the journey from affiliation, abjured attachment, the soft-landing in the printless snow-where of farewell.

A SIDELIGHT ON FIRST-PERSON BEING: NOTES ON "ONE"

["One"] will enable [the self-conscious writer] to be impersonal and personal at once. He has repined at abstention from "I", or has blushed over not abstaining; here is what he has longed for, the cloak of generality that will make egotism respectable.   (Gowers 1968: 417)

To speak about oneself not at all is a very refined form of hypocrisy.   (Nietzsche, *Human, All Too Human*, §504)

When speaking of oneself (as, from time to time, howsoever reluctantly, one must), one says "one", deeming it more becomingly modest than "me", less forward (if one may continue) than a grammatically sound but deferential "I", which unassumingly assumes the very last place in any queue of pronouns and proper names. When (to resume one's thread) one says "one", under the circumstances, let us say, of adverting to one's duties or one's station, or to those among one's better feelings or deeper sighs that one expects others as sensitive as oneself to share, then one uses "one" in order to be partly effaced into the generality of persons, places and things.

One is, that is to say, a self no longer: or not, at least, one's own selfish, self-centred self. Rather, one is an instance, a place-marker, a mere unit, exhibiting an ideal modesty. One's presence to oneself is thinned by due acknowledgement of how, beyond the horizon of one's preoccupation with oneself, just how absent one is from others' preoccupations with their selves, from their thoughts and experiences and memories, from all the places of the world one does not haunt. These are places where (to be frank) one's self-light and self-delight pale in the boundless they-light, dissolve in the dusk of "them", and die in the night of an unimagined "they" whose reaches encompass all the centuries and sentences since sentience and sentences awoke and all the centuries of sentience and sentences to come.

In truth, "one" is not quite so simple, nor morally so pretty, as one might at first blush think. While, introduced as "one", one puts oneself forward but one also holds oneself back, one can still advance one's egocentric cause, although by indirection, strengthening one's hand by alignment with those – on the inside of the sash windows in the expensive rooms where the decisive conversations conducted in patrician accents between thick carpets and heavy chandeliers shape the world – with those (to resume after one's slight digression) who have enough breeding to know how to "one" themselves. "One", after all, is not nothing. One is not zero, and to speak of oneself as "one" is hardly an own goal since, at the very least, it brings one a little closer to one's queen.

Although designating oneself as "one" shows that one is pregnant with awareness of others, is blessed with a more rounded consciousness than those abrasive little upstart creatures picked out by "I"'s stabbing finger of self-indication or "me"'s sharp squeaks of self-assertion, one is not in reality what one seems. It is (one is sorry, even ashamed, to note) the breath of unreformed iotacism that inflates "one" so that it (you, me) may float with serenity and confidence across the cigar-scented air of the drawing room where quite the most tasteful and delightful discourses are to be found.

First-person, rising third, yes; mezzanine presence lit by absence, yes; but it is still oneself who speaks and this is not *despite* but *because* one knows, or pretends to know, that one is not number one and is thereby brought closer to the One, *the* One, the One of Ones.

18

"Honestly, I Think the World's Gone Quite Mad"

I heard someone say that yesterday. And last week. And the week before. An everyday occurrence, hardly deserving of an entry in the diary. Assertions that the world is mad – crazy, bonkers, a lunatic asylum – seem to roll off the tongues of all but the terminally aphasic and the pens and printers of all but the agraphic. One hears: "The universe is a madhouse", "Life's crazy", "and Everyone's bats on this barmy planet", "It's a mad world, my masters", "Modern societies are only the institutionalization of human insanity". Such is the range of this most handily available of all conversational ready-to-wears, this successor to "Virtue is its own reward", "East west, home's best", "Money can't buy happiness", "God is love" and other platitudes of earlier times. All general comment on the world is now destined, it seems, to terminate in *that* comment.

Where did it come from? Who was the first to think this unthinkable thought? Was it Heraclitus, perhaps, in a moment of embittered pride? I don't know and, for present purposes, it doesn't matter. What matters now is that it has percolated down from the philosophers, poets, visionaries and prophets through bishops and journalists and cultural critics, to television personalities, the writers of letters to provincial newspapers, and to the pundits in the lounge bar in my local pub. It is now pronounced in the most casual of circumstances and no longer seems to require the dignification of a pair of folded arms, heavenward-rolling eyes or a raised forefinger. The average father, the ordinary daughter, the conversationalist-in-the-queue, are obliged by custom to repeat themselves and each other in passing this global judgement countless times a year. Addressed to a stranger in a train sharing the experience of an unexplained delay, it is sure of a warm response of agreement. It never elicits blank incomprehension or embarrassment or provokes hostility: not one inhabitant of this putatively mad world has, to my knowledge, ever taken offence at it. It rivals in safe vacuity rude comments about the weather or disparaging remarks about the enemy in wartime. It may yet force "Hello" into second place and "Turned out nice again" should look to its laurels.

I was at a dance – straining to talk and listen – when this astonishing utterance first presented itself to me peeled of the glove of familiarity and its staggering peculiarity dawned on me. I had, it is true, felt uneasy about it for some time, suspecting that it might harbour layers of strangeness that through laziness I was allowing to pass unexamined and that this laziness was contributing to a wider obnubilation. As it turned out, it was not in a moment of especially intense mental effort that this strangeness revealed itself, but in one in which my habitual mode of half-attention had lapsed and I was unchaperoned by the usual flat self-awareness.

The band had repaired to the bar, leaving a disco to deputize for them. A record was playing itself. It had slightly unusual lyrics. Instead of being about love and so on, it was about distributive injustice and so on. The culminating lines of the refrain said something about a rich man smiling in his Rolls Royce while two-thirds of the world was starving and *the world was therefore quite mad.* Despite the frail logic of the lyrics, the record was a popular choice. It certainly got them out on to the dance floor and people not only jigged in the usual way but were incited to adorn the background jigging with extraneous movements. The tune was pretty good and the lines about the world going mad were accompanied by one of the catchiest bits of the tune and many of the dancers sang along with them.

My eyes alighted upon a very good-looking young man in a perfectly fitting dinner jacket and a maroon cummerbund who seemed at that moment to inject a supercharge of throwaway elegance into his jigging. His eyes were half-closed and his face, as he mimed along with the words, assumed that stylized agony – of concentration, of unhappy love or of nostalgia – that pre-war crooners patented as a way of dealing with their over-scrutinized faces while they devoted them to singing and which has become standard facial uniform of all singers, professional and amateur, and even mere sing-alongers, alike. I lip-read, lip-crayonned in his Cupid's bow lips, an inaudible echo of the song's denunciation of the madness of a world in which rich men had second yachts and poor children went without breakfast. The phrase about the madness of the world intensified the elegance he had already wrung out of "while two-thirds of this world is starving".

I went to the toilet to think. I at first misconstrued the impression the man had made on me. I connected it with those cost-free thrills of left-leaning theoretical disapproval I enjoy when I read in *Country Life*, while awaiting my turn at the dentist, that a charity ball in aid of the third world (more recently, and optimistically, renamed the developing world) has turned out to be one of the most exclusive events of the year. This was a mistake. I am not that inwardly coherent; and, besides, the feeling occasioned by the young man's elegant mime was remote from any objections I might have for certain manifestations of capitalism. The funny feeling that had led to my time out from the dance floor had no power-base of theory to support it and certainly no off-the-shelf political surface. It did not revive either the inchoate political sympathies or ethical pomposities that had recently died on me; and it was, as a consequence, much more undermining of the self of that moment and seemed to belong with an estranging solitude that made the chill echoes of the gents even chillier and more echoing. Unlike the *Country Life* sentiment, it was not susceptible of counter-argument and liable to peter out into a stale awareness of my own stupidity reflected in the predictability of my facile opinions.

That the feeling aroused by the man in the cummerbund singing about the madness of the world was indeed different from my youthful quasi-political tantrums of impotent and theoretical distaste (anger is too strong), and in fact from any feeling I had experienced before, became evident to me when it recurred.

I had opened a tabloid newspaper left behind on a train with the intention of looking at a picture of an escaped hippopotamus squeezed between columns of one-sentence paragraphs. My eye was distracted by the editorial about an inch to the left of the hippopotamus's right buttock. The theme of the editorial was of no interest to me. It was probably about social security scroungers and a nation that was headed canine-wards. What seized my attention was its conclusion: that the world, for some reason, was *going [quite?] mad.* A flash of strangeness lit up my world – or myself at least – as if in silhouette; and then the feeling was gone and I found myself in determined pursuit of it, "the widow" as Gerard Manley Hopkins said so beautifully "of an insight lost". (In his beautiful last poem "To R.B.", his friend and advocate Robert Bridges, Hopkins describes himself as "the widow of an insight lost", the insight being "the fine delight that fathers thought".)

I set my imagination to work. I pretended that the assertion had been written down by someone who actually believed it was true. I imagined a man or woman in a newspaper office, troubled by all the things that trouble people who work in newspaper offices – the timing of the journey to a loo, the slowness at which the clock moves, the significance of certain noises next door, the meaning of so-and-so's meaningful glance, the arrangements for picking up the children – coming to the conclusion that the world is mad, taking ten or fifteen seconds to type it into the machine, and then carrying on with something else. I imagine that someone, wearing a new jumper that had attracted a certain amount of favourable or unfavourable comment, taking saccharin rather than sugar in their coffee because of the long-term health benefits, preferring Manilow to Mahler any day of the week, actually recording the opinion that the world has gone mad and then carrying on as before. In the midst of a busy, perhaps irritating, perhaps gratifying, Tuesday, someone notes that the world has gone mad. And then, because the telephone is ringing, turns to other things.

This did not restore the vanished feeling. One would have to be something of a romantic even to entertain the idea that a person will state that the world is mad only because he or she actually *thinks* it to be so. The writers of editorials for tabloids, after all, do not write out of thought processes but in response to a professional opinion-peddler's daily obligation to produce copy. I therefore pursued other lines of enquiry. I envisaged the process by which the thought, or at least the sentence, had passed to my consciousness from that of the writer, or typewriter. I thought of the typing and the corrections and the word counting and the modifications and the subediting and the editing, of the discussion about the layout (resulting in "mad" – or in the misprinted northern edition "mud" – being located so close to the hippopotamus's buttock); of the problems with the electronic compositing machine (resulting in the already noted "mud" for "mad"); and of the process of distribution (a long chain of lorries, vans, of wholesale and retail outlets, held together by the world of backs and hands and shoulders and legs and arms) necessary to bring the statement, in accordance with which the whole world was certifiable under the Mental Health Act 1983, to someone's front door, to this train and to my attention. I allowed myself the luxury of a tableau: two men, one with a pencil lodged in the space between his pinna and the temporal bone of his skull, enjoying the well-earned break of a cup of tea together after having heaved out of a van approximately 15,000 assertions that the world has gone mad – or (if we are north of a certain line) "mud".

Nothing ignited. I turned, therefore, to wondering whom the writer of the editorial felt that he or she was addressing. He or she must have considered the assertion not to be one that would irritate the average reader on account of its obscurity (as would have "the world as experienced linguistically is a hyperspace of mutually conflicting categories"); or upset the readership on account of challenging cherished beliefs (as would "the British Empire was nothing other than a money-making racket"). Editors must ensure that newspapers contain only what their readers think they think already: the cost of transgressing this rule is a fall in circulation that no one would be prepared to risk happening in the maddest of mad worlds. They must know that their readership is of such a nature that, when its paper states that the world is mad, neither its sense nor its sensibilities will be upset.

And this at once raises a problem.

How, in a mad world, can anyone be sure that there are so many sensible people out there to address? It is not as if the readership of a tabloid is carefully selected: next to membership of a crowd in a street, it is the least exclusive club in the world. Anyone who can afford £1, or who eats chips, or who has a bottom to wipe, is qualified to join that privileged group of people who will feel doubly privileged for being able to have the private view of the buttocks of a hippopotamus and who will be invited to concur in the judgement that the world has gone mad.

If a man asserts privately that all Cretans are liars and he is a Cretan himself, then the worst that can happen is that a few philosophers will try to drive themselves out of their minds with the paradoxes thus exemplified and the foundations of mathematics may be badly shaken, although sums will still add up and accountants' lives will be unaffected. If a man makes a similar statement publicly and his audience is Cretan, then the consequences may be more serious: he may start a riot and may have to flee for his life. So what of an editor who allows his paper to announce to the world at large that the world at large is mad? Does he spend the next day in hiding? Or – for the memory of tabloid readers is long – the next two days?

My attempts to recover the sense of strangeness occasioned by the editorial had, it seemed, ended only in empty questions remote from that sense. I could not, however, shake off the feeling that I had stumbled upon the offshore island of a great continent of presupposition, the exploration of which would alter my reading of the world

I woke into every day. This feeling was closely connected with whatever it was that made it impossible for me to converse with anyone about anything of a very general nature – even people with tongues less stupefied by the habit of immediate reactions than the laptops of newspaper editorialists – without feeling uneasy and a bit empty.

In the days that followed (as conventionally days do), I debated some of these secondary questions in the privacy of my skull. The paradox of the editor's relationship to the world, to the readership, he appeared to be insulting was easily resolved. The relationship in question was not dyadic but triadic. The editorial spoke to each reader individually about the world (out there, beyond said reader) as a whole. In the context of this rather personal address, each reader could forget that he or she was part of that world, that the world was composed of individual readers such as himself or herself. The mad world is a collective of the others – and it is these who are insulted – while the reader is spoken to in confidence. Since no reader can see, or imagine, the other 3,000,000 simultaneous readers, the illusion of being personally addressed is sustained.

The principle is rather similar to that which governs the relationship between the male reader and the page-three beauty. When he enjoys the exclusive view of the toplessness of the day, he forgets that his pupils are but one out of a million pairs of pupils dilating to the same stimulus. Like the dog in Cesare Pavese's poem "Instinct" ("a dog reasons the way he sniffs, and the smells that he gets are for him"), he believes that all the scents are addressed personally to him. Likewise, notwithstanding the rather easygoing procedures by which they have been selected, the readers of the editorial feel confided in as belonging, like the editorialist, to the remnant of sanity in a mad world. They are individuals and, as such, are part of the "we" who are entitled to pass judgement upon the "they".

Given that opinion writers must know how many readers their newspapers have (their personal standing being linked with the circulation figures) they must also know that they are talking to millions of individuals who will regard themselves as exempted from the general condemnation of millions of individuals. Indeed, it is their sanity, and their inchoate sense that the world is mad, that is being appealed to. Does this not imply that they must also *know* the world to be less crazy than they are asserting? How otherwise could one expect to find 3,000,000 readers a day, 3,000,000 perfectly sensible, ordinary citizens? Or is it possible that some of these readers simply lack insight and that, although they agree with what they have been told personally, they are in fact part of the collective madness?

This is quite possible and another newspaper editorial made this clear to me. A rumour was abroad, so the item said, that a certain prominent person (pictured on the opposite page) had been enjoying intimate relations with a beautiful woman (pictured below) who was not his own but somebody else's wife. The editor did not approve of such rumours and reported this one only to illustrate his condemnation of other newspapers that thrived on rumour-mongering. Until I had read about it in the editorial, I had been unaware that the rumour was abroad. Further enquiry revealed that the newspaper had in fact modestly omitted to mention that its own reference to the rumour amounted to exclusive coverage. Decrying the deplorable practice of rumour-mongering had simply been a pretext for reporting the rumour. Now it is obvious that someone who reports that there is a rumour to the effect that X is the case, not only reports that there is a rumour but also mongers it. Equally obviously, when it is a newspaper that reports a rumour, if it is the first on the case, the catchment population for the rumour is multiplied many thousand-fold. Since these things are so obvious, how is it possible publicly to enact that which one is at the same time condemning without being self-condemned? The answer must lie in the peculiarly ambiguous relationship between the reader and the writer when the text is a newspaper or some other mass-produced document available to an unrestricted readership. The ambiguity is rooted in the fact that the text is public and addressed to "anyone", whereas the reading of it is private and the reader is personally addressed. This enables readers to forget that they are but atoms of the collective anyone that constitutes the readership.

I was faced at this juncture in my deliberations with several temptations. For example, I could have consulted *Being and Time* and thought about *Das Man*: the "they" that is asked to keep off the grass and would never been seen in public doing such-and-such and dies and never encounters itself in authentic being (discussed at some length in Martin Heidegger's *Being and Time*: "*Das Man*" – the they – "is an existential and belongs as a primordial phenomenon to the positive constitution of Da-sein" [1996: 121]). And I could have dwelt on the invisibility of newspapers who tell us things and do not see themselves as constructing, creating, multiplying – as to merely uncovering – the things they tell. But I did not succumb to these temptations; or not at least in those weeks when I was thinking most intensely about the claim that "Honestly, I think the world's gone quite mad". I was too driven by the sense that I had not yet got to the bottom of things: continents, wrapped in the fogs thickening inside my laziness-curdled mind, were, I felt sure, drifting by undetected; although this was countered by the feeling that there might only be some stale metaphilosophical conundrum lying at the bottom of it all. Perhaps the editor of a newspaper who told the world at large that it was mad as casually as if he or she were "Wishing all our readers a Merry Christmas", was committing the kind of blunder – pragmatic self-refutation – that philosophers had discovered to inhere in certain sceptical philosophical positions that, in order to be argued for and communicated, must assume the existence of those very things (external worlds, other minds, etc.) that they deny. Or, rather less glamorously, doing what he or she does when he or she determines that the paper shall purvey sexually titillating stories about the rich and famous from the standpoint of a rather severe sexual morality stated in columns that have to tread round the curves of the topless model of the day.

For a while nothing happened. The questions I asked myself about this remarkable claim were not really questions at all but only the empty shells of questions. The real questions remained unasked, unfelt. I was very busy and my job, which carried heavy responsibilities, worried me a lot.

It was at work, however, when, a decade or so later, the question recurred to me. I had finished my bolted sandwiches and was talking to the nurses prior to an outpatient clinic. Our conversation lasted longer than usual because the first patient of the afternoon had failed to turn up owing to a muddle over transport.

I found the conversation a bit dispiriting: neither useful nor entertaining. Someone had mentioned a television programme that none of the rest of us had seen; and this provoked a discussion, sustained mainly by a slight querulousness, consisting only of conflicting general statements. I felt a wider hopelessness than the conversation – which was only a time filler after all – warranted. Post-prandial hyperglycaemia, with associated lassitude, and the fact that it was the Monday of a ten-day week (I was on duty the next weekend) added to the dreary knowledge that none of us took the views of any of the others seriously enough for anyone to influence anyone else's opinion on anything. We were all out of our depth – or out of our reach – and none of us was able to substantiate to any level of certainty the kinds of things the discussion seemed to oblige us to assert. I was aware of our collective ignorance, appropriate to a collection of nobodies holed up in some undistinguished province (planet, country, region, hospital, department) of the universe. Beneath my irritation was a heart evacuated by my sense of absent expertise. Collectively we lacked intellectual self-sufficiency; none of us could form an adequate idea of the world conceived at the level of generality we prompted each other to aspire to in our conversation. Evidence-based our desultory nattering was not: even our desperately inadequate reach far exceeded our grasp.

It was, in short, a pretty ordinary conversation. Just before it dwindled into a yawning return to work, it swerved into strangeness: *apropos* of the fact, pointed out by Eileen, the outpatient sister, that a single pair of the designer trainers her grandson wanted could cost more than the annual wage of a child working in the sweatshops where they were made, the outpatient sister, folding up her unread copy of a tabloid and with it her contribution to the conversation and, by implication the conversation itself, said, in something between a shrug and a yawn, "Honestly, I think the world's gone quite mad". I knew that if I did not get to the bottom of this strangeness now, I should lose sight of it forever.

Accidents favour the prepared mind, as has often been said. A certain amount of unconscious preparation had been taking place in my life. A couple of weeks before, I had been reading a book on Thomas Mann. It tried to summarize what he stood for, what he meant, what his wider significance was. This had led the critic into a discussion of Germany and of Europe. The critic stopped short only at a précis of the entire world – although he spoke unabashedly of "the modern world". And I had heard on the television yesterday – the day of an "important" football match – that "the country was holding its breath". All in all, I was feeling a little sensitized to impossibly general statements. When, that morning, I read a fiction reviewer talking about "the plight of modernity giving way to the plight of postmodernity", I was moved to mutter my standard riposte: "There you go again, summarizing the world in a few randomly chosen words".

After the clinic, I went to a pub to think. No music. Far from the nearest gassing conversationalist or smoker. I dealt with the surface elements first. The manner in which Eileen had asserted that, in her honest opinion, the world was going "quite mad" (the force of the "quite" being ambiguous – an intensifier, equivalent to "entirely", or a softener, equivalent to "fairly" or "partly") seemed to suggest a deep, even stale, familiarity with this remarkable, unthinkable thought: it had long since lost its power to take her by surprise. The faint air of satisfaction (or the air of faint satisfaction) with which she said it reminded me of the manner in which certain people announce that, over the years, they have become "cynical" (or "quite cynical"). It is the satisfaction of one who has at least seen the world for what it is and had her original suspicions confirmed. It was also the satisfaction of someone who has executed a conversational trope with convincing fluency, so that it looks autochthonous rather than aped. And finally, the satisfaction of taking possession of the entire occasion by being the one to wind it up with a closure that it is difficult to trump.

So much for the surface. I now attempted to enter the depths. For this, I ordered a second pint. I dismantled the sentence and studied its component parts, an approach that had occasionally yielded results. "Honestly", "I", "think", "world", "quite", "mad": what universes of meaning were sealed into these words, what fragrances had gone into compounding their now-stale semantic aroma, as familiar as the smell of old clothes and cigarette smoke of the upper decks of the bus of my childhood! And yet, in the utterance I had taken away with me to unpack, they were mere tokens adding up to a communicative act somewhere (as noted) between a shrug and a yawn, that dismissed something halfway between the world and our time-filling conversation. I put the words back together.

That someone should be able to derive such ordinary satisfaction from using such an extraordinary verbal gesture implied the existence of a very stable, largely sane world. If the world truly were mad, one would hardly expect its raving denizens to refer to this fact merely as a way of closing off an ordinarily unsatisfactory conversation. Only in a sane world of fulfilled expectations behind and of reasonable certainties ahead could one opine in this easy way. Only in such a world would it be possible to have opinions about the world, and derive such opinions from disparate things such as the price of children's trainers, the social security system or the inequitable distribution of the fruits of the earth. They most certainly did not belong in a world in which it was commonplace for one's next-door neighbour to try to eat one's earlobes with a knife and fork; in which one's little toe burst out laughing at a joke in poor taste; or in which, occasionally, lamp posts slyly formed themselves into the name of one's maiden aunt as a kind of warning.

My thoughts returned to the obvious point that a mad world would be an unlikely place for the assertion that the world is mad because such a world would be without insight into itself, if only through lack of a standard of sanity with which to compare itself. The strangeness of Eileen's statement boiled down rather disappointingly to the problem of how a senseless, pragmatically self-refuting utterance, monstrously outreaching the possible experience or even knowledge of any speaker, could occupy a respectable place in every conversationalist's repertoire. It was dafter than the assertion that the world is entirely water, which at least had the virtue of not being self-contradictory, yet Eileen would have been offered counselling, tablets or worse had she tried to achieve closure with that claim, which secured Thales' reputation.

I felt the chilly languor of the after-lunch conversation return and I decided to go for a walk. As I had already tried the pub, I ended up in my local public library, with the aim of finding the Thurber piece about the man who used to collect general statements. He commended this as a hobby to others: they cost nothing, required little maintenance, made no mess on the floor and so on.

I failed in this quest so was available to be blown off course by the poetry section where (as luck would have it, but then luck favours …) I came across this line from a poem in Lallans by Hugh MacDiarmid: "Ae weet forenicht i' the yow-trummle" ("The Watergaw", in MacDiarmid 1970: 17). I fastened on one word: "yow-trummle". It refers to a particular time of the year: the spring, when the sheep are sheared. "Yow", it hardly needs to be said, stands for "ewe"; "trummle", less obviously, means "tremble". So the month of May is captured by a remarkable double metonym: the trembling that signifies the sheep's demeanour while it is being sheared; and the month by one of the activities that takes place during it. The word cast a dazzling light on the power, scope and ingenuity of metonyms that we use to help us to get our mind round things; how, as Claude Lévi-Strauss said, we individually and collectively make the world our own thing; or make our own, familiar world in the interval between the darkness before and the darkness after.

I was helped over the threshold by another chance encounter in the library. I was pretending to read a copy of (I think) the *Observer*, when I alighted upon a piece in which the columnist (that is to say, someone whose views are available in a form in which the vertical dimension exceeds the horizontal) started by expressing the fear that what he was about to say would brand him as "an unhip harrumpher in the shires". What he had to say was of no interest; but the notion of someone entertaining such a fear was very much to the point on which I felt myself closing. The most obvious thing to say is that the danger of being thought of as (a) unhip, (b) an unhip harrumpher and (c) one in the shires is an egregiously abstract danger. But there are less obvious, and more germane, considerations.

Think of the notion of a "harrumpher". This is a generic type of person reduced to, defined by, a sound – not quite verbal, not quite non-verbal – it is deemed likely to emit when it is provoked by something (rather abstract) of which it disapproves. The sound is most typically heard when the organism in question is located behind a newspaper in a variety of particular settings. The reduction is further inflected by the importation of "shires": the enshired harrumpher is the canonical type of a character whose supreme expression includes a dog-toothed-pattern hacking jacket, and the terrible glare of Evelyn Waugh directed at a grammatical error and/ or the modern world – or the former as a symptom of the degraded state of the latter. The editorialist was locating himself in a rather rich part of the hyperspace of meanings we construct together, in order to anticipate how he might be seen by unspecified others themselves reduced to confused glares at him.

I had a breakthrough. The strangeness of the claim that the world was mad was not especially peculiar to that particular claim. It was something it had in common with countless other statements that crop up in almost every conversation. For we are obliged to live almost permanently beyond our cognitive and experiential means. The words of our least-considered remarks take us far beyond what we can accurately claim to know or to have experienced. Linguistically we outrace our knowledge, which itself takes us far beyond our experience, our imagination, even ourselves. Think of this: we talk, chat even, about the *world*. We humans, atoms of sentience, utter or mutter or splutter sentences that reach out for spaces, and we imagine we grasp them, that vastly outsize us; statements that are pregnant with the implication that we can transcend, see and pass judgement on those vast spaces.

The dancer, the two editorializers, Eileen my nursing colleague and the poet Hugh McDiarmid had all cooperated in helping me to see the misery and glory of articulate human consciousness: the tabloid awareness we need to mobilize in order to survive as full participants in this world. For a moment I trembled ewe-like before this thought: that the world into which we all reach, is only a virtual world, woven out of utterances that exceed what anyone can experience; that words alone generate and perpetuate the echoing vastness in which speaking consciousnesses overreach themselves in speaking about it.

I was almost tempted to imagine that this collective world of ours does not exist independently of language, even as an idea in someone's mind. I shrank from that thought. I knew where it led: the higher stupidities of postmodernism. There was a serious element of truth in the thought but it was not wholly true and therefore boringly not wholly serious. Even the world spoken of in the newspapers has some truth in it and mind-unencompassable events, such as the Gulf War, do not have a merely intra-linguistic existence.

Nevertheless, there is a sense, I felt as I walked out of the library into the sunshine, that through our articulate consciousness our every moment drains away from us into a universe that outsizes us: that we are perpetually hollowed out by huge spaces of virtual existence, triangulated by words such as "world", "these days", "people", and so on. And because of this, there was no especially culpable absurdity in the appropriation and dismissal of these spaces, these elsewheres, with more language, as "mad". There was nothing special about Eileen's ability to cast a casual lasso round The All as she terminated our pre-clinic conversation: The All was the mere creation of the reverberation of others' words in her mind. Indeed, this was a necessity if her consciousness was to be deployed in a shared world and yet not drowned. Must she not support herself on commonplaces (not so different from John Wilmot, Second Earl of Rochester's "bladders of philosophy") that are on loan and yet are hers because *she* has said them out loud (just as a joke we repeat becomes part of our sense of humour)?

Watching the children on the swings in the park with their infant cries and staring at the trees provoked by the breezes into a many-tongued discourse that precedes meant meaning, I was aware that I had come up against sticky philosophical questions about the ontological and epistemological status of articulated reality, and some equally non-philosophical questions, such as this one: what kinds of creatures are Eileen and myself such that statements of the kind "Honestly, the world is quite mad" rescue our consciousness, and return it safely to its own back garden, to a clinic where the sense of the world seems safely under control and consultations won't suddenly deliquesce into delirium? That a seemingly confident assertion that the world is (quite) mad should create a pocket of sensibleness seems as paradoxical as that a hammer should be singled out as a healer of sore heads or a whirlwind be chosen as a place of repose.

So I hadn't got to the bottom of what was troubling me with promises of revelation but I thought I had got as far as I could for the present. At any rate, I paused at this thought (which cannot be sung, editorialized or chance-remarked, but goes like this): the world doesn't make overall sense; but if this is taken to mean that the world is quite mad, what a mysterious world it must be and what people it must have in it to speak it thus.

Not so catchy, perhaps, but nearer the truth.

19

The Librarian's Voice

An end-of-October Wednesday afternoon, forty or more years ago, in the great-domed reading room of the reference library. The light sipped by the indoor spaces through the cupola, a glass nipple on the massive breast of the dome, is fading. Five o'clock: the old age of the day and the youth of the evening. Outside, in the mist-bloomed streets, the lamps will soon go on, extinguishing by their greater intensity the winter sunset, already squeezed to low lintels of blood red and orange, a disregarded fading brightness above the noise and lights of the streets.

The librarian – tall, thin and balding, horn-bespectacled, toothbrush-moustached, besuited – is talking softly. His voice is curdled with whispering, glinting with few sibilants, but mainly dry and crumbly, biscuit-grey, dusted with echoes. The thread of his meaning is lagged with a fluff of sound: around the core of sense, twilights and penumbrae of meaninglessness or of not-quite-sense. His suit is far from the distant sun.

"Language is the dwelling place of Being". At least, there is a mist of human meaning over things. And a mist of meaninglessness over meaning. The mist-echo of sound over the voice I hear and cannot quite understand. The mist over the book before me: a sleep-mist over the mirror of consciousness, over the thoughts that come and go like trees across far meadows lost in fog and chill. All that I have missed; and the time and places when and where I myself shall be missed; and the longer times and wider places when and where I won't.

Our human voices capture the air, shape it and then lose it. The voice that fades. These words fade as soon as they are spoken. So many flakes into the great seas of silence. Frail tokens fluttering into the dark. It is in language that Being makes its dwelling". We breathe that we may make sense, speak sense, send fragments of our minds into others' minds, and add mist to others' mistiness. Our meant meanings cross the small spaces and there dissolve into other meanings and are lost in distractions. Mist, missed, dismissed.

The library encloses the librarian. His spoken voice among so many written voices on the shelves, among those silent but unsilenced voices spread over a million, ten million pages, a frozen chorus awaiting the furrowed brows that will waken them to the echoless, soundless voice of the thinking mind. The enduring voices.

The sentence before me seems firm, as I sit in front of my book, awaiting the revelation, distracted by the librarian's voice, by his sounds that refuse to become meanings. Today (forty years on), before the library closes and I go out into the city mad with rush-hour traffic, I shall – I am determined – finally understand this sentence, and so understand what it is to be here, to be me, to be this.

Forty years on and the revelation still escapes me. Forty years that librarian's voice has survived to come to me intact, cupping a fragment of my youth in the vessel of a moment from his middle age. The human voice, weak straw in the wind, wisps and whispers, has enclosed the universe in its lattices of meaning. "Language is the house of Being".

20

Against the Promethean Libel

Technology is ... the mother of civilizations, of arts and of sciences.
(Dyson 2004: 270)

As I look round this room, at the bed, at the counterpane, at the books and chairs, and the little bottles, and think that machines made them, I am glad. I am very glad of the bedstead, of the white enamelled iron with brass rail. As it stands, I rejoice over its essential simplicity. I would not wish it different ... my wish for something to serve my purpose is perfectly fulfilled ... Wherefore do I do honour to the machine and to its inventor.   (D. H. Lawrence, *Study of Thomas Hardy*, quoted in Dyson 2004: 123)

Human smartness has been reviled for too long and by too many people who have benefited from it. The chorus of disapproval grows ever louder. For some, *Homo faber* is a heartless, spiritless fixer. His most recent manifestation – *Homo technologicus* – is despised as a zombie, his soul at best a many-layered anorak, at worst a vacuum dressed in the uniform of a brutal gaoler of the soul of his fellow men. An exploited exploiter, he is but a cognitive cog in the inorganic jungle of an interlocking machinery of gadgets and laws he has made his living space. The button-pressing existence that passes for his life makes his very self a console of pressed buttons. His passionless passions enable him to enact even violence without feeling flames of the anger scorching through his body. The effluent from his most peaceable pursuits violates the earth, threatening to reduce it to boundless desolation. His legacy will be a planet as lifeless as the other mineral wastelands orbiting in space, with the addition of a heap of rusting machinery and fragments of monuments to the history of mankind lost in the amnesia of matter.

Such views, which were particularly prevalent in certain circles in the second half of the twentieth century seem to have passed the peak of their popularity. It may have been that the commentators who expressed them happened to notice that the machines they despised had made life safer, warmer, better nourished, healthier, perhaps more fun – at least for themselves – than existence in the pre-machine age. They may even have paused to reflect that their views were being set down on, printed by, distributed with the aid of, a multitude of machines; and that what facts and factoids they had invoked to support their views had also been delivered to them by networks of machines. Or it may have been that opinions repeated often enough acquire the status of unassailable truths, then look like truisms, and finally no longer seem worth repeating. At any rate, the jeremiad caravan has moved on to other things. Some, such as concern that the sum total of increasingly frenetic activities by an increasing number of humans will render the planet uninhabitable, are entirely reasonable. Man-made climate change is a reality, it will have catastrophic consequences if not checked, and we need to do much more about it both locally and globally. The solution, however, will lie with more imaginative, more ingenious, more prudent and more sophisticated use of technology. A return to nakedness before nature or a regression to crankier machines seems unlikely to offer a solution to our present, and impending future, problems. In addition to the leadership able to awaken, and to direct, a collective will to save the planet, we will need more, and better, and better deployed, machines. This is why it is still worth addressing technophobia head-on – as I shall do in this essay – and also then indirectly by celebrating the revolution in consciousness necessary to start the technological revolution and open up an ever widening distance between us and nature.

At the heart of technophobia is the deep-rooted belief that smartness will bring comeuppance: a belief that has highways and byways. The byways are populated by domestic disapprovals of cleverness, the put-down of little smart alecs by reference to those smarty-pants into which their smart asses are placed, and the linking of brilliance, arrogance, head strength and tears before bedtime. These put-downs draw on a nexus of interchanges between the notions of cleverness and dangerousness (or even wickedness) captured in the single Greek word *deinos*, which word brings us to the most ancient and ubiquitous strain in technophobic thought: the myth of Prometheus, who stole fire from the Gods.

The Promethean myth is, like many myths, intricate and ambiguous and its coherence rather like that of a dream. (I have relied here on the account in Hammond & Scullard [1970], which had been happily dozing on my shelf undisturbed for nearly a decade.) Most crucially, when Zeus hid fire away from man, Prometheus stole it and brought it back to earth. He was punished for this and for other things; his other impieties are not our concern here and the nature of his punishment is of interest mainly to hepatologists. The most important aspect of the myth is that the theft of fire was not an unalloyed benefaction. Zeus punished mankind by, among other things, inventing woman to create confusion. The first of her kind – Pandora – delivered in spades, letting out all evils from the storage jar where they were kept.

Prometheus not only stole fire but he was the supreme craftsman; indeed, he taught man all the arts and sciences. The finest work of this master-craftsman was man himself, whom he fashioned from clay, possibly with the help of Athena. This extraordinary aspect of the myth captures the intuition that the arts and sciences make humankind what it distinctively is, so that whoever creates the former essentially creates the latter. This notwithstanding, Prometheus could not shake off the reputation for being a source of danger. Indeed, his character is entirely non-moral as the supreme trickster.

The Promethean libel that whoever delivered technology would bring sorrow has lived on as the bad smell of *hubris* hanging around human aspiration. Translated into modern parlance, the collective smart alec that is the human race, believing that it could seize hold of, and shape, its own destiny – rather than consigning itself to the hands of God or Fate – and gain mastery over nature, was always doomed to tears before bedtime and the bedtime of humanity was always going to be apocalypse. The Australian poet A. D. Hope's "Prometheus Unbound", in which the destruction of the earth by nuclear weapons is seen as the inevitable, even logical, consequence of the original theft of fire, is a succinct expression of the Promethean libel. According to the poem, it was Prometheus' continuing punishment, after his release from the rock to which Zeus had bound him, to discover an earth blasted by a nuclear holocaust:

> … to wander wide
> The ashes of mankind from sea to sea
> Judging that theft of fire from which they died.
> (Hope, "Prometheus Unbound", in Enright 1980: 17)

To see, in short, the consequences of what he had done.

The sentiments, although brilliantly expressed, are insufficient because of what the poet doesn't mention: why it is that we have technology in the first place and how things would have been for us had Prometheus failed to snatch fire from the gods. Pre-technological existence is grubbing in the dirt with one's bare hands and the short, brutal, "world-poor" lives of beasts. Yes, there is still brutishness in civilized human life, and the expression of that brutishness is often amplified by technology (spears are more destructive than teeth and bombs than claws), but it is not ubiquitous and ever present as it is for many animals, for whom life is a matter of kill or be killed. Human violence is episodic – there is peace as well as war; and localized – there are fields that are not battlefields, and the slaughter of other beasts is not infrequently sudden, humane and in abattoirs.

Smartness may seem like cleverness that stings; but even in war it may hurt less than dumbness. Smart bombs and smart sanctions are unpleasant (what, after all, is the physics of a "smart explosion"?) but are no more so than the blunt instruments used by all animals and pre-modern humans. The behaviour of the Aztecs, the war manners of the Mongols and the events in Rwanda in the 1990s (where the main weapon of destruction was the machete) demonstrate how the scale and intensity of brutality does not necessarily correlate with the sophistication of the technology of war, notwithstanding the howling misery of the hundred thousand (off-stage) casualties of the Gulf War of 1990, the first war where the victors tried to reduce the whole beastly business to computer games. (For a persuasive account of the gradual pacification of humanity in the recent technology-intensive era, Steven Pinker's monumental *The Better Angels of Our Nature* [2012] would be difficult to improve on.)

Let us, then, give technology its due for gradually changing human life from an ordeal of bodily effort (of gruellingly exerted physical power and wearying precision) and bodily pain, and an endless repetition of the same tasks and the same cycles, to a way of being whose contents are increasingly chosen from within the deepening soil of the self as opposed to being inflicted from a largely hostile outside. This change is far from complete and has been achieved to a varying extent in different parts of the world. While it would be over-optimistic to think that the ordeal of power (heaving, dragging, carrying) and its successor ordeal of precision (stitching, carving) and the ordeal of repetition, when these give place to machine tending, will finally lead to a work-free Utopia, an appropriate gratitude and a proper perspective requires us to acknowledge just how far down this, prior to us untravelled, road we have already gone. (There is more on this hobby horse in Tallis [1995e: esp. pt I; 1999a: pt I, ch. 3].)

In the beginning was the artefact and then came the smartefact as we moved ever further from reactions based on sentience to actions founded in knowledge. Even the earliest artefacts had built into them a kind of smartness, a knowingness, a relationship to nature that was unprecedented in the animal kingdom.

And so we come to Prometheus' gift: fire.

It is hardly surprising that, of all the technologies, the control of fire not only has priority but also remains the most pervasively present in our lives. Controlled fire ignited human culture, has sustained it, and has driven its growth and development. Prometheus' theft not only symbolizes mankind's seizing control of human destiny from the gods but also taking control of warmth and light from the sun and removing it from the realm of chance. Prometheus took over the stewardship of fire from Nature as well as from the deities.

For billions of years, chance ruled the manifestations of fire on earth: it blazed only when lightning struck and the flammable matter of the planet was set alight. It was a mere 400,000 years ago that hominids started to use fire routinely: for warmth, for light, for cooking, to assist hunting, to clear forests of underbrush, and eventually to create other artefacts such as clay pots. They could not, however, control it or even summon it up at will. It was not until 10,000 years BP – a mere *Augenblick* in the history of the universe – that fire-making techniques became reliable. Even then, it was often easier to keep the fire alive permanently than to reignite it as required. No wonder, then, that fire was haunted by myths that were somewhat at odds with the emerging secular spirit of *Homo faber*: the gods were allowed a foothold in the flames of their involuntary gift. The keepers of the flame tended a technology that was also the presence of the spirit. And, since Nature herself was a fire, fire was not only a dialogue between peoples and their gods, but also a mediator between the profane and the spirit world.[1]

Just as the hand is "the tool of tools",[2] so fire is the master technology, the father of all technologies. Prometheus' successors studied its laws – its causes, its behaviour, its effects, how it could be wooed and extinguished, and the ways of transforming it into more subtle versions of itself – and by this means were enabled to harness it to human ends unforeseen by the primitive gods of primitive mankind.

If there is a master strand to the history of technology it is the history of the metamorphoses of fire.

For many thousands of years, the only way to create fire (as opposed to passing it on) was by means of friction: wood-on-wood and flints. And then, less than 200 years ago (in 1827 to be precise), the phosphorus match was invented. Although the principle of friction was still in play, the wooing of fire became a little more abrupt: fewer caresses were needed to bring the action to a climax; every strike was a lucky strike. The aptly named "Lucifer", the bearer of flame, made Lucifer – Prince of Darkness and rival power to the gods – available to order at any time and any place and extended the realm of his rival power.[3]

The pace quickened. In the decade that followed, Michael Faraday made those discoveries that would in a very short time open up a distance between the creation and emission of the heat and light and the business of burning fuel. The generation and storage of electricity at will enabled heat and light to be posted down wires to wherever heating and illumination were wanted. By this means, he contributed as much as any other individual to making the cold places of the earth warm, the hot places cool, the dark places light. His contribution was beautifully summarized by his biographer James Hamilton:

> Archaeologists have shown that East Africa was the cradle of human being; 21 Albemarle Street [the address of the Royal Institution, Faraday's base for most of his scientific life], where so many natural phenomena came to be understood and harnessed, may quite justifiably be seen as the cradle of human well-being.   (2002: 272)[4]

Courtesy of Faraday and his generation of scientists, the key story in the tale of *Homo faber* – the increasingly precise control of the occurrence, intensity and manifestations of fire –reached a crucial phase. In the Age of Electricity, which began on Monday 29 August 1831, the theft of fire from the sun was finally secured and humans were able to create summer days even in the midst of nature's winter nights. Lives were gradually uncoupled from the habits of the sun. Domesticated fire itself was on the way to becoming increasingly flameless, although even now there is still some way to go. The Age of Machines, of those autonomous tools, needed fuels more pliant and compliant than brushwood and peat and coal. Controlled fires in fossil fuels powered the actions of engines and more elaborate machines driven by engines.

How subtle now are the ways of fire and the paths by which it is disseminated and contained! Consider a battery – a tight wad of heat and light, a flame wound round and round itself like a roll of paper – which carries fire as its folded possibility, and so makes lightning something that can be carried in a pocket. Consider how heat and light can be switched on and off with the flick of a switch. Consider how we can separate the brightness from the heat of fire so that we can safely light our way without setting fire to everything that lies in our path. Consider, in short, the distance between the smoky, sputtering rush-light and the pocket torch! Consider how circuitry conducts lightning fire through every crack and crevice of our plicated, imbricated, nook honeycombed lives. The metamorphoses of fire in human hands are truly more wonderful than the *Metamorphoses* of Ovid.[5]

Most dramatic of all has been the gradual displacement over the past century of electrical by electronic technology. Of all the metamorphoses of Ovid, none can compare with the transformation of the sun's uncomprehending fire into text on a screen. Heat and light have been yet further removed from the vagaries of flames, and the minutely adjusted journeying of transformed sunlight down conduits millionths of a millimetre in diameter, has created a virtual fire that is the bearer of information, a cold fire that flickers on tens of millions of video screens.

This magical transformation of fire in the innumerable computational devices that serve every single moment of our days, this exquisitely controlled passage of lightning through human artefacts, reflects and respects an essential truth about our bodies: that although they are creatures of the light and the heat, consumers and radiators of energy, this is only in the service of something quite different from energy, namely, the maintenance of the body's form in the face of a natural tendency towards formlessness. In the computer, it seems as if the Promethean enterprise has come to final self-understanding: information, revelation in text-light, as the most refined blaze of fire. For what Prometheus stole from the gods, along with hot fire, was the cold fire of knowledge and know-how.

The stolen, regulated, shaped, transported, cultivated flame is the artefact of artefacts. Prometheus, we humans – warm, lit, clothed, housed, fed, healthy, protected, informed, leisured, and future-orientated – we salute you!

NOTES

1. Fire was a direct means of communication with the gods and the mode of transport of transmissible gifts: burnt offerings. Sometimes the gift was a wretched beast or even more wretched human, sometimes merely something to pleasure the gods' nostrils. Perfume comes from "*per fuma*": "by smoke". The use of perfumes began with the burning of incense to carry prayers to heaven. Body-worn perfumes have become increasingly important as heaven is sought increasingly in the bodies of our conspecifics.
2. More precisely, Aristotle wrote: "For the most intelligent of animals is the one who would put the most organs to use; and the hand is not to be looked on as one organ but as many; for it is, as it were, an instrument for further instruments" (*Parts of Animals* 687a). Tallis (2003a) is, in part, an extended commentary on this passage.
3. Jules Verne puts the Lucifer in rather mixed company among the new technologies of his lifetime, along with "detachable collars, cuffs, letter paper, stamps, pants with free legs, the overcoat, the opera hat, the ankle boot, ... the metric system, steamboats on the Loire, ... omnibuses, tramways, gas, electricity, the telegraph, the telephone, the phonograph!" (quoted in Fernandéz-Armesto [2013]: 3–4).
4. For a long period towards the end of his life, Faraday dreamed of exploiting a putative connection between gravity and electricity, a notional "gravelectricity". Had he succeeded, he would have co-opted the burden of being to the purposes of being. He would have made of the force that weighs us down forces that would work for us; and so rescinded Adam's curse and counteracted the Fall.
5. All the more magical for being, unlike the transformations in Ovid's *Metamorphoses*, literally rather than merely symbolically true.

21

Reimagining the Wheel

> When a man wanted to imitate walking, he invented the wheel which
> does not look like a leg. Without knowing it, he was a Surrealist.
> (Guillaume Apollinaire, *Les Mamelles de Tiresias*,
> "Preface", quoted in Brandon 1999: 10)

First, a harmless fantasy: that what follows is a conversation; we are
in a pub; the television is off; no one is talking about Manchester
United; and everyone, with remarkably few exceptions, is struggling
to get a handle on the dawn of human consciousness, trying to work
out how this particular world – of pubs, pub conversations, televi-
sions and Manchester United – ultimately factored itself into being.
A harmless fantasy, but a fantasy nonetheless, and I have therefore
retreated to a rather ill-lit corner of the pub where the televised roars
of approval and dismay, echoed and amplified in the real shouts of
telly-watching drinkers, are muted below the threshold of distraction, and I can think to myself in solitude.

I am going to be brief, because I have limited time: the match
is scheduled for ninety minutes. Also, since I have a bit of a selling
job to do, I shall have to find a new angle, notwithstanding that the
point about wheels is that they do not have angles or (since circles
are arguably a continuous angle) no distinct angles. My angle, I suspect, will be that the invention of the wheel – simply as a thing that
moves by rolling – was nothing: nature served it up ready-made. If
we want truly to reimagine the wheel, and think about how rolling

was expropriated on behalf of trudging, stumbling, staggering, malnourished mankind, we need to award the palm to the man, the tribe, the epistemic community, that invented the *axle*.

A last preliminary, before the whistle is blown for kick-off: I must acknowledge the arbitrariness of alighting on the wheel. Anyone seeking to capture the mystery of the dawning of human consciousness out of animal awareness, anyone trying to reach, via twenty-first century intuitions about the earliest artefacts, those intuitions that were alive in the first phases of the passage from animal sentience to human knowledge, is spoiled for choice. Controlled fire, the hand axe and the lever compete with the wheel for examination.

Fire is rather remarkable in itself. An elusive but far from abstract entity, somewhat between a process and a thing, made to serve our comfort, it would be a contender had it not already had its rightful share of attention (*vide supra*).

The hand axe has a claim on our wonder, if only because it faces two ways at once, being addressed simultaneously to the bodies that grasp it and to the material world that is indirectly grasped through it. "Hand axe", "hand-axe", "handaxe" emphasize different aspects of the union between man and nature in the former's unending project of manipulating nature to his own ends.

The lever, too, is a deserved recipient of our astonishment and an appropriate occasion for gratitude towards those visionaries who were able to project the principles incarnate in their own jointed limbs into the world beyond the body, and by this means to magnify their capacity for shaping the world in dim accordance with the lineaments of needs perhaps not yet fully formulated as desires or reasons. It is an early, perhaps the earliest, amplifier.

If we have settled upon the wheel, it is only because, since reinventing the wheel is the very paradigm of fruitless activity and therefore despised, the duty of reimagining it – placed upon those who would pay due tribute to the ingenuity of their forebears – is likely to be skipped.

The act of reconstruction and of restitution naturally begins with thinking of the observation of things that roll: in the first instance (comparatively) mossless stones. The wheel was perhaps born of inchoate ideas awoken by an avalanche, although it would take some time before the penny would drop (or roll) and many hundreds of generations would live wheel-less lives, paying the full whack of effort for the necessary movement of their bodies and their young, and their goods and their means-to-ends over the surface of the earth.[1] Round stones, anyway, are a long way from wheels, for all that we may fancy them as balls that, unlike wool, unravel not their substance, but, with undiminished substance, an imaginary line tracing their trajectories and linking their present, past and future locations.

Stones are not, of course, the only things that roll on this earth. The most striking examples, the ones that must have screamed "Discover me!" loudest to the unheeding minds of the unwheeled, were probably logs. Rolling logs, however, tend not to occur naturally as often as unrolling ones. Trees occur naturally and, when they have died, their trunks may be deemed logs. But fallen trunks, natural logs, tend in their state of nature to be cluttered with branches. These obstruct fluency in rolling. It is possible that the emergence of the sleek logs we now know on the face of the earth would have awaited the use of trees for other purposes: shelter, firewood. Even then, one can imagine quite a few branchless trunks rolling down hillsides before someone suddenly thought that that rolling might be turned to human advantage and human beings found themselves on a roll.

While early technological developments were not the children of lonely inventors "outwatching the Bear", isolated by their higher-order puzzles, but emerged as new practices growing out of the old, midwifed by the collective, one might still imagine *someone* spotting the general principle: that dragging things from point A to point B (one of the main occupations of early man) would be greatly eased if friction could be bypassed by turning the trajectory into a series of spirals that had a more provisional relationship to the ground. By changing "moving things from A to B" from a dragging business to a rolling one, no one part on the surface of the object would have to be pulled over the recalcitrant surface of the planet. And this is close to the principle of the wheel, except that the latter incorporates something more complex than mere rolling, as already hinted. The object to be transported is allowed to make only mediated contact with the surly, sticky earth; and the mediator touches it at a vanishingly small point that agilely eludes friction. By this means, the control that characterizes trudging is combined with the ease that characterizes sliding.

The first application of the principle of the wheel – without an axle – was not probably entirely happy. The block of stone or slaughtered mastodon was placed upon a rolling raft of logs whose fore and aft members continually changed place: an extremely laborious process. Even so one can imagine this zeppelin predecessor of wheeled transport being repeatedly discovered, forgotten and rediscovered, but ultimately failing to commend itself to hominids weary of log-rolling. What was required was a leap of the imagination and another leap of the imagination until the necessary nexus of supporting technology had been invented.

The leaps would have to be gigantic. Unlike, say, the hand axe or the lever, the wheel has no intuitive relationship to the ur-tool of the human body instrumentalized by the hand, as the epigraph from Apollinaire at the head of this essay highlights (and see Tallis 2003a). Nothing in the human body truly rotates. There is no possibility of a complete, continuous 360° spinning of any part with respect to any other part as the basis for its advance from "here" to "there". The ball-and-socket joints of the hip and shoulder – the closest analogue of the wheel – tether the limbs to the torso and are therefore not truly wheel-like. To put this more precisely, there are no *axles* in the human body, and for good reason: the blood vessels would soon become knotted like a domestic telephone cable and the blood supply to distant parts cut off with disastrous consequences.

The human imagination had, therefore, to look outside the human body to conceive of the wheel. Mankind had to do something no other sentient creature does: look dispassionately at the world in itself; at an objective world with which its body engages. In short, it would have to wake up out of the wakefulness known to other creatures equally busy. Only thus might humans intuit tools that are not projections of their own warm flesh.

The obstinate reader, resistant to the spirit of the present enquiry, might invoke somersaults, log rolls and even cartwheels, executed by the human body acting as a whole. Since the grass-flattening and handprints this may leave are too evanescent to enter the fossil record and be displayed in cabinets in museums, we have to remain agnostic. If people wish to see gleeful little hominids rolling down ancient declivities as a step towards human rotaculture, so be it. Our speculations about the early steps permit many rival pathways to be entertained. The fact remains that there can be no greater imaginative leap than that which led to *the axle*. The suggestion that a cart is simply the combination of a gigantic cupped palm and four ball-and-socket joints must be set aside as the desperate strategy of those who want to narrow the gap between humans and beasts or humans and their bodies.

This leap of imagination must also have been a leap of faith (rather like Richard Goldschmidt's "hopeful monsters" in evolution[2]) because the early developments, the first steps, would bring doubtful rewards. A wheel alone, a log-slice – howsoever beautifully fashioned – would deliver nothing, except perhaps a little recreation after hours. Only when it was attached via axles to a large people-holder or goods-holder such as a cart, which in turn would have to be furnished with handles (or something like this to guide it), would there be any significant payback. For the wheel to be of any use, in other words, several technologies would have to converge. Beasts are an optional extra,[3] but one thing is mandatory: a device to connect the wheels to the rest of the vehicle in such a way as to keep them securely in place without impeding their ability to roll freely.

And so to the heart or hub of the matter. I am talking about the axle, without which the wheel is just a fat wooden medallion commemorating a technological cul-de-sac.

The invention of the axle is perhaps the profoundest creative moment in the history of rota-technology, indeed, in the entire history of technology after the expropriation of fire. It involves all sorts of indirect thinking of the kind that fire husbandry, levers and hand axes do not require of us.

There is so much to be said about axles, I shall have to be selective. First the fundamental principle. The axle may be immobile in what is known as "the object body" while the rest of the wheel rotates around it; or it may rotate inside the object body as it follows the movement of the wheel. In either case, the distance covered against friction is greatly reduced compared with the distance against friction covered on the ground. If an object is dragged 10 metres, there are 10 metres worth of friction to be overcome. If an object is wheeled 10 metres, and the axle has a circumference twenty times less than the circumference of the wheel, then there is only the equivalent of half a metre of friction to be overcome.

So much for the principle. Here are some further thoughts – rather hurried, as we seem to be getting close to the end of the second half of the match:

(a) An axle has length as well as a circumference. In it, the length and circumference of the proto-wheel, the log, are separated. More precisely, the long axis of the axle fulfils the function of the length of the log while its roundedness is assigned to the wheels, separated by that length, at each of its ends, where the essential, executive rolling is done. If that is difficult to grasp, how much more difficult it must have been to envisage.

(b) The axle separates the supportive function of the log from its rotatory function. Rolling therefore lifts dragging off the ground and, to some extent, off its back; or dragging is lifted off rolling's back.

(a) plus (b) thereby allows one to avoid the problems incurred by the log-rolling zeppelin earlier described.

(c) An axle's rolling is of a rather special kind. In one version – where it is fixed to the rest of the wheel – it does not roll with respect to the wheel. Like the wheel whose rolling it follows, it rolls with respect to the ground and, more importantly, with respect to the slot through which it passes in the vehicle. This combination of stillness (with respect to the wheel) and rolling (with respect to – for example – a cart) translates the rolling movement of the wheel into the linear movement of the vehicle. The wheel's forward motion presses on the axle, which in turn presses against the cart, which thereby makes its creaking way towards its destination. The axle is both a fluent translator (of circular into linear movement) – ensuring that the cart does not cartwheel – and a transmitter of movement.

(d) Thanks, in short, to the axle, motion is passed from one component of an artefact to another. In this composite artefact, we have the beginning of a machine and, perhaps (as the cart runs away down the hill out of control), the first hint of autonomy in artefacts and the first twinge of a distant future in which tending more or less autonomous artefacts will be the greater part of the work of mankind.

What follows, after these initial acts of genius that exploited rolling in the transportation of the bodies and goods of humans that have hitherto only walked, run and jumped, are mere details. Here are a few:

(a) Harnessing animals to "cartefacts" by means of yokes and bridles and reins and, later, of non-living sources of energy (steam, electricity, petrolic explosions), bridled and reined in by millions of patentable ingenuities, resulting in engines and a variety of horseless (and oxless, and bullockless) carriages. In its wake, will come the theory of the training, breeding and caring for horses; of manufacturing, tuning and looking after engines; and much else besides.

(b) Modification of the wheel to make it:

(i) lighter without sacrifice of strength and durability (the hollow wheel with its hub, spokes and rim);

(ii) protected against damage from the roughness of the travelled-over earth and less likely to transmit a complete transcript of the road's jagged outline to the traveller's sore bottom and his aching, shaken bones. Hence metal hoops – analogous, perhaps, to horseshoes – solid tyres, pneumatic tyres. Worn rubber goes proxy for sore feet; concern about blistered soles give way to worries about illegally shallow tread. People become passengers and travelling becomes physically passive.

(c) Insertion of wheels within wheels, such as ball bearings: a throwback to those first rolling stones. Their superior fluency – reflecting their purer roundness (even smoothness), their comparative resistance to warping and their equable crowding – limits the extent to which the friction between the rotating components of the vehicle squanders energy that should be devoted to achieving human goals. An alternative approach employs lubricants – the ultimate in finely divided bearings – that insinuate themselves between the axle and all those parts that have to act upon, and move with respect to, other parts.[4]

(d) Laying down journey-ways that are modifications, indeed formalizations, of the immemorial footpaths and hoofpaths between dwellings and hunting grounds, shelter and watering holes, such as to make them suitable for wheels. Our human tracks become (i) wider, (ii) smoother, (iii) firmer, (iv) more robust: these are the desiderata shaping the long evolution of people-ways from the parted vegetation and foot-burnished earth of our beginnings to the six-lane concrete and tarmac interstate highways of today. An interesting by-product of this is that human dwellings increasingly come to line lattices of streets and these are linked by roads that are drawn in an ever tighter mesh over the face of the earth.

(e) The spread of the wheel, and the rotatory principle, into every corner of human life: animal-, wind-, water- and (later) fuel-power drive all sorts of wheeled servants of direct and (ever more) indirect human needs, harvesting human purpose from the restlessness of the earth. Quornstones and windmills enslave wind and water to pre-digesting food. Rotating sails play with the air and change its wild fidgeting into useful energy (wind turbines), create vortices that draw flying machines forwards (propellers), and generate breezes that cool subjectively over-heated bodies and prevent objective overheating of machines (fans). Eventually the rotatory principle is translated to a more abstract cyclical one – as in the steam and petrol engines – and to iterative processes that come back again and again to what seems to be the same place, although it is not the same place, as in computation.

Another shout indicates full time. The score is level. Since there *has to be a result*, I am granted a little extra time to pay tribute to the protean device that takes so much effort out of the motion of *Homo sapiens*, that self-moved mover, that wilful creature who more than any other is the origin of his own actions and the architect of his life. And to glance sideways at the transformations of the wheel: steering wheels, which turn manageable rotations into means of directing otherwise uncontrollable land bound, seagoing and airborne vehicles; the spinning wheel, which turns fleece into yarn; the fly-wheel, which harvests motion in times of plenty to release it when the going is not so good; the capstan, which magnifies the muscle power of sailors pulling on ropes, cables and hawsers.

Although there are individuals whose smooth trundling some-times seems like self-wheeling, the difference between walking and wheeling is absolute. Wheeling is halfway to flying, as anyone knows who has just learned to roller-skate with confidence or who has at last mastered a bicycle. A car, when we first drive out by ourselves, offers the same sensation: all cars – not just those that criminals metonymically call "wheels" – are getaway cars, except when they are obstructed by everyone else's getaway cars. Even where one is self-propelled (as in cycling), the comparatively effortless motion of wheeling, as one oscillates between activity and passivity, between groaning legwork and blissful submission to the gravitational field, makes it a kind of dream-walking. The wheel, in short, *liquefies* motion: *Homo rotationis* drinks space rather than (as does poor footsore, body-sore *Homo ambulationis*) bites it and chews it over.

All praise, then, to the wheel, this second greatest of the blessings humanity has bestowed upon itself, that has turned so much of human trudging to gliding and freed us to dream of wings. The story of the wheel rolls on forever.

But it is time to apply the brakes. For the game is over. I can already anticipate the result: one team won and the other team lost. It doesn't matter either way, because there are deeper things that unite man than Man United.

NOTES

1. And until very recently in some parts of the world: "My fellow passengers are only the second, perhaps even the first generation of Africans fortunate enough to be conveyed to their destinations. For thousands and thousands of years, Africa walked. People here did not have a concept of the wheel, and were unable to adopt it. They walked, they wandered, and whatever had to be transported they carried – on their backs, on their shoulders, and, most often, on their heads" (Kapuscinski 2001: 1; the essay from which this passage was taken was first published in the 1950s). There are many reasons for the failure of the wheel to penetrate much of Africa until recently: the terrain much more naturally entangled (jungle) or sifting-slithery (desert) so that roads are more difficult to establish and sustain; the lack of roads made wheeled transport unattractive; the lack of wheels would in turn make roads pointless. This has made for the most sustained and extensive imaginable gridlock: a vicious circle that kept out the virtuous circle of the wheel.

2. Goldschmidt suggested that massive mutations, generating creatures with vastly different anatomical structures, might, very occasionally, be useful rather than lethal. He invokes these "hopeful monsters" as a way of getting round the difficulty of explaining organ development by the effect of selective forces on random minute mutations. Any organ must be the result of many millions of mutations, the first many thousands of which might not yield survival advantage. See Popper (1972: 281–4).

    The analogy with technology is not very strong but it is meant to highlight how the glorious achievements of *Homo faber* would not have been possible without a propensity to follow up long cul-de-sacs. The capacity of humans for making egregious mistakes and to stick with them is a necessary complement to the capacity for getting things right in the way that only humans can. Animals rarely make interesting errors. As someone once said, the aim in science should be to make as many mistakes as possible as quickly as possible. One should be prepared to bark up the wrong tree until it grows into a Sequoia from which one may have a vantage point on possibility. Idle curiosity, blue-sky research instinct, and the spirit of play are easy to underestimate in humans whom we conceive as being on the edge of survival.

3. Who, incidentally, was the genius who cottoned on to the idea of (a) using the beasts of the earth as beasts of burden and (b) enhancing the carrying capacity of those

beasts by attaching them to carts? The more one thinks about these obvious things – putting the horse before the cart – the less obvious they seem.

4. Lubricating is at least as important as glueing in the history of the world. Sometimes we need to enhance the coherence of things and at other times we need to ease the passage of things over or through one another. Sometimes the world is too rough and at other times it is too smooth.

22

Sail

Of Trades and Winds

> There is much that is strange, but nothing that surpasses man in
> strangeness. He sets sail on the frothing waters amid the south winds
> of winter tacking through the mountains and furious chasm of the
> waves. (Sophocles, *Antigone*, ll.332–7)

It is possible to imagine aesthetes, at a certain stage in the spiritual
development of humanity, for whom the phrase "trade winds" is a
union of opposites that falls just short of outright oxymoron. The
fresh air, acting out its freshness in a caressive breeze (more subtle
for being fingerless and more soothing for demanding no response)
seems the very antithesis of the narrow-eyed, clench-fisted, awareness shaped by peered-at-paper that is adumbrated by the word
"trade" when it is enunciated in a certain privileged tone of voice
elevated above the thing of which it speaks.

The opposition between good wind and bad trade, fresh air and
stale business, is, of course, unfair not only because winds wreck
lives as well as caress cheeks – and it is from such wrecking winds
that the (traded) goods of the world protect us – but also because
it is upon trade that we build the world within whose wind shelters
aesthetes are freed to formulate their abstract contempt. In short:
the perfectly manicured fingernails of the aesthete are erected upon
the nail-breaking work of the tradesman.

Why, however, might trade winds come to some Professors-of-
the-Taken-for-Granted (not the deepest thinkers, of course) to seem

an unhappy zeugma? Is it not in part because of the inward movement of trade: inland, deeper into the *urbs*, back from the harbour to
the market, from the street into the shop, from the front of the shop
to the back of the shop, to the sweatshop, the warehouse and the
dealing room? From such disadvantage points in the stale, cramped
places of business, the fresh and open winds – ocean breezes that
are the very paradigm of openness – seem especially remote. Their
remoteness is broadcast through a window jammed fast (the duration
of its fastness spelled in spiderwebs overwoven to milk) or the crude,
boastful talk and constricted certainties of the parody tradesman.
And aesthetes notice jammed windows (they have the free dispos-
able consciousness to do so) and deal in parodies that in fact demonstrates how refinement sometimes stupefies: the sharpening of some
sensibilities may blunt others; salon-wise may be street-thick.

This inward movement was also a journey from simple origins
– never quite as simple as they seem through the blurred eyes of
scholars with "notions" – to complex consequences. A nexus of
middle-men – assemblers, processors, packagers, distributors,
advertisers, financiers – makes trade into an Everglades of interlocking thickets. The sickly, overworked, woe-burdened clerk adding
up, checking and re-checking the column of figures by candlelight in
a freezing room in a cessed quarter of a city is doubly remote from
the open sea.

Let us, therefore, get down to basics.

The wind – as much when it freshens a child's soft cheek as when
it disembowels a house – is the very paradigm of the lawlessness
of a nature that is a law unto itself. This is why the wind seems to
poets to personify the essence of freedom (although a pedant might
point out that a process that is void of purpose and of consciousness can hardly be, or express, freedom). And yet, harvested and
concentrated, this lawlessness may propel ships across the face of
the earth, to far places beyond the edge of the world revealed to the
most advantaged gaze.

Stand where the land ends and the sea beckons with the vastness of its indifference to, its ignorance of, the tangled meanings

of the land-livers' lives. Let the nostrils of your eyes inhale the far blue. Listen to the breeze uttering the hush of distance into which all cries ultimately dissolve. The wind has come from a long way away. How shall we engage with its farness, and so as to turn it into distances covered, journeys successfully completed? How do we tether its meaningless energy to energizing our (temporarily) meaningful lives?

Of course, we may travel across seas by hitching a ride on currents. But currents unregulated by banks in the landless ocean are capricious. Indeed, the working life of currents is largely done when rivers reach the sea. The sea is their carefree retirement from defined identity. They are the very model of unreliability and consequently start and stop at locations that fall short of points of departure or points of arrival. And so we, who sense that there is more to life than the places where we came into being, for whom a horizon is a promise of new meaning, require another source of movement, which, borrowed and controlled, will change motion (in which all natural entities more or less voluntarily participate) into journeys – which only humans truly undertake.

Which is a roundabout way of introducing the link between trade and the wind.

The most important link between trade and wind is the sail.

The sail.

The sail harvests a natural process on behalf of a human purpose, turning the restlessness of the earth's outermost coat into fuel to bring hopes closer to fulfilment.

The sail is the basis of the busiest, oldest and most entangled interchanges between the natural world and human culture. And between the scattered tribes of the human race. So it has defined an entire way of being human for a significant portion of the human race since that extraordinary moment when animal hides were first raised aloft above the sea. And it classifies those human beings: they are sail-ors; and their central, defining, activity is sail-ing.

We all know how a sail works, or think we do. The hurrying air presses against the obstruction of the canvas. The canvas is pushed forwards. It is, however, attached to the mast, itself designed to elevate the sail to where it can get in the way of the maximum amount of wind, and the mast is attached to ship. The sail–mast–hull is a single coherent mass. The pressure on the canvas is thus translated into a pushing on the ship, which is thereby propelled across the water, whose sleekness makes even the rough-sided vessel a smooth transient.

There are numerous other interactions between sail, wind, boat and water, so that by tacking and beating it is possible to sail against, as well as with, the wind. I shall set these aside because I do not want to lose sight of the general mystery. The general mystery is how it is that we, who are part of nature, are able to subordinate natural processes to purposes that nature, being mindless, did not have in mind. How are we able to co-opt the insentient wind to being a partner in our enterprises, thereby making them the unwitting agents of our agency?

There is "nothing/ That surpasses man in strangeness". A human being, piece of nature, a "naturefact", creates an artefact, a sail, that enables another artefact, a boat, to act on behalf of general, in some respects quite abstract, human needs: the transport of artefacts, or raw materials out of which artefacts may be made, or stand-alone commodities that serve a multiplicity of fundamental, or acquired, human needs. Pots, raw silk, spices, salt, cross the oceans to be passed from stranger to stranger. How can it be that humans could rise above nature in order to operate upon it and, eventually, change the very face of nature itself? It seems like Baron Münchausen, lifting himself by his hair. And breaking the laws of nature is not on the cards, that's for sure. The laws of nature are, by definition, unbreakable. Besides, we pieces of nature depend on nature's laws being 100 per cent unbreakable, that we may rely on a long series of actions – such as a year-long voyage – to result in an anticipated outcome.

A philosophical digression beckons. Those who wish may skip the next few paragraphs and instead meditate upon how the sea entered the thinking of the Greek philosophers, so much so that the earliest of the great ones – Thales – proposed that the world was composed entirely of water. Perhaps he was thinking of seawater when he brought metaphysics down to earth and had the pivotal scientific thought that everything might be a manifestation of some fundamental substance rather than an emanation of a god or a cluster of gods. (The suggestion that he was trying to sign the universe with a derivative of his own name – Thalassa for Thales – may be set safely aside.)

The digression leads directly to John Stuart Mill, who saw the way through our otherwise mysterious ability to suborn nature to our purpose. "Though we cannot emancipate ourselves from the laws of nature as a whole", he argues:

> we can escape from any particular law of nature, if we are able to withdraw ourselves from the circumstances in which it acts. Though we can do nothing except through laws of nature, we can use one law to counteract another. According to Bacon's maxim, we can obey nature in such a manner as to command it. Every alteration of circumstances alters more or less the laws of nature under which we act; and by every choice which we make either of ends or of means, we place ourselves to a greater or less extent under one set of laws of nature instead of another. ("Nature", in *Three Essays on Religion*, quoted in Aiken 1956: 152–3)

The "useless precept" that we should follow nature could be rescued if it were changed into a precept to *study* nature: "to know and take heed of the properties of the things that we have to deal with, so far as these properties are capable of forwarding or obstructing any given purpose". Then "we should have arrived at the first principle of all intelligent action, or rather at the definition of intelligent action itself" (*ibid.*: 153).

The idea that we can place ourselves in circumstances in which one law of nature acts rather than another is, of course, not as clear as one might like. Given that, as Mill says, humans "have no power but what the laws of nature give them – when it is a physical impossibility for them to do the smallest thing otherwise than through the laws of nature" (*ibid.*: 152) – it seems as puzzling that human purposes should be served by their *using* the laws of nature as that they should require breaking them. How, except in accordance with the laws of nature, might one come to be in the favoured circumstances? It would be like part of a stream seizing hold of a current in that stream to guide its descent. One cannot manipulate the laws of nature from within and, given that we are inside nature, there seems therefore no way, period, of manipulating nature in such a way as to exploit them to serve one's purposes. Even if we accept that several laws of nature are working at any given place and that one has a range to choose from, there is still a problem of how it is that we can *choose*, utterly immersed as we are in the laws of nature.

What is missing here is an account of how it is that we can place ourselves in those desirable circumstances that will ensure that the laws of nature will work for us rather than against us. What seems to be required is that we should be able to approach one set of circumstances as if from outside all circumstances: access it through a choice between possibilities. And so we ask: where is this outside to be found? Where does possibility awaken in a world of actuality?

These are deep waters. I have tried to navigate them elsewhere – where I find the necessary "outside-of-nature" in the "am-soil" that grows in the one animal that knows that it *is* the body that it is (see Tallis 2003b, 2004b). That animal, *Homo sapiens* – more specifically *Homo sapiens sapiens* – possesses *itself* in an identity that creates a point of departure in the natural world of which it is a part. For the present, we may take away the idea that the sailing ship, which turns wind into the servant of trade, floats on profound cognitive, as well as marine, depths, noting meanwhile for our friends who have returned from the satellite session with Thales, that *our compact with nature requires us so to serve her as to command her.* The sail is the instrument of that commanding service, subordinating the restlessness of the second most elusive of nature's elements to human endeavour. Courtesy of its sail, the ship takes advantage of what nature serves up and bends it – or bends with it – to achieve human ends. The sail weaves one of the most densely drawn and busiest interchanges between natural forces and human intentions.

Our attention has drifted a little from the wind to the sails that it fills. There is another knot to be tied before we reach our destination and achieve our goal of repairing the schism the thoughtless have opened up between beautiful winds and supposedly ugly trade. We have seen how the wind acts as the co-partner of trade. We have not, however, arrived at an adequate idea of its role in shaping the earliest filaments of the worldwide web of globalized consciousness: how the general patterns of marine adventuring are laid down in such a consistent fashion as to end up as arrows or lines on a chart inspected on a bridge or on an atlas patiently transcribed in the suburban bedroom of a homeworking schoolchild. If we think of the pointed sail, or the mast, as a stylus, it helps us to pose the question: how did writing on air become incised in the collective conscious-ness and the customary pathways of mankind?

We have arrived at the beautiful notion of the trade wind.

If trade winds astonish, it is above all because they should not exist at all, since weather is the paradigm of the unbiddable, the untamed and the uncaged. But there are patterns even in weather. Weather differentiates to climates. The seasons with their more-or-less predictable heatwaves, storms, monsoons arrive with greater punctuality than the trains operated by certain rail companies. And there are habits of the atmosphere that, notwithstanding formless-ness and mindlessness of the air, have outlasted all human monu-ments. Trade winds – "Winds that emanate from one prevailing direction" – are largely dictated by the presence of pressure systems due, for example, to the higher pressure of the tropics compared with the equator. Permanent habits of the air: the trade winds that blow across the globe and stick to their paths for thousands of miles and millions of years. They are older than the flight paths of migrat-ing birds.

"Trade" originally meant "track" or "journey", and the most por-tentous of the trade winds – which has carried the greatest number of hopes to their fulfilment or destruction, and mingled most densely with intentions – is the massive airflow that passes westwards and points a little downwards in the direction of the equator. This is the fair wind that carries ships and their freight westwards across the Atlantic from the West African coast to the Americas and across the Pacific from the Americas to Australasia.

It is because of this fidelity of the wind to its own habits that great and sustained human purposes are possible. The swollen-bellied sails symbolize the conception that took place in the port of origin that will culminate in delivery in the port of destination ("When we have laughed to see the sails conceive/And grow big-bellied with the wanton wind"; *A Midsummer Night's Dream* 2.1). Thus are remote places, with different cultures, linked. They mingle or are kept fiercely apart. New modes of consciousness, born of new understandings and misunderstandings awaken. Utterances translated in minds, on lips and on paper, assist the transmission of ideas and technologies, along with new kinds of friendship, new more complex, organized and larger-scale hatreds. And diseases. The Black Death, which cut deeper than any other event into the European consciousness of the past 1,000 years, was imported by sailors riding the trade winds. And syphilis, which had a profound impact, although a slow-burning, long-lasting one, was introduced by sailors who had introduced themselves into sexual partners at both ends of their voyages. Peoples are most profoundly connected by copulation (rape, marriage). My genes – the possibility of the person who is thinking all this now – were assembled by trade winds.

All hail, therefore, to those long, long breezes that have blown through history and, in virtue of their comparative permanence, have been the winds of change. And to the unique cooperation between wind and man, between the least and the most developed elements on the earth. And to the notion of attaching a piece of cloth to a mast to make the wind, careless of everything, permit us to travel over the seas, so that we may populate the world with realized possibilities. Thanks be to "The tall thought-woven sails, that flap unfurled/Above the tide of hours" (Yeats, "The Rose of Battle", in Yeats 1950: 42).

And damned be those who have forgotten where they have come from, the ingrates who cannot see how the dust and dailiness of trade could be linked with the openness and freedom of the wind. Or how the journey from the open sea, from spectacular tropical sunsets to smoggy city dawns, from the riding out of storms to the careful totting up of figures, was a step on the path to our freedom from want.

23

Mad Artefacts

I want to think past two items by the surrealist artist Méret Oppenheim. They are the famous fur-lined teacup and the marble sugar cubes. I want to argue that they reveal only what ordinary artefacts should say to us.

First, the fur-lined teacup. A nice joke, of course. And perhaps it does undermine our notion of essence, even of the fixed essence of artefacts that wear their essence on their sleeve (otherwise they wouldn't be much good). Maybe, maybe not. If this is what they are about, they do not really say anything that isn't, to the properly tuned brain, shouted out by the run-of-the-mill ceramic-lined, earthenware cup. The truth is, human reality is supernatural and consequently all human artefacts are surreal: they are transfigurations of nature.

Think of this. If the cup really was a transformation of the abstract idea of the palms of our own hands, the leap of the imagination that must have lain behind the *handle* by which we take hold of it is astounding. A human palm, lifted free of the hand and then fitted with a delicate little handle: now there's a work of art worth exhibiting! Better still, privately viewed, in the uncatalogued exhibition of artefacts that we have in our own homes, so that it won't be stolen from us (see Chapter 9, "The Shocking Yawn").

Our meditations on the wheel revealed how far transformations could go. The transition from space-nibbling legs to space-wolfing wheels, from leg-propelled body to engine-propelled automobile, liberated us from the constraints of carnal givens.[1] And, of course, the wheel was only the beginning of the story of *Homo faber*. Once our artefacts break with the model of the human body, components may be summoned from the four quarters of the earth. In this light, I would like to re-examine Oppenheim's other creation.

Her marble sugar cubes bring together a form and a substance that should not be brought together. Hence their charm. But for something a little more thought-provoking than charm, let's examine two things that *should* be brought together: a sugar cube and a pair of sugar tongs, united when a long-fingered, long-nailed hand transfers the former to a cup of tea, with dexterity and grace. (I locate this event in a well-appointed vicarage, sometime in mid-twentieth century, approximately 3.30pm on a winter afternoon when the silverware is laughing at the competition between the firelight inside and the December sky-light without.)

The cubing of sugar is in itself remarkable, allowing the amount of sweetness to be measured out with precision. Sugaring one's tea becomes a quasi-scientific exercise, with the material being doled out in standard units rather than in the nearly continuous (how nearly continuous depends on how finely divided is the sugar[2]) quantities of bagged sweetness. It underwrites the famous question whose *locus classicus* is the vicarage tea party, that paradigm of the temperate zones of the world: "one lump or two?" The notion that sugar should be cubed, that the silver bowl should be filled with unmarked dice, and that those dice should be destined to dissolve is odd in a way that is difficult to grasp hold of. And yet, in the case of Cuban sugar, overdetermined, as in a dream.

The cubing of Cuban sugar is particularly intriguing because it seems to solve no problems; indeed, it creates one. For in the appropriate, genteel setting the cubes may not be lifted by a hand exhibiting its prehensile skills. We are not monkeys and our naked hands could in theory contaminate the cubes that others may eat and so inflict an unwanted intimacy, or even worse, upon them. This admitted improbability is sufficient to sustain a custom that upholds a genteel way of life and a communal sense of self.

The solution to the problem of getting the cubed sugar to the poured tea marks the brief intersection between two very long journeys of two sorts of artefacts.

First, the cubes themselves. From formless sweetness in the cane fields in the tropics to its geometrical figures amid the crockery and the chintz is a long journey attended by much hard work and not a little hardship.[3] I can only guess at the conditions in the fields, in the holds of the ships, and in the warehouses at either end of the journey. I have a clearer idea of what I assume will be the rather better conditions in the lorries, depots and shops that the cubes inhabit on the last leg *en route* to the vicarage and of the relatively benign setting of the absolutely final phase of the journey, from retail shelf to shopping bag, to car, from pantry to silver bowl to drawing room.

The path taken by the sugar tongs is of equal length, although the relative contributions of space and of time (certainly more of the latter) are different. Its components – silver, nickel – have travelled from the far ends of the earth. After its birth, it wandered for over a hundred years from house to house, dealer to dealer, shop to shop, family member to family member, room to room. And here it is, clutched in the vicar's wife's hand, which pauses at stoop, selects its prey (absently while its owner talks about, let us say, the significance of a verse of the Gospel according to St John or the rota for arranging flowers in the church) and swoops.

As the tongs clutch the sugar with the miraculously judged precision that takes account of the weight and hardness of the cube and the coefficient of friction between nickel and the sides of the sugar, so that the little parcel is lifted without being crushed or dropped, the trajectories of the sugar and the tongs converge. There is the brief chiasma of the threads of spacetime, of the geodesics, already alluded to, after which their paths diverge. The tongs are laid down on the linen tablecloth, a pause in a sequence of short and long trajectories that will end who knows where or when. The sugar will dissolve in the tea (with the help of a little mauling from a spoon, whose stirring will cause the tea to mount up the sides of the cup, showing that the fixed stars are doing their work in defining the inertial frame of human activities); enter the tea-drinker's body along with the beverage whose flavour is commented upon with many favourable well-chosen adjectives between aliquots ingested with due regard to the etiquette of noiseless deglutition; and then be distributed in the body of the drinker with a precision of biochemical posting and sorting that beggars belief. At some time later, it will be called upon to do its bit towards maintaining the order of the vicar's wife's body and eventually die in that service into water and carbon dioxide.

The encounter between the tongs and the cube is as brief as the glance between myself and a tiny bemused baby at the chaotically busy international airport where I broke a several-thousand-mile journey a few hours ago.

NOTES

1. For the progressive disembodiment of our life and work see "The Work of Art in an Age of Electronic Reproduction" in the unreviewed, unbought and probably unread and uncited Tallis (1999b).
2. I like to think of a scale created out of the following points: crystal, granulated, caster, and icing. But not too hard because thinking of icing sugar does something I am inclined to call "setting my teeth on edge". This is one of the many properties of myself I do not understand, one of the many characteristics of being embodied-RT that RT stumbles into uncomprehendingly.
3. This said, the first sugar cubes were created by Jacob Christoph Rad in Moravia in the 1840s and the sugar was derived from beet. Subsequently, cane sugar was the main source. There is a monument commemorating this invention in Rad's native town Dačice. Needless to say, it consists of a sugar cube on a plinth, but it is made not of marble but of granite.

24

A Can of Beans

I could have chosen a can of soup but someone else has been there before me. By celebrating the look of the famous but under-regarded Campbell's soup can, Andy Warhol made it truly visible, perhaps for the first time. Rendering it with po-faced precision, and transplanting it to places far from the nexus of practical use, he peeled off the patina of familiarity that custom had laid over it like congealed tomato sauce on the cap of the ketchup bottle in a greasy spoon cafe. He invited us to contemplate its intricate artistry. A new light radiated into Wednesday afternoons from this, a quintessentially typical denizen of our ordinary days.

The trouble is Mr Warhol played the same trick with other commodities – Coca Cola, the face of Marilyn Monroe, and so on – and he did it again and again. His idea was then reproduced in a thousand magazines, catalogues, posters and so on: the very numerousness that, as is the way with daisies, had made the can seem uninteresting was reconstituted. Worse, the can, the image of the can and the idea of making an image of the can were wrapped in another patina of dullness even thicker than the carapace of disregard, born of familiarity, from which Mr Warhol had rescued it: a coating of

theory, for example, about the revelatory replication of the uncon-
sidered ordinary. In the end, Warhol–Campbell's soup can has been
buried under the theory of the representation of cans as an act of
postmodern art. The artefact has been lifted from the household
trashcan, the council tip, only to be consigned to a trashcan in the
tip of the cluttered, over-aware self-consciously contemporary mind.
My mind, for example, when it is sick of itself and of the twenty-first
century in equal quantities.

In order to scrape off this mess of second-order, third-order
and nth-order reflections that nag one to look at ordinary artefacts
through the supposedly liberating eyes of an artist extending our
notion of the work of art, one must dig more superficially. And when
the object of our attention is a can of beans, gold is soon struck: the
item is uncovered as a meeting place of disparate items fronting a
vast hinterland of ideas, assumptions and modes of being together.

Container, wrapper and contents severally and together reveal the
modern artefact as a standing realization of the surrealist notion of
"a chance juxtaposition of a sewing machine and an umbrella on a
dissecting table" (Comte de Lautréamont, *Les Chants des Maldoror*,
in Lautréamont 1978: 217). That the meeting on this occasion is not
the result of chance but of a countless multitude of intentions in no
wise diminishes its specialness. For intention is more mysterious
than chance, even the surrealist's ill-named "objective chance"; after
all, chance has reigned for all but a few million of the fifteen billion
years of the universe while the kind of intentions fulfilled in a can
of beans has been active in the universe only over the past few hundred years at most. As we shall discover, our can of beans realizes an
immense tapestry of intentions. They are woven more densely than
the silk threads in a luxury stocking: so densely that we shall need
to move slowly in order that we do not lose our way.

There is much to be noted about each of the three chief components – wrapper, tin, beans – into which, for the sake of order, we
have broken down our specimen artefact. Each of the trio breaks
down to further constituents worthy of detailed notice in their
own right; and these in turn yield numerous separately discussable

elements. Since my aim is not to be wearisomely exhaustive but to give life to the hypothesis that one can, more surely than in a grain of sand, find a whole world in the convergence of technologies, institutions, innovations and rituals that is a can of beans, a few selected observations about each of the three main characters will, I trust, suffice.

WRAPPER

The beans themselves I shall leave to the end, by which time we should have built up an appetite for them. Let us begin, as happens so often in real life, by reading the *wrapper*. The impressive list of ingredients broadcasts that in the darkness within are to be found materials drawn from what are quaintly called the four corners of this round earth. To these we shall address ourselves in due course. For the present, we shall stay with the wrapper. Several things are to be noted.

First, the very process of labelling deserves a little more attention than it usually receives. When Adam named the contents of the earth, he did not place those names, or their written forms, on the named object. There are several quite straightforward reasons for this. Most obviously, writing, which would eventually transmit the story of Adam's fatal misbehaviour to generations unknown to him, had not yet been invented. Second the named objects – goats, trees, water – were too numerous to label and, in the case of animals anyway, would not keep still enough to be labelled. While these reasons have a certain plausibility, they seem to miss the essential point: that the objects he named were self-evidently what they were; they uttered their own names. Name and nature were inseparable. They wore their essence on their sleeve (see Chapter 23, "Mad Artefacts").

Labels – names placed upon things – are required when it is not manifest what those things are; and it is not self-evident what they are when they are hidden – in packaging, wrapping – from the direct gaze. All that is directly visible is the wrapping. So BAKED BEANS is imprinted proudly on the wrapper, which may also note that said beans are served in tomato sauce.

In practice, not even this is enough. For names signify products and products are there to be bought and sold so that their survival through reproduction may be ensured. In this respect they are in competition with other products. As in Darwinian evolution, the fiercest competition is with the closest kin. Names are consequently modified as *brand* names. The brand name says "Sainsbury's Baked Beans": implicitly "Baked Beans Better than X's Baked Beans". It says "Buy Me" and "Buy Me in Preference to X's Baked Bean". When Adam looked round Eden, he saw all kinds of things but, as there was only one manufacturer – the devil's wickedness was limited to destruction rather than rival creation – there was only one strain of each. There was no need for brand names. In our fallen, competitive world of rival strains of commodities, the label is subordinated under the logo. The logo implies: "Buy me if you want quality". The name is embedded in a network of references linked up with advertisements, jingles, which amount to an entire mini-universe in the mind of the consumer, training her reflexes and appealing to many longer-loop components of her consciousness (of great moment in the case of clothes, where the label is what is bought and the clothes are merely a means of presenting the label – just as [according to Neo-Darwinian theory] an organism is simply a means for ensuring the continuing existence of a particular kind of genetic material). Sustaining the presence of this universe, even in its micro-reflection on the wrapper, mobilizes an army of papermakers, colour consultants, dyers, printers, typographers, creative artists and factors of glue. So there is no natural limit to what we may say about the wrapper or what it may prompt us to say. A self-denying ordinance is required. I shall confine myself to two further comments.

First, the placing of the generic name of the object upon itself allows for a variety of interesting games. We are in the world of self-reference, close to the famous dizzying *mise-en-abyme* of the sauce bottle that has a label showing a man holding a sauce bottle whose label shows a man holding a sauce bottle whose label in turn

.... There is no *mise-en-abyme* here (although the link with heraldry through the notion of the pedigree of the product is interesting) but something just as vertiginous. The application of a token of a word-type upon a token of a thing-type is almost a parody of the justly reviled "labelling" theory of language.[1] It does not, however, give succour to that theory because the name-placed-on-the-thing works only because it is part of a complex system of language (and verbal acts) such that even the stark "BAKED BEANS" on an unbranded tin (perhaps scribbled in felt pen on its conveniently writable surface) unpacks as the less stark "These are beans" or "Herein are beans". The single word is effectively a telescoped sentence: at any rate, a compressed communicative act. For the labels are not merely part of "a word heap", just as the contents of a supermarket are not just a thing heap. (Not even in pile-'em-high-and-sell-'em-cheap Netto.)

This mode of intersection between language and space, between fields of meaning and physical extendedness, which enables us to touch the verbal token as literally as we touch the object, is a recovered simplicity that belongs to a very late and sophisticated stage of language. Hardly surprising, therefore, that it creates interesting opportunities for exploiting the relationship between words and their referents, as when recently (to digress a moment) I saw on some sacks the following words, printed in varnish or tar on hemp: "NOT REUSABLE. NO DEPOSIT". This was an answer located precisely at the place where the question might arise, on the very object that may not only prompt the question but is also its referent-answer!

Nowadays, it is customary to include on the wrapper not only the name of the commodity within but also a picture of that commodity. Unsurprisingly, the picture is usually somewhat flattering: hence, the baked beans will be snapped in favourable lighting, with individual beans catching the ambient light in such a way as to look ravishingly tasty. They will be in a carefully selected bowl – classical, tasteful but not showy, lest the beans are outshone – and a spoon or forkful of them will be lifted from the main mass to make the customer's salivary glands secrete with the imminence of savouring. To intensify the sense of the presence, or imminent presence, of

281

beans and to heighten the otherwise indifferent (hurried, bothered, going-through-divorce, on-the-edge-of-a-nervous-breakdown) consumer's appetite for them, the image of the forkful will encroach on the part of the label that announces that here are indeed beans. The neat yellow border will be interrupted by a heaped up promise-of-pleasure; geometry and discourse will give place to the carnal senses; the iconic label, in short, will compete with the verbal one, representation with reference. Just how complicated is that?

Very complicated indeed, but there is much more complication to come. The wrapper is densely populated with iconic, referential and abstract signs. There are: heating instructions, in variant forms depending upon whether a traditional cooker or a microwave is to be used; lists of ingredients; comparisons of nutritional contents with those of other kinds of beans; detailed biochemical information about calories to be derived from various protein, carbohydrate and fat components; boasts about the quantity of fibre (without any guarantees as to the volume and loudness of flatus to be triggered by the contents); and warning-hedged advice about what to do when the can is opened and the contents exceed immediate requirements. The information samples a huge variety of kinds of human knowledge and draws upon a hidden Everest of implied human practices.

Remarkably, we have far from exhausted the contents of the wrapper. There are also:

(a) a Freephone number corresponding to a customer careline (for those who are interested in trying a bit of bean-customer-care);

(b) a statement, without an explicit subject – athough it is manifest through the implied deixis of the location of the written sentence – to the effect that the beans have been produced in the UK for X's Supermarkets;

(c) a note of the liability status of the firm in question ("LTD"), the address of the firm (for those who are thinking of a pilgrimage or a surrealist *dérive*) and the internet address of the same – www.X.co.uk;

(d) a reassurance, next to a logo combining a magnet and a portrait of a tin, that the tin is made of recyclable steel, to pre-empt the possibility that any pilgrimages to Holborn might be fuelled by Green rage;

(e) a Bridget Riley miniature – a barcode – encoding the name and nature of the commodity on which it is stamped;

(f) and two enigmatic alphanumeric codes(probably not addressed to me but possibly crucial in some kind of emergency) < 00332071 > and PO819.

Given that every product attracts liability to the producer, in order that the reader – of this book or that label – may rest assured that each assertion and instruction on the wrapper will have been subjected to a scrutiny considerably more microscopic than the rather casual observations of the present tour, it is not surprising to find a disclaimer or two among the declaratives. The nutritional information, for example, applies only if "heated as per instructions" and the can once opened must be kept refrigerated and eaten within twenty-four hours: a suspiciously rounded period of time that suggests that the laws of tort rather than those known to biochemists have been in the driving seat. The heating instructions are also qualified: "All cooking appliances vary in performance, these are guidelines only". This places the blame for underheated or overbaked beans precisely where it should be: with the disaffected customer. The densely packed surface of the wrapper will have to be continually updated in the light of an evolving world of claim and counter-claim. The wrapper not only says "Bean" and "Top quality beans fitting in with a desirable style of life" but also anticipates the mother who decides that her child has been irreversibly brain damaged as a result of eating one bean or the owner who wishes redress for injury to the dog's tongue when it licked the contents of an opened can.

Disappointingly, the chatter on the wrapper on the can next to me does not include the reassurance that the wrapper is itself made out of 100 per cent recycled paper. The nearest we get to deictically guaranteed self-reference is the aforementioned subjectless sentence asserting the recyclability of the steel in the can. This, at any rate, must be the right moment (since we are about to move on from the wrapper to the can) to reflect once again on the remarkable existential grammar of such labelling information. We are so used to objects that talk about themselves, or have frozen, self-referring speech acts posted on their external surfaces, we hardly notice this feature. And yet it is no less striking than the bottle in *Alice's Adventures in Wonderland* that, despite being tongueless, lacking agency and being void of a self- or sustained first-person perspective, says "Drink Me" to anyone whose eyes alight upon it.

That is why the polite suggestions as to how to dispose of the can dressed so smartly in its wrapper is so fascinating. The advice is sometimes supported by iconic representations of an idealized or stylized litter basket with an idealized or stylized unisex individual lobbing the can into it. (Such precision in the way the object specifies the details of its own disposal reminds one of the instructions of a couple of recently deceased members of the Royal Family as to how their passing should be marked.) Equally thought-provoking is the trademark earlobed with the trademark sign that implicitly warns that it – the trademark – is registered with the authorities, is the intellectual property of the trader, and must not be expropriated by imposters. I could go on – perhaps I have done already – but the point is clear: the meeting of such disparate things – cooking instructions, advice about disposal, fair trade warnings and so on – and the wattage of self-reference (the trademark referring to itself, the can giving instructions for its mode of entombment) – makes the chance meeting of an umbrella and a sewing machine on a dissection table a rather low-intensity event.

TIN

The wrapper broadcasts the contents of the can and, at the same time, comments on it. Although the wrapper is intended to render unhidden the beans that have been hidden by the tin, it is itself another layer of concealment. That is why we have taken so long to reach our second component: the tin in the tin of beans.[2] (The tin, it is probably not necessary to remind anyone, is plated with, not made of, tin. The tin should be called a tinplated-steel. The magnet next to the recycling motif betrays this.)

Dispensing baked beans in hurled dollops from a central vat (in, for example, the aforementioned Holborn) is logistically incompatible with the way modern life is organized. Besides, it would present the manufacturers and distributors with all sorts of difficulties in addressing transport, hygiene, quality control, quantity control, issues. Those who regret the ubiquity of packaging – boxes, packets, jars, bottles, cases, cans, blisters seem to some to dominate the distinctively human contribution to the landscape – cannot deny that some kind of container/dispenser is necessary. As the experts would agree, selection of suitable containers can be as important as formulation of foods for long-term storage and for the prevention of changes in colour, flavour, odour, texture, and nutritional content with consequent staling, rancidity and lethal invasion by bacteria. Naked heaps of beans would sooner or later be portioned out among other creatures, large or small, with whom we share the animal kingdom in which we live. It is nice pleasantry, therefore, to imagine starting with a blank sheet and going through the considerations that would lead to the inevitably conclusion that beans should be in cans.

Boxing would be unsatisfactory because of the permeable sogginess of the foodstuff in question and the peculiar vulnerability of a wet food to corruption. Jarring would seem acceptable and so would enclosure in plastic containers. (After all, three-bean salad is.) So there must be some other reason why baked beans are indissolubly associated with tins or (as they are more usually called cans). The overwhelming argument, I suspect, is that beans are in cans because they always have been in cans. Or beans must always be canned because they always have been canned. This is an empirical assertion that is beyond the knowledge base that lies to hand, so I shall not pursue this question any further. If it is true, however, we should pay tribute to Sainsbury's and Heinz and others for this

285

modest contribution to the coherence and stability of the world and for, in this slight fashion, applying the brakes on a human world that is in runaway mode, in the grip of an accelerating rate of change.

The canning of beans – with a speed that does not threaten quality control – is an extraordinary feat about which I have little to say, so humbled do I feel by the achievements of technology.[3] I note only a few things. The material out of which the cans are made is a mixture of the eponymous tin and two other metals. The choice of this alloy has been influenced by reasons of cost and of malleability and of suitability to be the bearer of beans: keeping all the flavour in, keeping all the dirt out, and preventing them mating in the darkness with the sauce with toxic results.

The relationship between the human race and tin and, even more, tin alloys has been no passing affair. The combination of tin and copper – bronze – defined an entire epoch in the evolution of humanity from its animal origins. The use of tin as a coating for other metals goes back to the Romans, who used tinned copper vessels for cooking. The tin coating of iron sheet to form tinplate – in lanterns, plates and goblets – has a much shorter history, beginning in central Europe about 500 or 600 years ago and spreading outwards from there. The date that bears most directly on our present preoccupations is one celebrated by Tchaikovsky in his famous *1812 Overture*. This was the year when Napoleon (who had observed that an army marches on its stomach and was faced with a starving *Grande Armée* that, for the most part, marched into the ground) invaded Russia, and also, rather more importantly, the year when food canning was introduced and packaging became the prime use of tinplate. It is nice to speculate that the explosions in the *1812 Overture* alluded to the effects of the canned food on the invading force, but it seems unlikely.

The cylindrical "tin" sits very satisfactorily in the hand and may form a convenient missile. Since this is not its primary function, it has to be opened: its contents have to be got at. More ingenuity is required for this purpose. As Karl Popper pointed out, every solution to a problem creates a new problem-situation. The levering-knife, using the handy (non-accidentally so) rim as a fulcrum (the diagram of forces is beyond my recollected physics), that is a can opener is a miracle of intermediate technology, even if one sets aside the ingenuity of wall can openers, wheeled versions and so on, and other varieties that are regarded as commonplace in our blasé household. Even more compelling is the new ring-pull, built into the can itself. The two steps – lifting the tab and pulling back the top (which has a built in leak-proof weakness in its attachment to the remainder of the can) – are actually spelled out in diagrammatic form on the can itself: another twist in the fiendishly plotted tale of self-reference of which the can is the hero.

The purpose of the can is to permit the storage, preservation and distribution of the beans. Since can-makers are machinists and metallurgists and not bean-processors, nor are they graphic artists and paper-makers, the coalition of talents, of arts and crafts and sciences and technologies, that convenes in this can of beans is extensive. And we have not even considered the warehouse men, the lorry-drivers, the garage mechanics, the cardboard-box-makers (in which platoons of cans are meta-packed), buyers, stock-controllers, shelf-fillers, managers and so on who watch over the process from the growing of the beans to the moment when the can, presented to the decision field of the weary, distracted shopper, is selected and bought.

BEANS

We have not yet said anything about that without which the wrapper and the tin would be somewhat pointless: the beans themselves. To those inclined to complain that we have reached the final act and have so far had *Hamlet*-without-the-prince, we can only bow in acquiescence. Enter Hamlet, but accompanied by a retinue of supporters. As the wrapper proclaims, beans form only 49 per cent of what is to be found in the darkness within. For what we have bought is:

BAKED BEANS
in Tomato Sauce with Sugar and Sweetener

Tomatoes constitute 27 per cent of our purchase; and water, sugar, modified maize starch, salt, onion powder, ground paprika, spice extracts, herb extracts and "sweetener: saccharin" contribute unspecified percentages of the rest. In short, there is an international congress of edibles and preservatives in the darkness of the can and each delegate has its own retinue. Farmers, moneylenders, millers, truckers, speculators, traders, shippers, dealers, importers, warehouse workers, tasters, packers, distributors and retailers will all have had their hand in one or more of the many items declared on the label. Lawyers, food inspectors, health-and-safety experts, quality controllers and chemists, too, will have had their say.

Each of these is deserving of our attention but only the key character will receive it because I have a life of finite duration and you, reader, have a rather more finite patience. It will be noted that none of the beans in the can is mouldy, dirty or discoloured. This is not a matter of luck but the result of the work of the automatic baked-bean sorter. The beans *en route* for the can are required to run the gauntlet of magic eyes. These send out beams of light that blindly finger every single bean. If the visual echo, detected by the magic eye, is dull, a computer triggers a device that sends out a puff of air which, awaiting the faulty bean further down the track, ruthlessly pushes it off the track. In large canneries, up to 60,000 beans may be sorted this way in a second. (I owe these facts to a lovely book: *How is it Done?* [Reader's Digest 1992].) This step in the process brings more characters into the picture: physicists, software writers, photo-electronic wizards, mechanical engineers and so on.

Which prompts a final reflection. Baked beans are the archetypal food for campers, consumed round the campfire upon which they may have been cooked. The open air, the traffic-free quiet, the call of the owls and the uncombed informality of the flames may lead to the impression that the campers are closer to nature. No such thing. The discarded can in the midden and the beans in the pan carry between them a huge mass of the civilized world. And this is betrayed by the fact that even the anticipated, or commented-on, emissions that the beans traditionally foster are citations with complex histories and a *locus classicus*: the very expensive, self-referential Hollywood movie *Blazing Saddles*.

It is not for nothing that children pronounce "human beings" as "human beans" and "bean" and "been" are homophones. So much of the past of humanity is incorporated into the contents of that "humble" (to wobble from prose into a voiceover for a moment) commodity. To suggest, however, that humans do not amount to a hill, only a can, of beans would be to draw precisely the wrong conclusion from this extraordinary story.

NOTES

1. This is the so-called Fido–Fido theory of language, which no one, I suspect, has espoused, but which it is great fun to mock. Essentially, this view, that the meaning of a word is an object, holds: that (a) words are nouns standing for concrete objects – they are names; (b) that reference is achieved by pronouncing the name of the concrete object in question; and (c) that discourse is essentially directly achieved reference. Wrong, wrong, wrong. Not that we know what is right, right, right.
2. At the risk of wearying – or further wearying – the reader, I note that the can's discourse about itself does not end with the wrapper and the description of how it should be opened. Its under surface contains a dot-matrix-printed date: "APR 2014". This signifies the approximate time (and from this distance – 2013 – such blurredness seems non-culpable) at which the instructions given elsewhere on the can become invalid. It also has some more opaque inscriptions: "L 89SL", "2114 16:45 12.9", which may or may not record when this can was sealed and by whom, so that any enquiries into outbreaks of bean-borne diseases or other untoward events might be completed with a full account of by whom and when. (For an enthralling story of such an inquiry, dependent upon comparable opaque inscriptions, see Levi [2000].)
    And even then the story is not over. Remember the customer care line?
3. I read the other day – in the Trinity 2002 Issue of *Oxford Today* (p. 24), which had been enjoying a ten-year asylum in our loft – that on average yoghurt travels 3,500 kilometres before it ends up in a supermarket. More relevant to our present preoccupations, the same article notes that a Coke can – pressed in seconds – actually takes nine months in total to make. The contrast between the nine months in preparation and the second of pressing is analogous to the contrast between the brevity of intercourse and the *longeurs* of pregnancy.

Ink

The Artefact of Artefacts

For several millennia, writing meant handwriting and, most of the time, ink and pens and penning. A century or so ago, typewriting started to nudge aside handwriting; a couple of decades ago, typewriting began to be replaced by word-processing. For the preceding 4,000 years, inscription was mainly by means of a dampened stylus. The dip-in – reed or feather – bore most of the burden of the scribes' inscription. The overwhelming history of the world's accounting has been carried by quill pen and ledger; thinking has been inseparable from inking. Only very recently have ethereal spreadsheets been booted to a thousand ephemeral discarnations on screens.

Just before the stylus started yielding ground to the keyboard, the pen came to its highest expression. The fountain pen had a complexity unknown to the reed and the quill, being differentiated into the barrel, the cap, the teat-like rubber ink store and the nib. And, as is the way with things (or at least so Schopenhauer informs us in *The World as Will and Idea*) the most perfect outward expression is invariably the harbinger of decline. The beautiful pen with which Max Planck wrote his famous paper of 1900 inscribed the writing on the wall for the pen: out of our understanding of black body radiation came quantum mechanics; out of quantum mechanics came semi-conductors; out of semi-conductors came microprocessors; and, before long, letters were more often alphanumeric characters, bytes stored on a magnetic medium and glowing on a video screen, than trails of dark ink on a light page.

Now that computerized information technology is in the ascendant and we can download information in gigabytes from the internet and we text our friends and email anyone at all at the touch of a button, we must not forget the original information technologists upon whose shoulders we stand: the handwriters, the calligraphers and the frozen-fingered rap-knuckled cacographers who unpacked their dreams on pages, who recorded and transcribed; the tribe of scribes, the clerks and thinkers and literary artists who documented and preserved the shared knowledge and growing collective consciousness of the human race.

All praise to these drones to whom it was not open to Xerox, tape or incise on disc the combinations of characters that filled their working days. Praise, too, to the pen and paper: none of us, after all, has failed to access a handwritten page because of a system failure or a forgotten command and never has a pen crashed, wiping out hundreds of pages of text. The worst disaster, short of fire and flood, is bounded by the scope of a blot of ink. Even the leakiest pen cannot cancel years of work.

Ink has survived the decline of the pen relatively unscathed. It remains a necessary partner of the computer and the email if "hard copy" is needed, and hard copy is always needed. (The paperless office remains knee-deep in paper.) It has had its metamorphoses, of course: typing ribbon (with the early Xeroxing courtesy of carbon black); characters tattooed through the pointillist action of the dot-matrix pins; and micro-hoses painting the letters on the page in response to an exquisitely modulated stream of million-per-second instructions.

These have proved the most enduring of the trails we have left behind us. They have outlived the stone-prints left by falling boulders; and the paw-prints of beasts. And our footprints in the earth, our paths, are melting snow-prints by comparison. Our most truly human spraint is abstract meaning, captured in a drop of blackness, pulled out to a line. All praise then to such carefully spilt ink: to the line taken not for a walk but (cursively) for a run. How much more fluent is the ink-charged pen than a chisel trying to get stones to record speech.

All praise to the pen teasing out a drop of ink into words, clauses, sentences, paragraphs. I like to think of the nib, the stylus, as a sail leaving a black furrow in the white sea of the blank page, wakening a voice in the silent place of the unexpressed, creating the routes that eventually become our shared map of the world. A voice, yes. But one whose words move further and further from the mouths, from the sore tongue and the fillings in the teeth; further from bodies; from the accidents of bodily place; from accent and volume and scent. (Although they have to return to bodies to fulfil their purpose, reviving out of hibernation thoughts that may or may not be recited.)

Ink is the artefact of artefacts. Diagrams, pictures, equations, regulations, letters patent, institutions – that underpin the growth of technology – are inked. The pen's arrhythmic dance unravels the ductile darkness of the ink to a quinkled, esoteric shade of light; thought-light that the sun (drying characters it does not comprehend) remotely lit. It is the dark heart of the light – light's being known, the inmost gleam of light.

Justifying the Search

I

How, then, shall we escape the shanty burrows of busyness, the dithering dapples of occupation and preoccupation, attraction and distraction, burning the dew from self-presence?

How to incise a permanence on this space that sleeves our passage through time to the end of time, space that so briefly assumes our shapes, and in that brief assumption still confounds our forms with its own rococo of turbulence – cross-rolls, knots and varicosities – a litter of grace notes garnishing the architectonics and harmonics of intention with consequence and inconsequence, reminding our minds of the opacity of the world to our minds, the intractability of matter to our embodied will?

How shall we resist those cancellations that heal the air behind us and render streets and fields innocent once more of our imprint, as we, and ours, and all we made and marked, and hugged and held dear, wrinkle out of being to an unbeing, untethered to any private wake of absence?

II

Shouting is not the deft or apt retort to the jabber of process and gossip of event, to the tales, and tales of tales, simmering and soaking through the networks of the hours. Screams are as impotent as thick and dusky whispers, sound-hedges glistening with sibilance, and nested with hairballs of meaning and dunnock-like fidgetings of sense. Likewise, a deliberate silence, rebuking by understatement the rustle of passage, as it dies into nobody's noise, proving thereby the constancy of evanescence.

III

Our unanswered questions justify the ache that justifies the search: the hunt for words, for voices – neither loud nor quiet, but tuned to whatever verberation is most ourselves and most in tune with the great world in which we have found ourselves – that will imprint mordant memory on the noise-pocked silence after our passing, iterating that we were *This*: that we stopped the light and cast shadows; that we made and suffered happening; and that our folded thoughts and intuitions, touching and painting the twin-panelled nothingness of the no-longer and the not-yet, seemed almost to grasp our coming and stay our going, as if shimmers could be arrested to flowers embroidered, unfading, on the silk of time itself.

IV

Alas (and of course), there are no such words, no such voices, nor any tone of voice, to finesse a flight from the closing fist of the forces that first forged and fathered us, the dumb collisions of the boulder-grained though innocent enemies of our delicate delight.

And yet, even the Grandmasters of Disenchantment may believe that there is, or will be, someone, somewhere, who will uncover a muffled music of meditation, a melody stitched from scattered notes not entirely damped even in the narrows of abstraction, that will melt the penitentiary locked and barred by the habit of Habit and bolted by the master-habits of indifference and despair. A music muffled but still tingling in strait-laced and earnest propositions, well-formed formulae and dun syllogisms, barked into ranks by martinet connectives; a music not wholly missing from those heath lands of the mind, where sour, thin soil and sifting dust-grey dunes are tufted with dry words whose spines rasp the minds that think them.

Yes, even a calcified metaphysician, a withered sentence-factor, may dream of a marvellous, unwavering cry that will arrest the unregulated "whoosh" of the hours skeltering from "will be" to "was", frogmarching each thinking "I" to oblivion; will arrest the varnished vanishment of time, whose instants are like a mouse's-tail-down-a-hole eluding the prehensile pinch of little fingers, a snake of water through a crack, an edge of smoke; and release a buried song of thought, harmonizing the tassels of sadness and of joy, and all the vectorless cut grass the senses harvest; and so orchestrate this inexplicable gift of consciousness to its own idea of perfection.

V

And believe, although our destination will remain the predestined, that we shall, from time to time, in this journey that digests tomorrows to yesterdays, burst upon a transfigured Wednesday, that we shall move among its scattered occasions, ourselves transfigured for unrepealable moments of hope, of lucid delight, and, in absolute waking, unaching *be*.

References

Adluri, V. 2011. *Parmenides, Plato and Mortal Philosophy: Return from Transcendence*. London: Continuum.

Aiken. H. D. (ed.) 1956. *The Age of Ideology: The Nineteenth Century Philosophers*, New York: Mentor.

Alston, W. 1997. "Searle on Perception". Unpublished manuscript.

Aristotle 1993. *Metaphysics*, C. Kirwan (trans.). Oxford: Oxford University Press.

Aristotle 1984. *Parts of Animals*, W. Ogle (trans.). In *The Complete Works of Aristotle: The Revised Oxford Translation*, J. Barnes (ed.). Princeton, NJ: Princeton University Press.

Austin, J. L. 1962. *Sense and Sensibilia*. Oxford: Oxford University Press.

Bach, K. 2007. "Searle Against the World: How Can Experiences Find Their Objects?" In *John Searle's Philosophy of Language: Force, Meaning, and Mind*, S. L. Tsohatzidis (ed.), 64–78. Cambridge: Cambridge University Press.

Barnes, J. 1982. *The Presocratic Philosophers*. London: Routledge.

Barthes, R. 1978. "Waiting". In *A Lover's Discourse: Fragments*, R. Howard (trans.). New York: Hill & Wang.

Bayne, T. 2012. "How to Read Minds". In *I Know What You're Thinking: Brain Imaging and Mental Privacy*, S. Richmond, G. Rees & S. J. Edwards (eds), 41–58. Oxford: Oxford University Press.

BBC News 2002. "Hirst Apologises for 11 September Comments". http://news.bbc.co.uk/1/hi/entertainment/2268307.stm (accessed February 2014).

Benn, G. [1961] 1971. *Primal Vision: Selected Writings*, E. B. Ashton (ed.). New York: New Directions.

Bergeron, K. 2010. *Voice Lessons: French Mélodie in the Belle Epoque*. New York: Oxford University Press.

Bergson, H. 1911. *La perception du changement; conférences faites à l'Université d'Oxford les 26 et 27 mai 1911* [The perception of change: lectures delivered at the University of Oxford on 26 and 27 May 1911]. Oxford: Clarendon Press.

Berlin, I. (ed.) 1956. *The Age of Enlightenment: The Eighteenth Century Philosophers*. New York: Mentor Books.

Blackburn, S. & K. Simmons (eds) 1999. *Truth*. Oxford: Oxford University Press.

Bowie-Sell, D. 2013. "Graham Ovenden Prints Removed from Tate". *Telegraph* (4 April). www.telegraph.co.uk/culture/art/art-news/9970830/Graham-Ovenden-prints-removed-from-Tate.html (accessed March 2014).

Brandon, R. 1999. *Surreal Lives: The Surrealists 1917–1945*. London: Macmillan.

Bray, C. 2012. "Jackson Pollock by Evelyn Toynton – Review". *Observer* (26 February). www.theguardian.com/books/2012/feb/26/jackson-pollock-evelyn-toynton-review (accessed March 2014).

Call, J. & M. Tomasello 2008. "Does the Chimpanzee Have a Theory of Mind? 30 Years Later". *Trends in Cognitive Science* 12(5): 187–92.

Carnap, R. 1959. "The Elimination of Metaphysics Through Logical Analysis of Language", A. Pap (trans.). In *Logical Positivism*, A. J. Ayer (ed.), 60–81. New York: Free Press.

Cave, P. 2007. "With and Without End". *Philosophical Investigations* 30(2):105–26.

Caws, M. A. 1997. *The Surrealist Look: An Erotics of Encounter*. Cambridge, MA: MIT Press.

Churchland, P. 1988. *Matter and Consciousness: A Contemporary Introduction to the Philosophy of Mind*, rev. edn. Cambridge, MA: MIT Press.

Dantzig, T. [1930] 2007. *Number: The Language of Science*. London: Plume.

Davidson, D. 1982. "Rational Animals". *Dialectica* 36: 317–27.

Davidson, S. 2004. "What Thought Requires". In his *Problems of Rationality*, 135–49. Oxford: Oxford University Press.

De Pierris, G. & M. Friedman 2013. "Kant and Hume on Causality". In *The Stanford Encyclopedia of Philosophy* (Winter 2013 Edition), E. N. Zalta (ed.). http://plato.stanford.edu/archives/win2013/entries/kant-hume-causality/ (accessed February 2014).

Dennett, D. 1991. *Consciousness Explained*. New York: Little Brown.

Dennett, D. 2003. *Freedom Evolves*. London: Allen Lane.

Dennett, D. 2012. "Sakes and Dints". *Times Literary Supplement* (2 March): 12–14.

Dennett, D. 2013. "Kinds of Things: Towards a Bestiary of the Manifest Image". In *Scientific Metaphysics*, D. Ross, J. Ladyman & H. Kincaid (eds), 96–107. Oxford: Oxford University Press.

Derrida, J. 1988. *Limited Inc.* Evanston, IL: Northwestern University Press.

Devaney, M. J. 1997. *"Since at Least Plato ..." and Other Postmodernist Myths*. Basingstoke: Macmillan.

Dorment, R. 2000. "Million-pound Man". *Telegraph* (26 April). www.telegraph.co.uk/culture/4720541/Million-pound-man.html (accessed March 2014).

Dowe, P. 2008. "Causal Processes". In *The Stanford Encyclopedia of Philosophy* (Fall 2008 Edition), E. N. Zalta (ed.). http://plato.stanford.edu/archives/fall2008/entries/causation-process/ (accessed February 2014).

Dummett M. 1973. *Frege: Philosophy of Language*. London: Duckworth.

Duncan, A. 2012. "Snowman Creator Raymond Briggs: Grumpy Old Man or Great Big Softie?" *Radio Times* (24 December). www.radiotimes.com/news/2012-12-24/snowman-creator-raymond-briggs---grumpy-old-man-or-great-big-softie (accessed February 2014).

Dyson, F. 2004. *Infinite in All Directions*. New York: HarperCollins.

Eagleton, T. 1998. Review of M. J. Devaney, *"Since at Least Plato ..." and Other Postmodernist Myths*. *Times Literary Supplement* (2 January): 2.

Eliot, T. S. 1963. *Collected Poems 1909–1962*. London: Faber.

Enright, D. J. 1980. *The Oxford Book of Contemporary Verse 1945–1980*. Oxford: Oxford University Press.

Fernandéz-Armesto, F. 2013. "All Things Possible". *Times Literary Supplement* (18 October): 3-4.

Feynman, R. 1986. "Cargo Cult Science". In *Surely You're Joking Mr Feynman!*, R. Leighton (ed.), 338–46. London: Unwin.

Frith, C. 2007. *Making Up the Mind: How the Brain Creates Our Mental World*. Oxford: Blackwell.

Galbraith, J. K. 1971. *A Contemporary Guide to Economics, Peace and Laughter*. Boston, MA: Houghton Mifflin.

Gale, R. M. (ed.) 1968. *The Philosophy of Time: A Collection of Essays*. London: Macmillan.

Gardiner, J. E. 2013. *Music in the Castle of Heaven: A Portrait of Johann Sebastian Bach*. London: Allen Lane.

Gardiner, P. 1963. *Schopenhauer*. London: Penguin.

Gleick, J. 1992. *Genius: Richard Feynman and Modern Physics*. New York: Little, Brown.

Gowers, E. (ed.) 1968. *Fowler's Modern English Usage*, 2nd edn. Oxford: Oxford University Press.

Graham, G. 1998. "Mind and Belief in Animals". In his *Philosophy of Mind: An Introduction*, 2nd edn, 65–86. Oxford: Blackwell.

Hamburger, M. & C. Middleton (eds) 1962. *Modern German Poetry 1910–1960*. London: MacGibbon & Kee.

Hamilton, A. 2012. "Still Dotty About Damien Hirst". *Independent* (16 January). www.independent.co.uk/arts-entertainment/still-dotty-about-damien-hirst-6289982.html (accessed February 2014).

Hamilton, C. 2001. *Living Philosophy: Reflections on Life, Meaning and Morality*. Edinburgh: Edinburgh University Press.

Hamilton, J. 2002. *Faraday: The Life*. London: HarperCollins.

Hammond, N. G. L. & H. H. Scullard (eds) 1970. *The Oxford Classical Dictionary*, 2nd edn. Oxford: Clarendon Press.

Harrell, E. M. 1996. "A Report from the Front of the 'Science Wars'". *Notices of the AMS* 43(10): 1132–6. www.ams.org/notices/199610/comm-harrell.pdf (accessed February 2014).

Harris, R. 2003. *Saussure and His Interpreters*. Edinburgh: Edinburgh University Press.

Harris, W. 1998. "Multiculturalism and Cultural Warfare". *Philosophy and Literature* 22: 497–515.

Heidegger, M. 1978. "What is Metaphysics?" In *Basic Writings*, D. Farrell Krell (ed.), 91–113. London: Routledge & Kegan Paul.

Heidegger, M. 1996. *Being and Time*, J. Stambaugh (trans.). Albany, NY: SUNY Press.

Hitchens, C. 2008. *God is Not Good: How Religion Poisons Everything*. London: Atlantic.

Hope, A. D. 1972. *Collected Poems 1930–1970*. Sydney: Australian Poetry Library.

Hume, D. [1748] 1975. *An Enquiry Concerning Human Understanding*, L. A. Selby-Bigge (ed.), P. H. Nidditch (rev.). Oxford: Clarendon Press.

Hume, D. [1739, 1740] 1985. *A Treatise of Human Nature*. Harmondsworth: Penguin.

Kafka, F. 1995. *Franz Kafka: The Complete Stories*, N. N. Glatzer (ed.), W. Muir & E. Muir (trans.). New York: Schocken.

Kant, I. [1781] 1964. *Immanuel Kant's Critique of Pure Reason*, N. Kemp Smith (trans.). Basingstoke: Macmillan.

Kapuscinski, R. 2001. *The Shadow of the Sun*, K. Glowczewska (trans.). New York: Vintage.

Latour, B. 2004. "Why Has the Critique of Science Run out of Steam? From Matters of Fact to Matters of Concern". *Critical Inquiry* 30(2): 225–48.

Lautréamont, Comte de 1978. *Maldoror and Poems*. Harmondsworth: Penguin.

Lechte, J. 1990. *Julia Kristeva*. London: Routledge.

Levi, P. 2000. *The Periodic Table*, R. Rosenthal (trans.). Harmondsworth: Penguin.

Lewis, D. 1973. "'Causation". *Journal of Philosophy* 70: 556–67.

MacDiarmid, H. 1970. *Sangschaw*. In *Selected Poems*, D. Craig & J. Manson (eds), 1–2. London: Penguin.

Malcolm, N. 1972–73. "Thoughtless Brutes". *Proceedings and Addresses of the American Philosophical Association* 46: 5–20.

Malik, K. 2000. *Man, Beast and Zombie*. London: Weidenfeld.

Mallarmé, S. 1886. "Preface". In R. Ghil, *Traité du verbe* (Treatise on the Word), 5–7. Paris: Giraud.

Matthews, E. 2002. *The Philosophy of Merleau-Ponty*. Chesham: Acumen.

McDowell, J. 1996. *Mind and World*. Cambridge, MA: Harvard University Press.

Mellor, D. H. 1995. *The Facts of Causation*. London: Routledge.

Merquior, J. G. 1985. *Foucault*. London: Fontana.

Mill, J. S. 1846. *A System of Logic*. New York: Harper.

Mill, J. S. [1865] 1979. *An Examination of Sir William Hamilton's Philosophy and of the Principal Philosophical Questions Discussed in His Writings*, J. M. Robson & A. Ryan (eds). In *Collected Works*, vol. 9. London: Routledge & Kegan Paul.

Nagel, T. 1974. "What Is it Like to Be a Bat?" *Philosophical Review* 83(4): 435–50.

Nagel, T. 1986. *The View from Nowhere*. Oxford: Oxford University Press.

Nagel, T. 2012. *Mind and Cosmos: Why the Materialist Neo-Darwinian Conception of Nature is Almost Certainly False*. Oxford: Oxford University Press.

Nietzsche, F. 1954. "On Truth and Lie in an Extra-Moral Sense". In *The Portable Nietzsche*, W. Kauffmann (ed. and trans.), 42–7. New York: Viking.

Norris, C. 1992. *Uncritical Theory: Postmodernism, Intellectuals, and the Gulf War*. Amherst, MA: University of Massachusetts Press.

Pavese, C. 1966. "Instinct", N. T. di Giovanni (trans.). In *Modern European Poetry*, W. Barnstone (ed.), 318–19. New York: Bantam.

Pearl, J. 2000. *Causality*. New York: Cambridge University Press.

Pinker, S. 2012. *The Better Angels of Our Nature*. London: Penguin.

Popper, K. 1972. *Objective Knowledge*. Oxford: Oxford University Press.

Povinelli, D. J. 2003. *Folk Physics for Apes: The Chimpanzee's Theory of How the World Works*. Oxford: Oxford University Press.

Price, H. 1996. *Time's Arrow and Archimedes' Point: New Directions for the Physics of Time*. Oxford: Oxford University Press.

Quine, W. V. 1960. *Word and Object*. Cambridge, MA: MIT Press.

Quine, W. V. 1969. *Ontological Relativity and Other Essays*. New York: Columbia University Press.

Quine, W. V. 1975. "The Nature of Natural Knowledge". In *Mind and Language: Wolfson College Lectures 1974*, S. Guttenplan (ed.). Oxford: Clarendon Press.

Reader's Digest 1992. *How is it Done?* London: Reader's Digest.

Richmond, S. 2012. "Brain Imaging and the Transparency Scenario". In *I Know What You Are Thinking: Brain Imaging and Mental Privacy*, S. Richmond, G. Rees & S. J. L. Edwards (eds), 185–204. Oxford: Oxford University Press.

Rilke, R. M. 1967. *Rainer Maria Rilke: Selected Works, Volume II Poetry*, J. B. Leishman (trans.). London: Hogarth Press.

Robinson, H. 1982. *Matter and Sense*. Cambridge: Cambridge University Press.

Roudinesco, E. 1997. *Jacques Lacan*. Cambridge: Polity.

Rovelli, C. 2008. "Forget Time". www.fqxi.org/data/essay-contest-files/Rovelli_Time.pdf (accessed February 2014).

Russell, B. [1953] 1992. "On the Notion of Cause". In his *Mysticism and Logic*, 171–96. London: Pelican.

Russell, B. [1912] 1959. *The Problems of Philosophy*. Oxford: Oxford University Press.

Ryle, G. 1954. *Dilemmas*. Cambridge: Cambridge University Press.

Safranski, R. 1999. *Martin Heidegger: Between Good and Evil*, E. Osers (trans.). Cambridge, MA: Harvard University Press.

Salmon, W. 1984. *Scientific Explanation and the Causal Structure of the World*. Princeton, NJ: Princeton University Press.

Sartre, J.-P. [1943] 2003. *Being and Nothingness*, Philosophical Library (trans.). London: Routledge.

Schaffer, J. 2013. "The Metaphysics of Causation". In *The Stanford Encyclopedia of Philosophy* (Winter 2013 Edition), E. N. Zalta (ed.). http://plato.stanford.edu/archives/win2013/entries/causation-metaphysics/ (accessed February 2014).

Schulz, K. 2010. *Being Wrong: Adventures in the Margin of Error*. New York: Ecco.

Searle, A. 2012. "Full Circle: The Endless Attraction of Damien Hirst's Spot Paintings". *Guardian* (12 January). www.theguardian.com/artanddesign/2012/jan/12/damien-hirst-spot-paintings-review (accessed February 2014).

Searle, J. 1983a. *Intentionality: An Essay in the Philosophy of Mind*. Cambridge: Cambridge University Press.

Searle, J. 1983b. "The Word Turned Upside Down". *New York Review of Books* 27 (October): 74–9.

Searle, J. 1997. *The Mystery of Consciousness*. New York: New York Review of Books.

Sellars, W. 1956. "Empiricism and the Philosophy of Mind". In *Minnesota Studies in the Philosophy of Science*, vol. 1, H. Feigl & M. Scriven (eds), 253–329. Minneapolis, MN: University of Minnesota Press.

Sellars, W. 1962. "Philosophy and the Scientific Image of Man". In *Frontiers of Science and Philosophy*, R. Colodny (ed.), 35–78. Edinburgh: Edinburgh University Press.

Serota, N. 2000. "Who's Afraid of Modern Art?" The Dimbleby Lecture. BBC television.

Servi, K. 2001. *Greek Mythology*. Athens: Erdotike Athenon.

Smart, J. J. C. 1955. "Spatialising Time". *Mind* 64(254): 239–41.

Smolin, L. 2006. *The Trouble with Physics: The Rise of String Theory, the Fall of Science, and What Comes Next*. London: Allen Lane.

Smolin, L. 2013. *Time Reborn: From the Crisis of Physics to the Future of the Universe*. London: Allen Lane.

Sokal, A. D. 1996. "Transgressing the Boundaries: Towards a Transformative Hermeneutics of Quantum Gravity". *Social Text* 46/47: 217–52.

Sokal, A. D. 1998. "What the Social Text Affair Does and Does Not Prove". In *A House Built on Sand: Exposing Postmodernist Myths About Science*, M. Koertge (ed.), 9–22. New York: Oxford University Press.

Sokal, A. D. & J. Bricmont 1998. *Intellectual Impostures: Postmodern Philosophers' Abuse of Science*. London: Profile.

Stebbing, L. S. 1958. *Philosophy and the Physicists*. New York: Dover.

Stroud, B. 2000. *Understanding Human Knowledge: Philosophical Essays*. Oxford: Oxford University Press.

Sturrock, J. 1998. "Poor Sokal". *London Review of Books* (16 July): 8–9.

Tallis, R. 1995a. *Not Saussure: A Critique of Post-Saussurean Literary Theory*, 2nd edn. Basingstoke: Macmillan.

Tallis, R. 1995b. "The Mirror Stage". See Tallis (1995a), 131–63.

Tallis, R. 1995c. "Preface to the Second Edition". See Tallis (1995a), x–xxiii.

Tallis, R. 1995d. "Words, Senses, Objects." See Tallis (1995a), 107–11.

Tallis, R. 1995e. *Newton's Sleep: Two Kingdoms and Two Cultures*. London: Macmillan.

Tallis, R. 1997. "The Philosophies of Consciousness and Philosophies of the Concept, Or: Is There Any Point in Studying the Headache I Have Now?" In *Enemies of Hope: A Critique of Contemporary Pessimism*, 327–51. Basingstoke: Macmillan.

Tallis, R. 1998. *In Defence of Realism*, 2nd edn. Lincoln, NE: University of Nebraska Press.

Tallis, R. 1999a. *Enemies of Hope: A Critique of Contemporary Pessimism*, 2nd edn. Basingstoke: Macmillan.

Tallis, R. 1999b. *Theorrhoea and After*. Basingstoke: Macmillan.

Tallis, R. 2000. *The Raymond Tallis Reader*, M. Grant (ed.). Basingstoke: Palgrave Macmillan.

Tallis, R. 2002. *A Conversation with Martin Heidegger*. Basingstoke: Macmillan.

Tallis, R. 2003a. *The Hand: A Philosophical Inquiry into Human Being*. Edinburgh: Edinburgh University Press.

Tallis, R. 2003b. "Human Freedom as a Reality-Producing Illusion". *The Monist* 86(2): 200–219.

Tallis, R. 2004a. *I Am: A Philosophical Inquiry into First-Person Being*. Edinburgh: Edinburgh University Press.

Tallis, R. 2004b. "Agency and First-Person Being". See Tallis (2004a), 285–329.

Tallis, R. 2004c. *Why the Mind is not a Computer*. Exeter: Academic Press.

Tallis, R. 2005a. *The Knowing Animal: A Philosophical Inquiry into Knowledge and Truth*. Edinburgh: Edinburgh University Press.

Tallis, R. 2005b. "The Cause-Seeking Animal: Agency and the Causal Intuition". See Tallis (2005a), 239–42.

Tallis, R. 2008. *The Kingdom of Infinite Space: A Journey Round Your Head*. London: Atlantic.

Tallis, R. 2010. *Michelangelo's Finger: An Explanation of Everyday Transcendence*. London: Atlantic.

Tallis, R. 2011. *Aping Mankind: Neuromania, Darwinitis and the Misrepresentation of Humanity*. Durham: Acumen.

Tallis, R. 2012a. *In Defence of Wonder and Other Philosophical Reflections*. Durham: Acumen.

Tallis, R. 2012b. "The Myth of Time Travel". See Tallis (2012a), 56–61.

Tallis, R. 2012c. "On (Almost) Nothing: Concerning Spatial Points". See Tallis (2012a), 81–7.

Tallis, R. forthcoming. *Of Time and Lamentation: Reflections on Transience*. Durham: Acumen.

Tye, M. 1986. "The Subjective Qualities of Experience". *Mind* 95: 1–17.

Ungaretti, G. 2003. *Vita d'un unomo: Tutte le poesie*. Milan: Mondadori.

Valéry, P. 1960. "Rhumbs". In "Tel Quel", *Oeuvres*, vol. 2, J. Hytier (ed.), 473–781. Paris: Pléiade.

Williams, D. C. 1951. "The Myth of Passage". *Journal of Philosophy* 48(15) (19 July): 457–72.

Wittgenstein, L. 1958. *Philosophical Investigations*, 2nd edn, G. E. M. Anscombe (ed. and trans.). Oxford: Blackwell.

Wittgenstein, L. 1961. *Tractatus Logico-Philosophicus*, D. F. Pears & B. F. McGuinness (trans.). London: Routledge & Kegan Paul.

Wittgenstein, L. 1974. *On Certainty*, G. E. M. Anscombe & G. H. von Wright (eds), D. Paul & G. E. M. Anscombe (trans.). Oxford: Blackwell.

Wolpert, L. 2003. "Causal Belief and the Origins of Technology". *Philosophical Transactions of the Royal Society of London* A 361: 1709–19.

Woodward, J. 2013. "Causation and Manipulability". In *The Stanford Encyclopedia of Philosophy* (Winter 2013 Edition), E. N. Zalta (ed.). http://plato.stanford.edu/archives/win2013/entries/causation-mani/ (accessed February 2014).

Wullschläger, J. 2012. "Beyond the Froth and Jargon". *Financial Times* (24 November). www.ft.com/cms/s/2/f7a76ada-2e63-11e2-8bb3-00144feabdc0.html#axzz2t0wHyqoy (accessed February 2014).

Wynne, C. D. L. 2004. *Do Animals Think?* Princeton, NJ: Princeton University Press.

Yeats, W. B. 1950. *Collected Poems of W. B. Yeats*, 2nd edn. London: Macmillan.

Index